Janus's Gaze

Janus's Gaze

....

ESSAYS ON CARL SCHMITT

Carlo Galli

Translated by Amanda Minervini

Edited and with an Introduction by Adam Sitze

DUKE UNIVERSITY PRESS Durham and London 2015

Originally published as *Lo sguardo di Giano*
© 2008 by Società editrice Il Mulino, Bologna

© 2015 Duke University Press
All rights reserved
Printed in the United States
of America on acid-free paper
Typeset in Quadraat and Quadraat Sans
by Graphic Composition, Inc.

....

Library of Congress Cataloging-in-Publication Data
Galli, Carlo, author.
[Lo sguardo di Giano. English]
Janus's gaze : essays on Carl Schmitt / Carlo
Galli ; translated by Amanda Minervini ; edited
and with an introduction by Adam Sitze.
pages cm
"Originally published as Lo sguardo di Giano,
2008 by Società editrice Il Mulino, Bologna."
Includes bibliographical references and index.
ISBN 978-0-8223-6018-6 (hardcover : alk. paper)
ISBN 978-0-8223-6032-2 (pbk. : alk. paper)
ISBN 978-0-8223-7485-5 (e-book)
1. Schmitt, Carl, 1888–1985—Influence.
2. Political science—Philosophy—History—20th
century. I. Minervini, Amanda, translator. II. Sitze,
Adam, editor, writer of introduction. III. Title.
JC263.S34G3713 2015
320.01—dc23
2015021377

....

Cover art: Collage by Natalie F. Smith using
detail of photo by Bogomyako/Alamy.

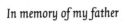
In memory of my father

CONTENTS

....

ACKNOWLEDGMENTS

....

Amanda Minervini would like to express her warm thanks to Adam Sitze for his wonderful editing work and continued inspiration. She also thanks Carlo Galli for offering prompt and useful clarifications. Adam Sitze would like to thank Alek Gorzewski and Laura Merchant for their insightful comments on early drafts of his introduction. He also thanks Diana Witt for creating the index for this book, work that was supported by a grant from the Amherst College Faculty Research Award Program, as funded by the H. Axel Schupf '57 Fund for Intellectual Life. Above all, he thanks Amanda Minervini for her scrupulous translations and discerning intellect, and Carlo Galli for his patience and counsel.

CARL SCHMITT:

AN IMPROPER NAME

Adam Sitze

1

The proper name, it must be said, has a curious place and function in the discourse of the history of political thought. On the terms of this discourse, a name like "Aristotle" does not designate a specific mortal being who lived and died in a particular place and at a particular time. Quite the opposite: it designates something in this mortal being—his thought—that exceeds his mortal being, and thus too his particular place and time. Even so, "Aristotle" doesn't refer equally to all of Aristotle's thought: political theorists typically use this name to designate the positions in The Politics and Nicomachean Ethics, not those in Quaestiones Mechanicae or The Souls of Animals. The name also can be used to refer to works not written by Aristotle at all. Converted into an adjective, "Aristotelian" refers to transmissible attributes that have come to be associated with Aristotle's thought—idiosyncratic conceptual habits or techniques that are common enough to be found reiterated in the works of others, and that with sufficient iteration can come to constitute a school (the "Lyceum") or tradition ("Aristotelianism"). This adjectivalization can go to such an extreme that some thinkers can come to be categorized more with reference to Aristotle's name than by their own (Aquinas, for some, always will be first and foremost a particular sort of "Aristotelian"). These descriptions, paradoxically, can even come to displace the objects they ostensibly only nickname. Certain passages in Aristotle's *Politics*, for example, have been said to be "un-Aristotelian." Still other works, meanwhile, which may not have been authored by Aristotle at all (such as *The Constitution of Athens*), have been attributed to Aristotle and reproduced under his name in his collected works. As a classifying device within the discourse of the history of political thought, in other words, the proper name would seem to operate not with the simplicity of Aristotelian taxonomy, but with the perplexity of Cantorian set theory.

All the more strange, therefore, that historians of political thought should make the proper name so central to their pedagogy. It's not uncommon to find entire anthologies and syllabuses organized exclusively with reference to proper names, as if knowing how to think were synonymous with knowing how to properly name thinking. In theory, it's not difficult to defend this practice: the proper use of the proper name in the history of political thought, it would seem, is to allow students to acquire an awareness of the sense in which their own thoughts are but "residues and abbreviations" of thinkers who thought before them. But in practice, this theory does not so much spur the genesis of thought as produce the most excruciating chronicles ("Plato begat Aristotle, Aristotle begat Cicero, Cicero begat St. Augustine . . ."), which seem designed to filibuster young thinkers into conceding that there is indeed nothing new under the sun. By turning thinking into something tedious, wearying, and even melancholic, this mode of transmitting thought achieves nothing so much as the complete deeroticization of thought: its unstated institutional function is to anesthetize curiosity, to tame an otherwise polymorphous *libido sciendi*. Defended as a mnemonic device for sustaining pious fidelity to lost objects, the proper name instead gives one permission for misreading and forgetfulness, allowing the student to forget everything in a given text except the one or two concepts that consensus and opinion, not to mention Wikipedia, attribute to a thinker prior to any reading, and thus qualify as memorable whether or not any reading ends up happening at all. Or else it becomes the opposite: an instrument for the obsessive and pointless accumulation of memory, for the excessive recollections of historicism, which unthinkingly seek to reduce the infinity of thought to the circumstances of a finite time and place. In either case, political thought that organizes itself with reference to the proper name—which is, let's be clear, almost always a patronym—comes to possess a testamentary function, and thence to arrange itself implicitly around forms derived from inheritance law. Scholarly disputes in the history of political thought thus come to resemble paternity suits in courts of law: "Plato, not Aristotle, is Aquinas's true father." A subtle but decisive irony: it would appear that the history of political thought depends for its intelligibility on forms that are not primarily political at all, but that are, more precisely and directly, jurisprudential—juridical forms that are authored by no one in particular, but that nevertheless govern the historiography by which that history arranges its authors; and that historians of political thought, more often than not, unthinkingly accept as unhistorical and apolitical necessities. Thought thus taught wilts on the vine that should allow it to flower, suffocated by its self-proclaimed stewards. As it functions within the discourse of the history of political thought, the proper name does not teach one how to think, only to categorize and to cite. It does not explain anything, as someone once said; it must itself be explained.

2

The political thought of Carl Schmitt presents a limit case of this peculiar dynamic. Especially in the Anglophone academy, where the reception of Schmitt lags behind that in other languages, to speak of Schmitt's thought is more often than not to produce an occasion for rhetoric centered directly on the sense and meaning of the proper name "Carl Schmitt" itself. One of the main points of reading Schmitt, or so it would seem, is to attach praise or blame to this name, to defend this good name from its accusers or to make a case against that same name. So powerfully entrenched is this premise today that even to name it *as* a premise—even to treat this approach to the reading of Schmitt as a debatable proposition, and not as a natural, self-evident, or inevitable necessity—would seem to miss the point of reading Schmitt in the first place.

And yet, far from being the necessary condition for a reading of Schmitt on Schmitt's own terms, Schmitt's proper name in fact inhibits the possibility of that reading. Consider, in this light, what is probably the very first attempt at a comprehensive introduction to Carl Schmitt in the Anglophone world. Titled "Observations on the Personality and Work of Professor Carl Schmitt," this four-page memo was composed in November 1945 by the jurist and political scientist Karl Loewenstein

(1891–1973), a student of Max Weber who claimed "thirty years of experience with Schmitt," and who wrote in his capacity as a consultant for the Legal Division of the United States Office of Military Government for Germany (the administrative body responsible for Schmitt's postwar detention).[1] Interpreted on strictly bureaucratic terms, Loewenstein's memo was a response to a request jointly submitted by Schmitt's wife and jurist Hans Schneider for the recovery of Schmitt's library, which Loewenstein had helped Allied forces sequester a month earlier on the grounds that it was an "invaluable . . . source of information on pre-Nazi and Nazi law and political science" ("about the most complete," Loewenstein noted, "I can imagine").[2] For the purposes of this discussion, Loewenstein's text is instructive for the way the category named in its title, "the Personality and Work of Professor Carl Schmitt," contains a symptomatic conflation—"personality *and* work"—that, in turn, explicates the horizon that implicitly governs the interpretation of Schmitt even today.

Loewenstein's memo opened by praising Schmitt in the most unconditional terms.

> I do not hesitate to qualify Carl Schmitt as the foremost German political scientist and one of the most eminent political writers of our time, comparable in influence on world opinion perhaps only to Harold Laski, though in the reversed sense in that Laski is the literary protagonist of democracy while Carl Schmitt, on the other hand, has become the leading authority on authoritarian government and totalitarianism. Broadly speaking he is a man of near-genius rating. He possess[es] . . . a vast and by no means sterile erudition, drawing from an immense store of factual information such constructive conclusions as have greatly contributed to the shaping of the things to come in the past. He is one of those rare scholars who combine learning with imagination; book knowledge with a realistic sense of what is possible in politics; scientific training with political versatility. Without doubt Carl Schmitt is the most prominent personality in the field of public law and political science Germany has produced since Georg Jellinek.[3]

Loewenstein's praise then took a very different turn. "To his and the German people's misfortune," Loewenstein then asserted, "Carl Schmitt abused his gifts for evil purposes."[4] To support this accusation, Loewenstein proceeded to produce an abbreviated biography of Schmitt's work and conduct under Weimar, ranging from his academic career (his appointment at the Handelshochschule in Munich and his rejection by the Law Faculty at the University of Munich) to his first marriage and divorce (Schmitt's application for which was rejected by the Catholic Church, an event which, in Loewenstein's view, turned Schmitt against the Church) and to his sudden turn to anti-Semitism after 1933. Schmitt, Loewenstein claimed, was

> the first and certainly the most influential of all German writers who enthusiastically joined the Hitler Government after it had won the elections of March 5, 1933. . . . His writings revealed him at once as an ardent supporter of Hitler's dictatorship which seemed to him the fulfillment and climax of his intellectual desires and for which he had prepared himself and his public by his scientific research and writings. Suddenly he became an enthusiastic anti-semite. . . . In April 1933 he published in the leading newspaper of Munich a vicious attack against what he considered the evil influence of the Jews on law and politics directed specifically against his benefactors [Stier Somlo and Hans Kelsen, two Jewish professors who helped Schmitt obtain his professorship at the University of Cologne]. Likewise he helped the Hitler Government in the drafting of its early anti-democratic laws.[5]

After drawing several direct connections between Schmitt's writings and Nazi policies, Loewenstein then praised Schmitt once again, this time for his international influence in France, Spain, and Latin America. "In due course," Loewenstein wrote, Schmitt "became the recognized authority on German law and political philosophy. . . . He is probably the most quoted German legal author of this generation, with the possible exception of Hans Kelsen. . . . Hardly any contemporary writer can claim for himself to have influenced his time to such an extent as Carl Schmitt."[6] But precisely because Schmitt was so influential, Loewenstein continued, it was essential not to neglect his prosecution. Schmitt's arrest, Loewenstein argued, "will be considered—and is so considered—by responsible Germans as an act of justice on the part of Military Government. His release, if such is contemplated, would constitute a blow to incipient democracy in Germany and to public opinion abroad. Particularly in such countries where Carl Schmitt is considered the standard authority of totalitarianism, his immunity from punishment will be rated as a victory of Nazism over Military Government."[7]

We should not overlook the surprising rhetorical form that begins to take shape here. For Loewenstein, praise of Schmitt was not at all the opposite of blame of Schmitt. It was its *counterpart* and *double*, if not also its very *condition of possibility*. In Loewenstein's view, the fact that Schmitt enjoyed such a strong international reputation was *also* a reason that Schmitt *could not but be* tried as a war criminal. Because Schmitt was so visibly and publicly acclaimed as an authority on constitutional law, Loewenstein reasoned, Schmitt not only must be prosecuted but also must be *seen* to be prosecuted. Surprisingly, however, something like the converse held true as well. Loewenstein's recommendation that Schmitt be prosecuted as a war criminal—a much harsher fate, needless to say, than denazification alone—nevertheless concluded by sounding a note that *also* could amount to *a defense* against that selfsame prosecution. Schmitt, Loewenstein argued, was such a craven opportunist, such a careerist, so devoid of substance or character, so thoroughly governed by his personal interests, etc., that he could be expected to function perfectly well as a democrat were he allowed to return to teaching under conditions of democracy. "It may be added in conclusion that Carl Schmitt if permitted to write and publish and teach would be perfectly capable of becoming as successful and ardent a democrat as he was a defender of totalitarianism. His political versatility is surpassed only by his ability to adjust his vast learning to that doctrine which seems most convenient of his personal interests."[8]

The true crux of Schmitt interpretation, Roberto Racinaro once observed, is the problem of Schmitt's occasionalism.[9] For Loewenstein, Schmitt's occasionalism was to be interpreted on grounds that were at once personalist and instrumental: Schmitt the person was such a tool that he would turn his work into a tool for use by whatever regime happened to be in power, up to and including the worst of the worst. But note well: at the same time that Loewenstein's interpretation of Schmitt's person and work served as grounds to accuse Schmitt as a war criminal, it also served as grounds for Schmitt *not* to be permanently banned from teaching.[10] On the terms of Loewenstein's memo, the strongest charges against Schmitt doubled as the best reasons to mitigate Schmitt's punishment: the accusation that Schmitt was a tool who allowed his work to be used as an instrument of totalitarianism was perfectly commensurable with a defense of Schmitt on the grounds that, precisely as a tool, his work equally might be useful for democracy.

Praise and blame, accusation and apology—Loewenstein's brief not only mobilized these antitheses as the definitive coordinates for the first Anglophone attempt at a comprehensive reading of Schmitt; it also revealed the sense in which each of these terms could pivot into its opposite. Holding these couplets in place—crucially—was the judicial form of Loewenstein's brief, which obliged Loewenstein to interpret the proper name "Carl Schmitt" as a "case" not only in an epistemological sense (an object of study) but also in a strictly juridical sense (as an object of legal action). Determined in this way, the question of interpreting Schmitt's work becomes indistinct from the question of passing judgment on Schmitt's person. For Loewenstein—as for many contemporary readers of Schmitt—the answer to both questions is clear: because Schmitt's work was complicit in or even justified an unprecedented crime, that work has the character of a criminal wrongdoing, a deed that can and even must be attributed to Schmitt's person.

Prior to this answer, however, is a series of unasked questions: what does it mean to displace the work of reading Schmitt with the very different work of *imputation*—of attributing a doer to a deed for the purposes of specifically legal judgment?[11] When the work of reading is preinterpreted in this way, what alternate possibilities for reading might we unwittingly abandon? On what other modes of reading might imputative reading foreclose? Once reading becomes juridified as imputation, needless to say, the possibilities for reading narrow considerably. On these terms, before one can read Schmitt's work, one must first decipher his person (to try to figure out whether he was a true anti-Semite, an evil genius, a Machiavellian opportunist, or simply a victim of his circumstances). But before one can decipher Schmitt's person, it's first necessary to interpret his work as evidence (cross-examining it for signs of guilt or innocence, good or bad intentions). Reading so construed silently assumes the form of a trial whose possible outcomes are at once *highly constrained* (a verdict of either guilt or innocence) and *indefinitely postponed*, such that scholarly commentary itself comes to assume the

form of a series of endlessly repeated appeals of prior verdicts. Juridified as imputation, reading never fully comes to a close; more to the
point, it never actually begins in the first place.

3

However neglected and even maligned by Schmitt scholars it may be,[12]
Loewenstein's memo nevertheless remains paradigmatic for the Anglophone reception of Schmitt: it outlines, with uncanny precision, the
deadlocks that continue to determine Schmitt commentary in English
today. Even and especially where contemporary readers of Schmitt oppose Loewenstein's damning conclusions, they do not seem to oppose
the terms on which Loewenstein read Schmitt. Then as now, the question of what it means to read Schmitt seems to be tantamount to the
question of whether or not judgments on Schmitt's "personality and
work" should be inclined more toward praise than blame, more toward
accusation than defense.[13] The intensity of debates over this question,
however, belies the underlying consensus that enables their seemingly
interminable persistence. All parties to the dispute seem to agree with
Loewenstein that the terms of epideictic and forensic rhetoric provide
the best or perhaps even the only coordinates for the interpretation
of Schmitt.[14] This consensus extends, above all, to include those who
attempt to avoid debates over Schmitt by trying to discover a sort of
liberal-technicist "golden mean" or "middle of the road" between praise
and blame, accusation and defense, as if one escapes the hermeneutic
difficulty of reading Schmitt by proposing that his work can be used
as some sort of a neutral "tool" by each after her own fashion.[15] To the
extent that the Anglophone reception of Schmitt accepts these terms as
the indispensable coordinates for any valid interpretation of Schmitt, it
unwittingly obeys the precedent established by Loewenstein's memo,
and renders itself vulnerable both to that memo's vicissitudes and to
its limits.

Nowhere is this more pronounced than in the symptomatic way citations of the proper name "Carl Schmitt" operate in Anglophone Schmitt
commentary today. Beginning with Loewenstein, "Carl Schmitt" would
be translated into English as a name for political thought that is as essential as it is unseemly, as imperative as it is unacceptable, as inescapable as it is immoral. In Schmitt's work and person, in other words, the

category of the proper name (understood as a classificatory operation internal to the discourse of political thought) would seem to become indistinct from the category of the improper name (understood as a name we experience as indecent or even intolerable). The unconscious dynamic set into motion by this indistinction hardly needs spelling out: operating both as a proper name and as an improper name, "Carl Schmitt" proves to be the source of an almost inexhaustible ambivalence—a hate that binds, that fascinates and paralyzes, that critics of Schmitt above all love to sustain.[16] Under the sway of this ambivalence, the strongest polemics against Schmitt also turn out to be the weakest critiques of Schmitt, since the very form of these polemics silently ratifies the content of certain works by Schmitt—most notably *The Concept of the Political*, in which Schmitt proposes antagonism as the substance of the political relation.[17] As a rule: the more polemical one's political relation to Schmitt, the more one confirms Schmitt's thesis on the concept of the political, and the more one realizes one can't live either with Schmitt or without him. Needless to say, the more that the improper name "Carl Schmitt" becomes normalized as a category within the Anglophone academe—moving from critical theory and political theory to international relations and geography—the more this deadlock of ambivalence is destined to intensify.[18] But the more this ambivalence intensifies, the more interminable becomes the reading of Carl Schmitt, and the more that interminability, in turn, becomes institutionalized as a normal state of affairs.

What's most interesting about this normalization and institutionalization, however, is how rarely its necessary condition is posed as a problem for thought. No Schmittian turn is possible, much less valid, without some prior understanding of what it means to read Schmitt on Schmitt's own terms, and as such to know what one is talking about when one proposes to categorize this or that argument, this or that concept, as "Schmittian." But even in the journals that now seem to be devoted almost exclusively to the Schmitt defense industry, to say nothing of those who polemicize against Schmitt, there seems to be little to no interest in the question that alone would generate this knowledge. Why?

The task of reading Schmitt within the horizon of his own self-understanding is more difficult than it appears. Read alongside one another, Schmitt's terms and concepts seem to form nothing but an incoherent maze, a jumble of shifting terms that veer from the archaic to the pragmatic, from the systematic to the oracular. What indeed is the relation between the idiosyncratic theory of "irruption" Schmitt sets forth in his 1956 *Hamlet or Hecuba* and the obnoxious defense of Raoul Malan he lays out in his 1963 *Theory of the Partisan*? Between the crisp decisionist thesis he formulates in his 1922 *Political Theology* and the critique of decisionism he offers in his 1934 *Three Types of Juristic Thought*? Between the systematic analysis of "constituting power" he outlines in his 1927 *Constitutional Theory* and the rambling rant he addresses to his daughter in his 1942 *Land and Sea*?

Given this jarring conceptual excess, many Schmitt scholars simply have abandoned altogether the ordinary but essential hermeneutic task of inquiring into the common horizon and specific unity of the Schmittian oeuvre. In the absence of this inquiry, the reading of Schmitt has taken place largely by way of *synecdoche*, where a handful of faddish but partial concepts (decision and exception, friend and enemy, *nomos*, etc.) stand in as names designating the essence of the cryptic and forbidding heterogeneity of the Schmittian oeuvre, and where Schmitt's own person becomes a synonym for a series of mutually exclusive political categorizations.[19] It is not uncommon these days for readers of Schmitt to interpret *Concept of the Political* in perfect isolation from *Theory of the Partisan* and *Nomos of the Earth*, to criticize the overt anti-Semitism of *Three Studies on Juristic Thought* and *The Leviathan in the State Theory of Thomas Hobbes* while withholding comment on the analytic taxonomies of *Constitutional Theory*, to reread *Political Theology* without reference to *Roman Catholicism and Political Form*, and so on.

To be sure, this haphazard approach to Schmitt rhymes perfectly with some of the most unshakeable habits of the contemporary humanities. A certain compulsory eclecticism—the analogue in scholarly interpretation to the eclecticism that is the "degree zero" of postmodern culture—sometimes seems to be the dominant, even default, school of hermeneutics today.[20] Applied to Schmitt, however, this approach results in a compartmentalization of the Schmittian oeuvre that is lacking in both sense and purpose. Picture a group of Freud scholars each writing separately about distinct problems in psychoanalysis (one on sadism and masochism, a second on the death drive and the pleasure principle, a third on repression and sublimation) but all without a single mention of the unconscious; or a set of Marxist thinkers taking on distinct questions within historical materialism (commodity fetishism, use value and exchange value, base and superstructure) yet without also referring to labor. Strange though it may sound, an arrangement of this sort seems to pertain in Anglophone Schmitt scholarship today. While many intelligent studies have appeared in recent years on various elements in Schmitt's thought (such as the exception and decisionism, secularization and political theology, the distinction of *hostis* and *inimicus*, the *nomos* and the *katechon*, and above all Schmitt's Nazism, his anti-Semitism, and his relation to the Weimar Republic), very few, if any, have attempted to put a name to the common hermeneutic horizon from which all of these elements gain their singular sense and force. In Althusser's terms, commentary on Schmitt has largely limited itself to the *thematics* of Schmitt's various texts, without pausing to pose the question of its *problematic*—which is to say, the question of the implicit questions to which the modalities of Schmittian thought are the explicit answer.[21]

In the absence of an inquiry of this sort, our reading of Schmitt encounters a host of interpretive aporias. Certain of Schmitt's writings call the conflation of war and crime into question;[22] and yet the accusation that Schmitt is a "war criminal" in many ways remains one of the dominant hermeneutic horizons governing the reading of Schmitt, both for those who seek to criticize him and for those who seek to defend him. Other of Schmitt's writings oppose the listless pluralism of modern liberalism;[23] and yet certain readers of Schmitt seem quite content to interpret Schmitt's oeuvre according to the eclecticism that is the hermeneutic equivalent of liberal pluralism. Schmitt's writings certainly contain polemics against the idea that technics could constitute a neutral standpoint outside of the conflicts of the political; and yet readers of Schmitt regularly seek to escape the polemics around Schmitt by claiming not to take sides in those polemics, only "to use" Schmitt's work as a "tool" or "lens." Certain elements in Schmitt's work point toward a general problematization of the concept of the "person";[24] this has not stopped the most fervent disciples of Schmitt from defending Schmitt on the basis of a clear and distinct understanding of the "person." Still other of Schmitt's writings begin to question the very idea of the proper name, not once but several times over;[25] and yet commentators on Schmitt for the most part seem to be self-confident about the obviousness and self-evidence of Schmitt's own proper name. Citations of Carl Schmitt today certainly are increasing; the same can't be said for self-consciousness about what it means to read Schmitt's texts on their own terms.

4

Carlo Galli's approach to the reading of Schmitt prepares the reader not only to enter these hermeneutic circles but also to exit them in the right way. Galli is best known for his monumental 936-page *Genealogia della politica: Carl Schmitt e la crisi del pensiero politico moderno* (Genealogy of politics: Carl Schmitt and the crisis of modern political thought). Written with a hermeneutic rigor and sustained analytic attention that reminded one reader of "the august tradition of the great philological monographs of the classics," Galli's *Genealogia* is quadruply systematic.[26] It is, to begin, a "historico-critical . . . reconstruction of the internal logic of Schmittian argumentation" that accounts for all of Schmitt's writings, in the mode of a symptomal reading, and that has as its aim a claim on the essence and basis of Schmittian thought from within its own immanent horizon.[27] Because no such reading could avoid paying attention to the crises to which Schmittian criticism is internal, Galli also engages in an "external contextualization" of Schmittian logic, discerning in the contradictoriness of Schmitt's texts the traces of select and pivotal events.[28] This contextualization is not, however, historicist; it does not seek to undercut the autonomy of Schmittian thought with reference to its determinants in its immediate cultural and political context. Galli argues that the fundamental crisis to which Schmittian thought is internal is not limited in place and time to the Weimar Republic or to Nazi Germany; it is instead an epochal crisis, the crisis of modern mediation as such. To support this claim, Galli situates Schmitt in the history of modern political philosophy, explaining how Schmitt inherits a crisis in philosophical mediation that begins with Hegel and Marx, reaches its turning point in Kierkegaard and Weber, and dissolves in Nietzsche.[29] In the process, Galli engages in a systematic overview of the secondary literature on Schmitt in German, Italian, Spanish, French, and English. The critical apparatus that results from this labor (Galli's footnotes alone take up nearly three hundred pages) does not, however, merely communicate bibliographic information; it adds up to a second book, an extension of Galli's earliest work on Schmitt, his 1979 "symptomal reading" of Schmitt commentary in Italy to Schmitt commentary worldwide.[30] Galli's *Genealogia* is, in short, a "gloss" in the best and strictest Bolognese sense of the word.[31]

    The central claim of Galli's *Genealogia* is that Schmitt's accomplishment was to have opened himself to, in order to radicalize, the crises that together constitute the origin of the modern epoch (where "origin" is understood as *Entstehunge* or *archē*).[32] Schmitt is consequently, on Galli's reading, a specifically genealogical critic of modernity: Schmitt's single-minded focus, according to Galli, was to grasp the origin of the strangely double-sided energy he perceived in the institutions and practices of modern politics. Schmitt's discovery, Galli argues, was that this energy derived from "an originary crisis—or, better still, an *originary contradiction*—which is not a simple contradiction, but, rather, the exhibition of two sides, two extremes," such that "the origin of politics is not, in either of its two sides, an objective *foundation* for politics, but rather its *foundering* or *unfounding* (*sfondamento*)."[33] The "political" is Schmitt's name for this originary crisis, this free-floating energy that undermines the very institutions and practices it simultaneously founds, that deforms the same political forms it produces, and that disorders the very systems of thought to which it gives rise. By fixing his gaze on this origin, Schmitt realized that modern political thought (and consequently too the liberal democratic institutions and practices whose modes of self-justification it grounds and sustains) is divided against itself in a nondialectical manner. At the same time that it emerges from and even implicitly feeds on a crisis it is incapable of resolving, modern political thought also accounts for this incapacity by suppressing the symptoms of the crisis, compensating for its own incoherence with ever more moralistic reaffirmations of the unquestionable necessity of its own explicit goals. The core problematic of Schmittian thought, Galli will consequently argue, cannot then be reduced to any one of the themes of Schmitt's various texts (the distinction between exception and norm, theology and politics, decision and discussion, friend and enemy, constituting power and constituted power, land and sea, limited and unlimited warfare, European center and colonial frontier, and so on). It is Schmitt's discovery that all of the forms of modern politics share a common trait, a birthmark that, in turn, attests to their common origin; despite the many and various differences between modern political thinkers—indeed as the silent but generative core of those differences—the epochal unity of modern political thought derives from its distinctive doubleness, its simultaneous impossibility and necessity, or, in short, its "tragicity."[34]

Developing claims he already had announced in 1979,[35] Galli argues that the specificity of Schmitt's genealogical insight into this "tragic-ity" derives from the *occasio*—the crisis—that is the kernel of Schmit-tian thought. Schmitt wrote at a juncture in European politics in which inside and outside, peace and war, civil and military, enemy and crim-inal were entering into the gray of a twilight, and in which a certain warlike polemicity was consequently emerging as the normal mode of being for political institutions and practices whose explicit and defini-tive aspiration was reasonable discussion, transparent representation, and rational mediation.[36] Instead of interpreting this crisis of repre-sentation from modernity's own various privileged points of internal self-understanding (the state, the subject, society, or reason), Galli argues, Schmitt instead sought to understand it with reference to the catastrophe from which modernity itself emerged, namely, the dissolu-tion of the specifically Christian form of representation that governed political order in medieval Europe.[37] To give a name to this lost form of representation—this peculiar and specifically imperial ability to em-brace any and all antitheses (life and death, Heaven and Earth, God and Man, past and future, time and eternity, good and power, beginning and end, reason and nonreason, etc.) in order to absorb them into one unified form—Schmitt took a term from the medieval Catholic thinker Nicholas de Cusa: *complexio oppositorum*. According to Galli, Schmitt un-derstood the *complexio* neither as a dialectical synthesis (a simple coin-cidence of opposites) nor as an eclectic relativism (a jumble of plural and variegated qualities) but rather as "a form in which life and reason coexist without forcing," a single hierarchy whose integrity derives, above all, from the way it reconciles and preserves many different, even opposed forms of life in the single "glorious form" of Christ's Person.[38] For Schmitt, Galli argues, the genealogical significance of the *complexio* is not theological but political: Schmitt is interested in the *complexio* be-cause of the way its mode of representation—the extreme publicity and visibility through which all opposites coincided in the immediate medi-acy of Christ's Person—in turn called into being a relatively stable and enduring political order.[39]

It is on the basis of this capacity for a mode of representation to con-stitute a political order (or what Galli calls "morphogenetic power") that Schmitt understands the Modern. With the events that together opened the modern epoch (such as the Copernican Revolution, the Wars of Ref-ormation, and the conquest of America), the *complexio* and the order of being it sustained no longer could be treated as a self-evident "given" that could be presupposed by political thought. In the absence of a coherent and integrative Idea in which opposites could coincide without conflict—indeed, under the unprecedented conditions of theological civil war in which the Person of Christ was no longer the basis of European *peace* but was now precisely both a source of and a stake in European *conflict*—political and juridical Power became disconnected from theological and moral Good, and the question of how to mediate opposing forces and qualities through representation suddenly emerged as an anxious and explicit question for political thought.[40]

According to Galli, Schmitt understands modern mediation to originate as an unwitting, precarious, and partial response both to this question and to the epochal catastrophe that occasions it. Modern mediation marks the attempt, on the part of a European subject who suddenly finds himself alone in the universe, to accomplish a set of morphogenetic tasks bequeathed to him by the *complexio*—such as the creation of order, the reconciliation of opposites, and the accomplishment of peace on Earth—but now without the support of a gestalt in which everything, however opposed, had its place—now, in other words, only through an ad hoc use of his own immanent powers.[41] In modernity, in short, the European subject is faced with the task of producing ex nihilo the political form, peace, and reconciliation it once could presuppose in the *complexio*. It pursues these aims through on the one hand instrumental reason (the mathematization and technical mastery of nature, up to and including human nature) and on the other through a new form of representation, which seeks to mediate contradictions between opposing forces but which also recognizes, without also fully realizing why, that its attempts at mediation are somehow already destined, in advance, to failure. The reconciliation of opposites the *complexio* achieved felicitously with reference to the Person of Christ is now the work of an unhappy consciousness, a person in the juridical sense who is capable of peace, reconciliation, and order only at the cost of a ceaseless and restless reflection on division and disorder.[42]

The State is modernity's solution to this predicament. In the place once occupied by the hierarchical *complexio* of the Catholic Church's "glorious form," Hobbesian political philosophy proposes the egalitarian simplicity of a new beginning—a revolutionary tabula rasa that articulates the rational necessity of peace, and establishes the impersonal laws of the State, through a manifestly geometrical deduction.[43] But the impersonal laws of the State can only produce political form and exercise morphogenetic power in an ungrounded manner, by presupposing the complete separation of Power from the Good. Indeed, the strength of impersonal law (its principled insistence on the formal equality of all persons before the law) is predicated on a displacement of the morphogenetic power of the *complexio* (a hierarchy centered on the Person of Christ). In the absence of a felicitous use of morphogenetic power, the State finds that law alone is insufficient for accomplishing the aims it inherits from the *complexio*, and discovers itself to be in need of supplements for its impersonal law. The State discovers this supplement by placing instrumental reason (which is to say, the neutralization of conflict through *dispositifs* of discipline, governmentality, and security, but also, if necessary, through the use of military and, later, police forces) at the service of repeated sovereign decisions that reproduce a semblance of the unity and integrity of Roman Catholic visibility and publicity by setting aside the impersonality of law (with its insistence on formal equality) in order to fabricate a public enemy, whose schema can then serve as the point of reference for the formation of the unity and integrity of a newly secular public.[44] In short, the State achieves the aims bequeathed to it by the *complexio* to the extent that it now includes exclusion.[45]

Both of these techniques, however, repeatedly undermine the end at which they aim. The State's attempt to create political form and maintain order through the use of force results in an "armed peace" that, in the concrete, amounts to a constant preparation for the next war, while its attempt to produce and maintain public unity and integrity through decisions on the identity of a public enemy constantly reintroduces into the internal space of the State a trace of the same unlimited hostility, the suppression of which is (as in Hobbes's elimination of the *bellum omnium contra omnes*) the main justification for the State's existence in the first place.[46] The means for resolving conflict within Christian Europe turn out to be plagued by a similar infelicity, only now acted out on a global scale: Europe attempts to expunge and expel the trace of unlimited hostility by instituting the *jus publicum europæum*, which creates an order of limited hostility (formalized warfare, distinction of criminal and enemy) within Europe only by demanding and justifying an order of unlimited hostility toward Europe's exterior (in the form of colonial conquest and genocide). In every case, in other words, modern political order discovers that it *must aim at*, but *cannot attain*, a set of goals—peace on Earth, mediation and reconciliation between opposites, the production of political form—that have been set for it, and indeed bequeathed to it, by the very form of medieval representation it also aggressively displaces. Modern political mediation therefore finds itself in a position where it can only fully legitimate its existence with reference to a set of inherited concepts to which it is also especially vulnerable. It discovers that it is fated to attempt a set of tasks (the ex nihilo creation of political form, peace, and reconciliation) that is both *necessary* (because the *complexio* is now missing, because opposing forces remain, and because peace and reconciliation provide the modern state with its raison d'être) and *impossible* (because, above all, in the thoroughly secularized modern epoch, there is no equivalent to the theological concept of miraculous creation; there is only making, fabrication, production—or instrumental reason, the work of *homo faber*).[47] To even approximate the realization of its inner aims—which are, to repeat, not its own, but those it inherits from the *complexio*—modern mediation seeks to forget the medieval origin that is at once indispensable for it and unsettling to it, and to that exact degree leaves itself exposed to destabilization by a genealogy written from a Catholic standpoint.

But though Schmittian thought is thus, indeed, for Galli, a Catholic genealogy of the Modern,[48] Galli also cautions that Schmitt's relation to Catholicism not be misunderstood as one of religious belief or even nostalgia. When Schmitt thinks the emergence of modern mediation with reference to its secularization of the *complexio*, he does not suppose that a return to the *complexio* is either desirable or possible.[49] Nor, on Galli's reading, does Schmitt really even mourn the passing of the *complexio*. Schmitt's achievement is rather to have occupied that standpoint *from which* a thoroughly secularized modern mediation genealogically derives its innermost aims, *through which* a thoroughly secularized modern mediation refuses to understand itself, and *to which* all of its institutions and practices are thus especially vulnerable.[50] Schmitt's idiosyncratic reading of the *complexio* is, in other words, a way to think the "origin of politics" outside of the standard points of self-understanding that modernity privileges in its own self-justifying historical narratives of its emergence. It is an attempt to name a crisis in which the old order (the *complexio*) has irreversibly dissolved and in which the new order (the modern State-Form) cannot accomplish the goals it inherits from the *complexio* (reconciliation and peace).[51] Schmitt does not, then, analyze modernity from the standpoint of a fully intact Catholic faith or ideology; nor does he really even presuppose that his account of *complexio* is accurate (which is why empirical or historicist refutations of Schmitt miss the mark). The *complexio* is simply the blind spot of modern mediation, that concept that enables us to grasp in genealogical terms the reconciliation that modern mediation must aim at but cannot achieve.

Here, indeed, because of the manifestly tragic character of the crisis Schmitt thinks, we may clarify the way that crisis finds its double in the critic. For Schmitt, the crisis that the *occasio* imposes on the thought and being of the critic is not the plentitude of an infinity. It is the poverty of a Nothing. It is the utter privation of order, an unsayable opacity internal to the critic's knowledge that is not a "trauma" in the psychoanalytic sense, but simply an absence of form-giving speech, the lack of any language that can resolve or even just describe the unprecedented crises of the Modern, the intrusion of the nameless into the order of the named. Indeed, it is this vacuum, this "inability to explain," that then serves as the inexhaustible resource for the prolixity of the critic's criticism. And while it would be tempting to make sense of this epochal crisis-event by calling it an *interregnum*, Galli does not, to my knowledge, do so in any of his writings, perhaps because this would be to use a juridical concept, and to give juridical form, to an experience and an event that, to the contrary, mark the *failure* of all juridical forms, both modern and medieval, and that consequently would be more properly characterized as an epochal anomie or, as Galli would later write, chaos.[52]

5

On Galli's reading, therefore, Schmitt's oeuvre amounts to a single metonymic chain, a single series of attempts to name a crisis that modernity itself cannot name: the real contradiction that is the origin of politics.[53] Schmitt's achievement was to have written *the genealogy of the political*, where "the political" is a name for an unnameable crisis, an originary contradictoriness, a "drift" (*deriva*) of terms that can only be understood with reference to its derivation from the obscure Void at the origin of modern politics, and where "genealogy" is the work of tracking the twists and turns the "political" silently exerts on the "schemata" or "figures" with reference to which modern theories, institutions, and practices try to attain stability and self-understanding.[54] What this genealogy finds is that modern politics acts out, without also remembering, the Void that comes into being when the constitutive crises that give rise to modern politics negate *the content* of premodern concepts (e.g., that Jesus is God) while also elevating *the form* of those concepts (e.g., the Sovereign Person).[55] Modern politics, it would seem, would rather *order itself around a void* than be *devoid of order*. The hallmark of modern politics, from this point of view, is what Galli calls a "coazione all'ordine" or a "coazione della forma"—a "compulsion toward order" or "compulsion for form" in which modern politics discovers itself to be governed by a "compulsion to repeat" in an almost psychoanalytic sense of the word. Not unlike the compulsions produced by the death drive,[56] modernity's compulsions for form and order spur its theories, institutions, and practices to try repeatedly to return to a lost state of equilibrium or homeostasis. And not unlike the death drive, modernity's various attempts to actualize its inherited schemata of premodern equilibria succeed only in introducing disequilibria and excess (*dismisura*) into its very own political forms: the more modernity's compulsion for form actualizes itself, the more it simply injects its own unthought—its genealogical origin in the Void—into the very forms it also seeks to stabilize, concretize, and order. For this same reason, the full or complete actualization of modernity's compulsion to form would—again, not unlike the death drive—end up zeroing out the forms of modern politics itself: unrestrained and left to its own devices, this compulsion would achieve only incoherence, deformation, and disintegration.

Schmitt sees the potential for this chaos; his thought is nothing other than the genealogy of this anomic drive (or, we might say, this "destituent power").[57] That is why Schmitt's thought can't be reduced just to this or that familiar keyword, stock formulation, methodological program, or popular antithesis, or derived from any one of his texts to the exclusion of the others. For Galli, "Schmitt" is a name for a theoretical gaze that's able to track the symptoms of the "compulsion for form" in modern politics, and to trace those symptoms to their genealogical origin in the Void that founded modern politics in the first place. It's a name for a theoretical standpoint that interprets modern politics not from the perspective of modern theories (where the Modern appears as a self-founding system in which reason gives birth to the very practices and institutions it also then judges), but as a *palimpsest*, a text whose emergence from the premodern renders the Modern constitutively non-identical with itself and permanently incomplete on its own terms. Far from being the name for a neutral "device" or "instrument," a theoretical "tool" to be used by a theorist who is implicitly figured as *homo faber*, "Schmitt" here then ultimately becomes a name for the irruption of the Void into theory itself. Better: "Schmitt" here becomes a metonym for a crisis of representation so acute that it recoils on thought itself, manifesting itself in a most unexpected way: in the inability of thought to give a proper name to its own most intimate potentialities and activities.

From this, in turn, emerges a counterintuitive account of Schmitt's Nazism. Under conditions of a neoliberal political economy, whose forms of self-justification compel us to make constant reference to the dangers of totalitarianism, discourses on Nazism tend to be more symptomatic than analytic.[58] The Anglophone discussion of Schmitt's Nazism is no exception. The prevailing reading of Schmitt's Nazism seems to pivot on the question of how to "periodize" Schmitt's Nazism, and as such more often than not dissolves into microscopic disputes over historicist and biographical details. To this reading, Galli offers a simple but bold hermeneutic alternative: there is only a single synchronic caesura that runs throughout Schmitt's entire oeuvre, a single "immanent risk" that marks *all* "phases" of Schmittian thought.[59] Galli draws out the dialectic of this risk by seizing on a remark by Schmitt in his preface to the 1972 Italian edition of *Der Begriff des Politischen*. There, after a short précis of his theses on the criterion of the political, Schmitt addresses the question of the hermeneutic horizon within which his theses ought to be interpreted. The impulse of his theses, Schmitt insisted, is scientific (*scientifico*), in the sense that "they do not make any move to situate themselves in the right and to push their adversaries into non-right. On the other hand, 'science is but a small power' [English in the original], and in the ambit of the political the freedom of independent thought always entails a supplementary risk."[60] It is essential to understand that even though, on Schmitt's own terms, this "supplementary risk" is antithetical to scientific thought as Schmitt understands it, there is nevertheless no way to rid or purify Schmittian scientific thought of that risk. The inconsistency of Schmittian science with itself—its permanent and constitutive openness to polemic, ideology, and propaganda—is utterly consistent with science in the Schmittian sense; it is the manifestation, in Schmitt's own criticism, of the crisis Schmitt thinks in and through his genealogy of the political, of his discovery that modern political institutions are radically incomplete in relation to their own attempts at peace, security, and reconciliation. "The objectivity of conflict," as Galli pithily stated in 1986, "implies the non-objectivity . . . of science."[61] Or, as he later would put it: "Schmitt's work is born in, and is characterized by, a polemical impulse and an existential positioning that are targeted and militant. It is thanks to this impulse and this positioning—and not despite it—that Schmitt is capable of a radical analysis of politics. . . . Ideology is the 'gate of hell' that leads Schmitt to knowledge of the 'political,' and it is the dramatic and irritating condition thanks to which Schmitt is not only an ideologue but also an important thinker."[62] If Schmittian "political science" is science not *despite* but *because of* its polemical and ideological character, then political science that is *not* plagued by the risk (and perhaps temptation) of its own polemicity is *not political thought at all*. It is thought that, to the contrary, *suppresses* the political, that stands outside the crisis it criticizes, that seeks to immunize itself from the crisis that the "political" itself is. Political thought that does not seek to immunize itself from the political, however, will suffer from a very different risk. It will share with modern politics a certain tragic susceptibility to dissolve itself from within. It will reproduce, now in the mode of thought, the constitutive risk that troubles all modern political institutions: it will be unable to become what it is without also supplementing itself with a polemicity that threatens to undermine its form, coherence, and integrity as thought. But just as political thought that fully *suppresses* its polemicity is not truly political thought, neither is political thought that fully *succumbs* to this immanent risk. By Schmitt's own account, it becomes something else: polemic, "an attempt to push its adversary into non-right," or, put simply, the epistemological equivalent of the destruction of the unjust enemy, the unbracketed hostility that Schmitt regarded as a plague on the house of the Modern.

This gives Galli a new and different way to avoid the paralogism that so often governs readings of Schmitt's relation to Nazism. According to this reasoning, if Schmitt was Nazi, then surely he was not a thinker; but if Schmitt was a thinker, then surely he was not a Nazi. It is, in short, inconceivable that one could be *both* a Nazi *and also* a thinker.[63] On Galli's reading, by contrast, the task of reading Schmitt is not to quarantine his Nazism to the period from 1933 to 1936 in order to liberate the rest of his work for neutral analytic "use" or even for leftist reappropriation. Nor is it, on the basis of a deeply ambivalent logic of taboo, to treat the whole of Schmittian thought as if it were tainted, as though Schmitt's anti-Semitism were somehow so powerful and mysterious in its ways that it is akin to a contagious and communicable disease, an incurable illness against which the only possible safeguard is complete and total immunization. It is to understand Schmitt's Nazism as the extreme actualization of a potential for regression and domination that is internal not only to Schmittian thought but also, as Horkheimer and Adorno argued, to the Enlightenment itself.[64] The immanent risk of Schmittian thought, Galli wrote in 1979, is "the risk of transforming scientific exposition into propaganda, of surrendering to the polemicity (polemicità) implicit in the discovery of the political in order to support, historically, a contingent political practice."[65] That, according to Galli, "Schmitt fell into this risk precisely when he 'used' the general form of the 'political' in a pro-Nazi sense" does not, however, mean that this development of Schmitt's thought was either necessary or inevitable.[66] To the contrary, Galli argues: "If it is true that Schmitt's Nazi phase fully realized all of the risks inherent in the structure of Schmittian thought, it is also true that this realization is ultimately a betrayal—both theoretical and practical—that does not occur necessarily or automatically, but that instead requires a conscious personal will, dictated primarily by opportunism, and academic and political ambition."[67] Here where Galli's understanding of Schmitt seems to be at its most "forgiving" (for having abstained from polemic), his immanent critique is in fact at its strongest, and his negative dialectical alternative to "imputative reading" becomes most apparent. Phrased in its sharpest possible terms, Galli's point is not only that Schmitt is personally responsible for his Nazism (he was not, in other words, "held hostage" by the Nazis) but also that Schmitt's evil is not to be sought in his thought, but rather in the immanence within his thought of what Hannah Arendt might call "thoughtlessness" (her later, more philosophical term for the "banality of evil").[68] Thoughtlessness is not the same as a simple lack of thought; it does not imply that Schmitt became a Nazi in a fit of absentmindedness. It implies that Schmitt's Nazism is the complete actualization of the polemicity that Schmitt could not fail to think if he was to remain loyal to his insight into the "political," yet to which he needed to resist surrendering if his insight into the "political" was to retain its character as thought. It is a sign that Schmitt's thought is nonidentical with itself. And this, in turn, has a startling implication: another actualization of Schmitt's thought is possible, one to which Schmitt the person would not consent, but to which his impersonal thought cannot but yield.

Can we then also say that Galli does for Schmitt's oeuvre what Lacan did for Freud's and Althusser for Marx's? Galli does, after all, perform something very much resembling a "return to Schmitt," explicating the textual principles on the basis of which alone the specific unity of Schmitt's theoretical formation may then come to light. But as distinct from Lacan's return to Freud or Althusser's return to Marx, Galli's re-reading of Schmitt is not, in the end, an attempt to retrieve or recuperate Schmitt's teachings. To the contrary, Galli's unprecedented philological labor culminates in a curt claim about the definitive and irreversible exhaustion of Schmittian thought in the global age. Galli's immanent critique of Schmitt—not only in the degree of its breadth and depth but also in the quality of its immanence—amounts to a test addressed to readers of Schmitt.

If Galli's scholarship is any example, it would seem that the fewer Schmittian texts we read (the more we limit our reading of Schmitt, say, to *Concept of the Political* or *Political Theology*, or more recently *Nomos of the Earth*), and the more carelessly we read these texts (the more our hermeneutic encounter with Schmitt's texts is limited to the extraction of keywords, formulas, or timeless and abstract "logics"), the more acutely we will suffer from the illusion that Schmittian thought is adequate for thinking through who we have become today, and the more we will prolong "Schmittian logic" past its own immanent expiration date. Galli's example also would seem to suggest that the converse is true as well: the more deeply and widely we read Schmitt's writings, and the more loyal we remain to the kernel of Schmittian thought in our own thought, the more we will realize just how pointless is Schmitt's thought in a present in which Schmitt's contradictory oeuvre no longer sustains a relation to the *occasio*—the emergence of modern politics—from which alone it originates.[69] In this case, the instrumentalist "use" of Schmittian thought in the global age not only betrays what was most alive in Schmitt's thought; it also allows us to comfort ourselves with the reassuring fantasy that coming crises will so resemble those of modernity that the critique of the latter will suffice for the critique of the former as well.

The true precedent for Galli's work on Schmitt, in this respect, is not then Althusser on Marx or Lacan on Freud. It is Adorno's "immanent critique" of Heidegger. Galli's achievement is precisely to have "re-liquified" the *occasio* that is the innermost core of Schmittian thought and that risks being "reified" to the extent that we limit ourselves to the instrumental "application" of Schmittian "logics."[70] His teaching is that it is ultimately *Schmitt's own thought* that obliges us to abandon the reification that anchors this consoling position. The challenge of Carlo Galli—the challenge of a post-Schmittian thought—is to read Carl Schmitt so completely, so carefully, and so loyally that we *therefore* turn to face a set of crises in relation to which Schmitt has, precisely, nothing to say.

6

In *Janus's Gaze*, Galli develops this challenge in a manner as under-stated as it is systematic. As distinct from his 2010 book *Political Spaces and Global War*, in which Galli treats Schmitt's thought as a point of departure for an analysis of the global age (which is also, for Galli, a post-Schmittian age), *Janus's Gaze* contains essays that, at least at first glance, seem to belong quite traditionally to the genre of the history of political thought (and in particular to the subgenre of Reinhart Kosel-leck's *Begriffsgeschichte*).[71] *Janus's Gaze* therefore opens with two chapters that explicate Schmittian thought from the interior of Schmitt's self-understanding, tracing Schmitt's thinking on the state and political theology as it develops throughout his oeuvre. At the structural center of the book, meanwhile, the reader will find two chapters that clarify Schmittian thought from the exterior of Schmitt's self-understanding, with reference to three thinkers—Machiavelli, Spinoza, and Strauss—whose names are each "improper" in their own way, and whose thought has been confused or even conflated with Schmitt's at various points in the history of Schmitt commentary. The intent of these four chapters is clear: to specify the sense in which Schmitt is a "classic of political thought,"[72] and as a means to that end to demarcate the precise line that distinguishes the inside of the Schmittian oeuvre from its outside. Implicit in these chapters, however, both as their condition of possibility and as their common horizon, the attentive reader will find the coordinates for a very new relation to Schmittian thought—one that turns away from the terms of epideictic and forensic rhetoric (centered on problems of praise and blame, accusation and defense) and toward those of negative dialectics (centered on the problem of the nonidentity between the identical and the nonidentical).[73] Only in the final chapter of *Janus's Gaze*, where Galli outlines the terms of Schmitt's desuetude in the global age, does this new relation begin to become explicit, and does it become clear that *the use* of Schmittian thought and *the abuse* of Schmittian thought are, increasingly, one and the same thing.

As the watchword for this unorthodox reading of Schmitt, the reader should bear in mind the name that provides Galli with the title of his book. For Galli, it would seem, "Carl Schmitt" is not actually the most felicitous name for the two-faced character of Carl Schmitt's person and work. For that purpose, Galli turns instead to an almost archaic figure, Janus, to whom Schmitt makes passing reference in his *Roman Catholicism and Political Form* to name the "diversity and ambiguity" of the Roman Catholic Church.[74] For Ovid, Galli reminds his readers, "Janus symbolizes the doubleness of things, the passage from inside and outside, and the transmutations and the determinations of the elements emerging from primordial chaos (and 'chaos,' don't forget, was Janus's old name)."[75] As such, Galli suggests, "Janus" is a fitting name for the unspoken core of Schmitt's genealogical inquiry into the "doubleness" or "contradictoriness" at the origin of modern politics.

Given the frequency with which Schmitt's name traps critics of Schmitt's work into becoming critics of Schmitt's person—or, more to the point, given the way that Schmitt's *proper name* also doubles as *an improper name*—the significance of Galli's displacement of "Schmitt" with "Janus" can't be underestimated. To nickname Schmitt's thought with a non-Schmittian name may at first seem but a small displacement. In fact, it accomplishes something quite significant: *it prepares the conditions under which thought becomes able to release itself from the obligation to treat Schmitt's name as the object of love or hate, praise or blame, accusation or defense.* It places thought in a position where it can relate itself instead to a certain doubleness or contradictoriness that's at once the very *signature* of Schmitt's thought and also *the dynamic by which Schmitt's thought passes into nonidentity with itself.* Thought thus oriented no longer has any need to constrain itself to undialectical oppositions centered on Schmitt's name (praise or blame, guilt or innocence, etc.). It instead becomes able to train its gaze on a very different problem—the doubling of the crisis and the critic—that is at once *the innermost operation of Schmitt's thought and the movement by which Schmitt's thought renders itself inoperative.*

As a specifically *negative* dialectic, the "non-Schmittian Schmittology" that emerges from Galli's reading of Schmitt may be clarified by distinguishing it from the more traditional dialectization of Schmitt recently undertaken by Jean-François Kervégan. For Kervégan, the purpose of reading Schmitt today is "to depart from Schmitt" in a double sense: to use Schmitt as a point of departure for one's analyses of the present, and *as such* to take leave of Schmittian thought.[76] Whatever else it may share with Galli's approach to Schmitt, Kervégan's reading is incompatible with Galli's on at least one crucial point. Whereas Kervégan seeks to negate Schmitt's thought in order to preserve it at a higher level, the dialectic of "passage" that Galli discerns in Schmitt's writings ends up leading to a very different conclusion: that today Schmitt's gaze has passed into its terminal phase, a phase characterized by its "outdatedness [*inattualità*] and disorientation."[77]

Informing this claim is an unusual concept of historicity that can be sharpened by putting Galli into conversation with two thinkers who already are well known in Anglophone academia. In his 1977 *Marxism and Literature*, Raymond Williams outlined a fourfold schema for the analysis of what he calls "epochs." In order to recognize the "internal dynamic relations" that specify epochs, Williams argued, it first of all was necessary to understand what he called the "dominant" of any given epoch. The "dominant," for Williams, is not simply a synonym for "hegemony," as is often assumed. It's more precisely the closed circuit by which institutions, practices, and traditions justify and explain themselves according to self-understandings that, circulating in culture, then come to reciprocally confirm those institutions, practices, and traditions as reality itself.[78] In order to understand the ways the dominant maintains its dominance, Williams argued, it was necessary to attend to two additional sets of self-understanding: those that are "residual" and those that are "emergent." The "emergent" (which is not the same as the merely "novel") designates the way "new meanings, new values, new relationships, and new kinds of relationships are continually being created." It is an experience of cultural inception that produces inchoate structures whose effects can be felt and experienced at the limits of a given epoch, but that have yet to be effectively named. The "residual," meanwhile, is what has been "effectively formed in the past" but "is still active in the cultural process, not only and often not at all as an element of the past, but as an effective element of the present." In this respect the "residual" is distinct from the fourth (and often-forgotten) element in Williams's schema: the "archaic," which is to say, "that which is wholly recognized as an element of the past, to be observed, to be examined, or even on occasion to be consciously 'revived,' in a deliberately specializing way."[79]

Glossed in Williams's terms, Galli's claim about the "outdatedness" of Schmitt's gaze amounts to an intricate claim about the place and function of Schmitt's thought in the present. Schmitt's great contribution, we might say, was to have interpreted *the dominant* with reference to *the residual*. Schmitt's insight into the "tragicity" of modern politics was grounded in a genealogical grasp of the traces of the premodern that remained active and effective within the Modern. Today, however, the apparatus of modern politics no longer can be described as dominant, having lost any aura of inevitability or necessity. That aura now has passed to the institutions, theories, and practices of the global, which at the end of Schmitt's life were only just emerging, and which today seem inescapable, self-evident, and necessary—they seem to be the natural and obvious form of reality itself. But under conditions where modern politics passes from the dominant to the residual, Schmitt's thought *also* undergoes a decisive shift: the coordinates with reference to which it orients itself, in turn, pass from *the residual* to *the archaic*. This shift does not imply that Schmitt's thought will cease to be studied and discussed; to the contrary, the more Schmitt's thought passes into the archaic, the more Schmitt's thought will be ceremoniously and ritualistically "revived" in highly specialized ways. What will change in this shift is something much more precise and intricate, yet also much more difficult to grasp: *the modality by which Schmitt's thought relates itself to the dominant.* Under conditions where the occasion of Schmitt's thought has become "archaic," any revival of Schmitt's writings will have been premised on the death of Schmittian thought—namely, its inability to touch any effective and active kernel in the present, its incapacity to interrupt the closed circuit that refers dominant institutions to the self-understandings that in turn affirm their continued existence, and its consequent deterioration into a one-sided gaze, an un-Janusian gaze whose *pars construens*—whose ability to tell the truth of the constitutive crises of the Modern—will then have become little more than an antiquarianism.

We may further clarify Galli's claim about Schmitt's "outdatedness" by translating it into the terms of a second text with which the Anglophone reader may be familiar: Theodor Adorno's inaugural 1931 lecture at the Frankfurt School, "The Actuality [*Aktualität*] of Philosophy." In this text, Adorno offers what at first seems to be a simple formulation of what it means for a philosophy to be actual. "Only out of the historical interweaving of questions and answers," Adorno proposes, "does the question of philosophic actuality emerge precisely." That question, he argued, has nothing to do with the distinction between maturity and immaturity (with reference to which the concept of actuality often is interpreted). It pivots on a very different question: whether there exists "an adequacy between philosophic questions and the possibility of their being answered at all."[80] On these terms, it would seem, the "actuality" of a philosophy would not derive primarily from its own qualities or powers, but instead from conditions that are extraphilosophical, even nonphilosophical, in character. A philosophy that is "actual" would be a philosophy that philosophizes under conditions that, in turn, allow for its problems to attain resolution. But if that is so, Adorno then suggests, then it may be the case that recent philosophy—contemporary philosophy—is not actual at all. Certainly, a philosophy would come to lack actuality if it were to close itself off to the questions posed for it by the experiences of its present. But philosophy also would come to lack actuality in another way as well. Under conditions where immediate experience has become so random and contingent that it no longer can provide any material to offer philosophic responses to philosophic questions, philosophy would become inactual not by *closing itself off from* the present, but instead by *opening itself* to the present—by trying to become adequate to a present that has become completely antiphilosophical, by posing only those questions that can be answered under conditions of a present that has become constitutively opposed to the very possibility of philosophy. Faced with such a situation, philosophy's only hope is to produce a philosophical reflection on the fact that, under conditions dominated by formlessness and anomie, philosophic form itself has become impossible. Philosophy's only hope, that is to say, is to understand the unanswerability of its questions not as a symptom of philosophy's obsolescence or inadequacy, but as a sign that philosophic self-questioning now *itself* must serve as a refuge for the "correct and just reality" that has been exiled from the present. Although philosophy may have missed the moment to actualize itself, it thus becomes actual nevertheless, but in a counterintuitive way: by producing philosophical self-consciousness of "the inactuality of philosophy" under conditions where antiphilosophic forces have so fully actualized themselves that those forces have come to be synonymous with experience itself.

This is an aporetic claim, to be sure, but parsing it will help the reader to clarify the concept of historicity informing Galli's claims about the "outdatedness" of Schmitt's gaze.[81] On Galli's reading, it should be said, Schmitt's questions were consistently unanswerable relative to their present. The actuality of Schmittian thought consisted precisely in its self-conscious inactuality, its ability to reactivate the traces of the premodern that subsisted at the limit of the Modern, to treat those traces as occasions to pose insoluble problems to the institutions, practices, and theories of modern politics. This is what Galli calls Schmitt's *pars destruens*: his ability to critique, demystify, and negate modern political forms.[82] If today, by contrast, Schmitt's gaze is "outdated," this is not because it has ceased to pose unanswerable questions. *It's because Schmitt's questions have become unanswerable in a new and different sense.* They are unanswerable not because Schmitt's works pose untimely questions that reveal the originary Void concealed in modern political forms. They are unanswerable because, in the absence of any self-consciousness that Schmittian thought is precisely the thought *of* that originary Void, Schmitt's works have ceased to pose *any question at all*: the primary mode of the relation between Schmitt and the present is no longer genealogy but now just "application." If Schmitt's writings have been able to bloom in the present, in other words, this is because the inactuality of Schmittian thought—its nonrelation to its own constitutive *occasio*—is securely in place as the prior condition and horizon for any possible reading of Schmitt today. The proof is in the pudding: Schmitt's thought has been integrated into the critique of the present today as little more than a disjointed series of faddish keywords, selective appropriations, isolated close readings, scandalous provocations, antiquarian intellectual histories, popular but reified formulations, or, worst of all, neutral methodological instruments. Under these conditions, Schmitt's thought is unanswerable not because it poses riddles that resist any answer, but because it is understood no longer to pose any unanswerable riddle in the first place. Far from disclosing the "tragicity" of politics in the present, Schmittian thought presents itself today as little more than a "tool" to be employed, as a series of disconnected and separable texts unified only by a proper name—a name that may be attacked by some and defended by others, but that all parties nevertheless agree to "use," as if it meant something.

7

In general, the Anglophone reception of Schmitt has proceeded along the lines prepared for it in advance by the standard use of the proper name within the history of political thought. According to this thoroughly taxonomic operation, thinking and categorizing are one and the same thing, such that good thinking and clean categories become synonyms. What this operation cannot think, however, is the way thinking so construed allows itself to be compelled by a form that is latently juridical in provenance. For Aristotle, it must be recalled, the juridical term that is translated into English as "accusation" is the Greek katēgoría, which gives rise to an English word that today seems altogether nonjuridical: "category." On these terms, to categorize is precisely to accuse, such that the work of categorization (attributing predicates to various beings in order to divide them up into species and genres) doubles as the work of legal judgment (attributing predicates to various beings in order to allocate praise and blame, innocence and guilt).[83]

Citations of "Schmitt," especially but not only in English, bring this doubleness to the surface: they excessively actualize the sense in which the practice of neutral categorization (of classifying thought with reference to the proper name) always already also hosts within itself the latent possibility for juridical accusation. From this perspective, in fact, Schmitt's name is in a category by itself. Here, after all, is a name that is so improper—so intolerable—that, for some, it even comes to exemplify the very paradigm of the intolerable itself—of evil that manifests itself, self-consciously, as philosophy. In the name "Carl Schmitt," therefore, we would seem to encounter a categorization that *so fully exemplifies the juridical form implicit in the practice of categorization itself* that it *leaves us unable to distinguish between categorization and accusation at all.* But where the taxonomic and the juridical enter into indistinction—where categorization begins to double as a form of accusation and vice versa—the work of categorization itself begins to short-circuit. In this instance, it's no longer possible even to categorize the category "category" itself. One can no longer sort out whether a category like "Schmitt" operates as a categorization or as an accusation, since "Schmitt" is both a categorization and an accusation—and therefore neither, since the conflicts of judicial proceedings are the very antithesis of neutral taxonomic classifications. Brought to bear on Schmitt's person and work, it would then seem, categorization becomes nonidentical with itself, passing from self-consciousness into unself-consciousness, and thus too beginning to exhaust its epistemological potential.

Faced with this dilemma, some readers might be tempted to scoff, snort, and carry on with business as usual, continuing to use the name "Schmitt" as if everyone knew what they were talking about. The history of philosophy, after all, has never assumed an especially philosophical relation to its presuppositions regarding history, and Galli's contributions are hardly likely to change that. Other readers, by contrast, might begin to doubt whether it is even possible to use this name in a fully self-conscious way—or whether, to the contrary, the proper use of Schmitt's proper name is to mark the constitutive limit of any use of any proper name whatsoever, up to and including Schmitt's, as a name for thought. For such readers, the proper name might cease to function as a classificatory operation, and might begin to emerge instead as a problem for thought itself—requiring us to think through the strange dynamic by which thought actualizes the potential for the proper name to not-be.[84] For these readers, the "improper name" might cease to function primarily as a synonym for an intolerable name. It instead might begin to serve as a metonym for a more radical set of phenomena, for the emergence of a set of experiences—call them "impolitical" or "impersonal"—that exceed both the horizon of modern politics and the lexicon of modern thought (up to and including thought that positions itself, as did Schmitt's, at the very limit of modern thought).[85]

Still other readers might protest: to divest Schmitt of his proper name is not at all to lance the boil of fascination with Schmitt. It's to absolve Schmitt himself, and as such to hush our consciences before a figure who, more than any other, clearly deserves our full fury. Nothing, however, could be further off the mark. The quietist reading of Schmitt is the reading that treats Schmitt as a touchstone by which we reassure ourselves of our own good names and clean conscience, at a moment in history where nothing could be less certain.[86] It's the reading that supposes thought's capacity for evil to be derived not from thought itself, but merely from thought's complicity with something supposedly alien to thought. This is a reading that ultimately assimilates the problem of Schmitt's impropriety to the classic theme of the political philosopher's complicity with tyranny—a theme in the history of political philosophy that's as old as the history of political philosophy itself, beginning at least with Plato's relation with Dionysus. But not only did Schmitt himself use this theme to rationalize his own relation to tyranny;[87] worse, this theme distracts us from a much more disquieting and intimate source for evil. Thought yoked to the proper name turns out to conspire against thinking itself: the more thought is named, the less thought is thought.[88] But the less thought is thought, and the more thought deprives itself of itself, the more thought gives itself over to its own privative modality, to its own deficit of existence—to its own immanent thoughtlessness. The path of least resistance, to be sure, is to let political philosophy's museum of improper names—Schmitt above all—reassure us that our own names, by contrast, remain proper. But even the most proper name hosts a potential that resists the distinction between the named and the nameless. Amorphous and aporetic though this potential may be, no thinking that neglects it will be able to resist what banality will leave in its place.

Janus is the ancient Roman two-faced god—the god of the Origin who can also gaze at the End. According to Ovid, who put him on stage in the first book of the *Fasti*,[1] Janus symbolizes the doubleness of things, the passage between inside and outside, the transmutation and determination of the elements emerging from primordial chaos (and "chaos" was, in fact, Janus's old name). It doesn't seem out of place to suggest an analogy between the doubled gaze of the mythical god and the political gaze of Carl Schmitt. The German jurist had the same ambivalent capacity to see the two faces of the "political," the same ability to grasp the passage from formlessness to form, from chaos to order, from war to peace, as well as their fatal reversibility, which is to say, the passage from form to crisis. Schmitt's theory—a "vision" that was, in his case, also an "experience"—was designed to fit with the double face of the Modern itself. It can face the simultaneous disconnection and co-implication between Idea and contingency that generates and shoots through the Modern; moreover, it can face both the epochal compulsion for order and the impossibility of that order. The wisdom of this twofold gaze allowed Schmitt to see in modern politics both God and the absence of God; it allowed him to think politics as that energy which at once establishes boundaries and transgresses them, which generates not only revolutions but also constitutions, which produces not only decisions but also forms.

Schmitt shared with Janus not only a two-faced gaze but also a two-faced nature: Schmitt was himself double, both in his historical praxis and in his theoretical proposals, suspended between deconstruction and construction, between respect for tradition and boldness. In his continuous oscillation between predictability and unexpected blows, between banality and sudden strokes of genius, between genealogy and ideology, between system and aphorism, between science and literature, Schmitt is an obligatory rite of passage for anyone who wants to think politics radically.

The bibliography on Schmitt is by now extensive and diverse, ranging from jurisprudence to political theory, from philosophy to the history of ideas. The numerous editions, translations, and collections of his works, the publication of his letters and the existence of specialized journals devoted to him, the many conferences, monographs, and essays that incessantly reinterpret his thought, the polemics that continually arise around his controversial intellectual and political activities, the formation, if not of "schools," then certainly of hermeneutic currents—all of this demonstrates that Schmitt has today become a classic of political thought (perhaps one of the last). His thought has taken effect in very different modes of reflection on politics, inside of Europe as well as outside of it, leaving a confrontation with his thought inevitable. Albeit with understandable delay, powerful academic apparatuses are now at work on his thought, producing good results with regularity and effectiveness.

All of this increased attention, though, does not mean that there is consensus on the key that can unlock Schmitt's intellectual work. Even in countries where the attention is more recent (such as the Anglo-Saxon academy, especially in the United States, and the Spanish-speaking world), Schmitt is seen both as a brilliant deconstructionist and as the disquieting father of all conservatives. His thought is valued for its critical edge, but it's also seen as reactionary and propagandistic ideology. It's possible to write about Schmitt in order to reject him as the inventor of "homicidal ideas" (not only during his Nazi phase, but also earlier), but also in order to delegitimize any nonliberal thought. Schmitt can also become the object of apologetic unquestioning belief, based on an appreciation of the perennial validity of his ideas. One certainly could place him in a sort of museum of ideas where, visited by specialists, he stays quiet while also remaining the disquieting specimen of a ferocious but now extinct age, in which danger predominated. On the other hand, one could treat him as a ladder that must be thrown away after use, or as a giant on whose shoulder one may climb to look further on.

Before specifying the mode of reading at work in this book—which follows the one I proposed in *Genealogia della politica*[2]—it's important to spell out another consideration. One doesn't do justice to Schmitt's thought by insisting that it be integrated peacefully within a general theory of politics (for example, as a contribution to the understanding of the role of violence and conflict in politics). With this, in fact, one misses its deepest significance, its disquieting and truly revolutionary side. To think politics, especially through Schmitt's categories, implies the awareness that what one is trying to measure touches, in reality, an incommensurable: the awareness, in other words, that the defined—the world of what is rationally knowable—lives alongside and coexists with the undefined and the undefinable (which does not, however, exempt one from seeking to distinguish each "according to its own principles").[3] The claim of this book is that the undefinability and incommensurability against which we struggle, but which at the same time also fascinates us, is the double-sided origin of modern politics. It is this origin, in other words, that accounts for the indetermination of Order, for the absence of God, for violence as the immanent destiny of the "political," and at the same time, for the modern compulsion to order. The tragic awareness of this origin, and the intellectual stimulant that results, is Schmitt's true legacy. His profound nonhumanistic humanity consisted in his announcement of the radical contingency, and at the same time the epochal necessity, of politics and of its knowledge.

....

There are two methodological devices that allow us to read Schmitt properly. The first is to distinguish his "doctrine" from his "thought." Schmitt's ideological side—which often leads him to attribute to various real historical entities (Jews, liberals, Anglo-Americans, pacifists, and so on) the responsibility for dynamics that logically are part of modernity—should be set apart from his theoretical capacity to radically touch upon the deep structure of the Modern. This is not, of course, a distinction between a mythical veil and a scientific substance: Schmitt's work is born in, and is characterized by, a polemical impulse and an existential positioning that is targeted and militant. It is thanks to this impulse, and this positioning—and not despite it—that Schmitt is capable of a radical analysis of politics. To read Schmitt, one must therefore know how to pass through the perilous path of ideology (enduring, along the way, disturbances and shocks) and to understand that precisely this sometimes precipitates concepts that, far from remaining stable or clear, are exposed to the structuring and destructuring power of the origin, of conflict, of chaos. Ideology is the "gate of hell" that leads Schmitt to knowledge of the "political," and it is the dramatic and irritating condition thanks to which Schmitt is not only an ideologue but also an important thinker.

Even though Schmitt certainly can be classified as authoritarian and traditionalist Catholic, as fundamentalist and antimodern, as belonging to the German right wing even before his Nazi phase, and to conservativism after that phase, his thought nevertheless can't be reduced to these categories. He can be grouped under these rubrics both because of his explicit will, and because of the objective articulations of his arguments; he can't because his thought treated his positions (which, in the concrete, sustained his thought as he sought to transform it into "doctrine") as a sort of propellant or occasion to do more—to arrive at the concepts, to grasp their contingent origin in conflict, to reach their constitutive epochality. It's in this gesture of radicality, which is sometimes only implicit, that we find the properly theoretical valence internal to Schmitt's performances. It's in this movement from ideology to concept and origin that we find the genealogical elements of the "system" that supports Schmitt's otherwise nonsystematic works. And it's for this reason that we, in turn, read him.

Given Schmitt's peculiarities and specificities, and given the true difficulty of deciphering this author beyond his apparent clarity, a second methodological device is necessary: Schmitt must be interpreted by difference, not by analogy or assonance. One should, in other words, underline what distinguishes him from other thinkers, rather than look for similarities. If one chases after the resemblances, one might end up (and this has in fact happened) assimilating Schmitt to the thinkers of the Frankfurt School because of his critique of parliamentarism, or assimilating him to Hayek because he distinguished between liberalism and democracy; one might also mistake him for a reactionary mystic of the *Reich*, or take him as one of the fathers of American political realism, or confound his decisionism with Benjamin's theological violence. Besides this risk, which is inherent to a strictly systematic exegesis of Schmitt's thought, there is also the risk of using Schmittian categories and methods for orienting thought and practice in the present.

The two essays that open this volume mainly deploy the first of these two devices, exposing the path that allows us to grasp the internal coherence of Schmitt's thought in its various phases and in its interweaving of thought and doctrine, of positions and concepts, of doctrine and genealogy. These chapters offer two comprehensive interpretations of Schmitt's thought on modern political form (the State) and its constitutive horizon (political theology as a particular reading of secularization). The third and fourth chapters deploy the second methodological device, distinguishing and differentiating Schmitt from those who are proximate to him and his beliefs. These chapters are dedicated to the complex relations between Schmitt and Machiavelli, and to the intricate interpretive bind that connects Schmitt to Spinoza and Strauss. The last chapter discusses the question of whether Schmitt's thought can help to decipher the global age—a crucial question, because deciding on it requires an evaluation of his thought as a whole.

The general thesis that governs this reading of Schmitt is that Schmitt's complexity is internal to the complexity of the modern epoch. Schmitt offers a political theory of the nexus—of the compulsion but also, at the same time, the impossibility—that links origin with form, energy with order (decisionism, the "political"). He also offers an antiprogressive epochal theory of modern history as secularization (political theology) and an antiuniversalist theory of political space as *nomos*. The result is a genealogy of the Modern—of modern European politics— that became possible during its early twentieth-century crisis. This is a genealogy that consists in grasping the other side of the Modern, in saying the unsaid (the origin) of its *logos* and narrations, in interpreting it not according to its customary motives (the conflict between subject, society, State, the ideological struggles) but according to the profound logic of its origin and its end. Schmitt's theory is, in this way, a double gaze on the double face of the Modern; but for this same reason, once his thought is taken outside of the horizon of European modernity, it risks losing its concreteness, losing contact with any genealogy, leaving only its doctrinaire side, exposing it to the risk of being reduced to obvious considerations on the necessity of the enemy and of order, on the bond between identity and hostility.

This is why, even though Schmitt's thought may appear suitable for the global age, dominated as it is by identitarian religious conflicts and by the compulsion to security, his ability to explain the dynamics of the present is actually poor and vague (aside from his enduring ability to demystify certain forms of universalism). Dragged to a space and time other than that of the Modern, Schmitt's concreteness is lost. By making reference to his categories, the present would appear as a lack and as disorder deprived of morphogenetic capacity. The force of Schmittian thought resides in its capacity to reach into the interior of any crisis—into the void internal to order—and grasp there the possibility of a new order, the constituent power of conflict. In the global age, by contrast, Schmitt can tell us only that conflict has become nonsensical, and that order is now little more than a conservative and restorative call to achieve what "must be." From the viewpoint of method, the movement that runs from ideology to concept, and from concept to genealogy, has vanished: we no longer can turn to the Janus gaze to frame the origin and the end of global phenomena and of the global subjects, which perhaps can no more be deciphered through modern "genealogized" concepts, and which wait instead to be grasped through a different sort of knowledge, with a different categorical approach—one that doesn't limit itself to the maintenance of chaotic, conflictual movements.

To conclude, if Schmitt's thought is the passage, seen from two sides, between order and conflict, and then again between form and crisis, then this passage shouldn't bring us back to its starting point. That would make it a labyrinth or maze, a place of loss and destruction, a tautological and pointless drift between Origin and End, between conflict and the exigency of order. Schmitt's thought is especially exposed to the risk of going nowhere when it's decontextualized with respect to the horizon of modernity. And this is why these essays aim not only to grasp the power of Schmitt's twofold gaze, but also to underline the necessity of surpassing him in order to move toward a new space—the necessity, in short, of posing the question of passing beyond the political theory of the passage.

Schmitt's distance from any political sensibility centered on the individual and its rights (and not just those of the private individual) rendered Schmitt's thought marginal relative to the liberal mainstream of modern politics. This was a fruitful marginality, since it enabled Schmitt to train a radically different gaze on the political logics of modernity. Today, however, the very different political logics of the global age consign this gaze to outdatedness [inattualità] and disorientation. Today, the question is not Schmitt's thought, but what exceeds that thought. After all, even a Janus gaze can't see beyond the end.

....

CHAPTER 1

SCHMITT AND THE STATE

Schmitt's confrontation with the problems of the State lasted his entire intellectual life. In this chapter, we'll discuss Schmitt's main attitudes toward the State in chronological sequence. We'll also discuss the different solutions he suggested to solve the crisis, starting from the assumption that although Schmitt's intellectual performance is indeed an extreme reading, it's not external to the dynamics of modern statuality.[1]

1. Introduction

In the first place, it's important to clarify that when Schmitt talks about the State, his point of departure is the concrete experience of the German State, which he lived with political passion and participated in intellectually. Beginning with the historical weakness of the German State and its *via crucis* [way of the cross] in the first half of the twentieth century, Schmitt analyzed the overall event of the modern European State, which he could not think except from a theoretico-epochal viewpoint, seeing it as the main aspect of political modernity. The specifically Schmittian analysis of the State is made up of the systematic interweaving of these levels—the politicological, the historical, and the theoretical.

Despite the importance of the State in all of Schmitt's political reflections, he never sees it as the "beginning" of politics, even if at times he does consider the State to be the center of politics. In general, Schmitt's fundamental disposition toward the State is ambivalence, as demonstrated by his tormented relationship with Hobbes,[2] whom he sees as the emblem of modern statuality. On the one hand, the significance of

Schmitt's complex intellectual performance consists in his understanding that in the twentieth century the State-form is no longer either the center of politics or synonymous with political order. Schmitt thought politics beyond the State, or before the State, in many different ways—ranging from the concrete experience of the destruction of the State through revolution to the crisis of parliamentarianism, from the central roles of the parties to the mingling of State and society, from the elaboration of the categories of exception, decision, and dictatorship to the concept of the "political," from his substitution of the constitution and constituent power for the State as key concepts of the political order to his deplorable Nazi adventure and his late concept of *nomos*. In each of these instances, Schmitt distanced himself from a reality and a conceptuality that were literally epochal. Schmitt's critique of the State *als ein konreter, an eine geschichtliche Epoche gebundener Begriff* [as a concrete concept that is bound to a historical epoch][3] is perhaps the most salient and constant of his critiques of modernity (one that he presents with special pathos in the late foreword to the 1963 edition of *The Concept of the Political*).[4]

On the other hand, Schmitt's juridical background left him incapable of doing away with modern statuality altogether, and unable to go radically beyond the critique of the crisis of the State in the twentieth century. Because the conceptuality of the Modern—which is also the conceptuality of the State—remained the horizon for Schmitt's nonetheless radical deconstruction, he never conceived of a politics completely detached from the State. The permanence within Schmitt's thought of two grand thematics—political unity and constituent subjectivity—together with his renunciation of the complete juridification, institutionalization, and rationalization of politics, thus position Schmitt's political reflections internal to the twentieth-century crisis of the State. In fact, the true outcome of Schmitt's thought is a paradoxical renewal of the political efficacy of the State that he obtained through the full acceptance of its instability—an "arationalistic" constructivism, if you will. Schmitt is thus a critic of the rule of law and of the liberal State, and, at the same time, a critic of the juridical positivism of the *Allgemeine Staatslehre* [general political science], which is to say, of the syntheses—between individualism and universalism, between juridical order [*diritto*],[5] power, reason—that the State-person claimed to realize. Schmitt attempted to revitalize the State by turning its liberal form—

which was, by then, already deformed—into a political and juridical form that now would derive its efficacy precisely by being aware of the powers that deform it. He conceived of a political order, that is to say, that would be able to recognize the disconnection in principle between form and reality—an efficacious order that would be mobile and not static, open and not closed, tragic and not pacified, transitional and not definitive. Even though this order would be foreign to the ideologies of legitimation elaborated by modernity (such as rationalism, liberalism, and progressivism), it nevertheless would remain modern—and, indeed, would be able to "restrain" the destructive dynamics of a modernity left to its own devices. For Schmitt, in other words, even though the State deserves to be mobilized and destructured, it also provided the efficacious political form that he acknowledges as having performed the task that would allow it to be defined as a *katechon*—a "force that restrains."[6] The function of "restraining," which was always difficult, became even more complicated in the twentieth century, so much so that the State could only continue to perform this function at the cost of a radical transfiguration of the State's own liberal form. In the wake of World War II, in fact, "restraining" became a function of order that Schmitt would view with nostalgia. It became a modality of the State no less important to Schmitt than those other modalities—such as deformation, relativization (which is to say genealogical historicization), and deconstruction—with reference to which Schmitt would both analyze and criticize the State over the years.

In his own way, therefore, Schmitt would touch on several of the main topics of twentieth-century juridical and political reflection on the State. Even if his thought is bound to a horizon that, in part, is no longer with us today, and even if his writings aimed at political objectives that surely diverge from ours, his reflections nevertheless remain an important testimony to the decline of the *jus publicum europæum*.

2. The State in Schmitt's Political Theory

I first will address the "theoretical" side of Schmitt's analysis, and then follow up by considering the "historical" and "politological" ones. This is a choice I make only for the sake of clarity: in fact, Schmitt's theoretical reflections are born from the exigencies of practice, and his philosophical reflection is born from a critique of the present.

2.1 During the first phase of Schmitt's thought, his Catholic viewpoint, which stood polemically against modern secularization, allows him to distance himself completely from the State. In his 1923 *Roman Catholicism and Political Form*,[7] Schmitt interpreted the State as the political form suitable for an epoch, modernity, that negates the traditional nexus between transcendence and politics (or, in the concrete, that criticizes the papal *auctoritas* and its mediation). In this sense, the State attempts to construct political order as a self-sufficient rational mediation, a contract producing a legal order, a technical artifice, an instrument of defense and domination that is at the disposal of the individual subject, with its rights and needs. According to Schmitt, however, the *ratio* of the modern State, which is independent from its *auctoritas* (from papal mediation, from relation with transcendence), is incapable of *repraesentatio*, which is to say, of the ability to form a public-political order that is open to the Idea (and that is hence too meaningful, complex, and concrete). Modern politics, of which the State is the proper form, does not then have a true public dimension. It is instead an ensemble of private subjectivities that believe themselves to be guaranteed by that State and that, together with every other modern ideology, are destined to anguish—to be annihilated by the triumph of technics. For Schmitt, this triumph is the true cipher and true horizon of modernity and of the State (whose origin he ascribes, in this phase of his thought, to Machiavelli). In his view, therefore, the Catholic Church is the custodian of politics, of unitary concrete form, of publicity, and of representation. The modern liberal State, by contrast, is unstable, nihilistic, incapable of any unity other than in abstract, and unable to produce a public sphere except other than at the level of the individual.

Even so, Schmitt does not plan to entrust politics to the Church: he is neither clerical nor a fundamentalist. Indeed, from the midtwenties, he will be critical of the ecclesiastical pretense—as of any other, whether of moral, economical, or of technical origin—to exercise a *potestas indirecta* [indirect power]. For Schmitt, politics pivots not so much around the Church and its triumphalism, but around the State[8]—provided, of course, that it be understood outside of its own self-interpretation.

2.2 In his 1914 book *Der Wert des Staates und die Bedeutung des Einzelnen* (The value of the State and the meaning of the individual),[9] Schmitt entrusted to the State the task of collapsing the transcendental Juridical Idea (which is, in itself, empty) into the contingency of concrete political praxis, which is to say, into the mediation between juridical order and power (which, in turn, is always in reality a "leap" or "decision"). But even though Schmitt thus assigns to the State a most crucial role, the State of which Schmitt speaks completely lacks any pretense to self-sufficiency, any presumption that it is the origin of order and politics. In Schmitt's view, in fact, the State has value only if it recognizes that it is not originary, only if it is aware that its mediation is imperfect, neither fully pacified nor completely immanent. The State has value, in other words, only if in the course of its own essential function—sovereignty—it recognizes the discontinuity between Juridical Idea and reality, between Juridical Order and Law, and only if it remains aware that *Macht* [Power], does not create *Recht* [Juridical Idea] but simply renders it effective by applying it to the concrete case. For the young Schmitt, the State with its power does not then create juridical order; to the contrary, State power realizes a Juridical Idea that precedes it. The State is thus instrumental, but without also becoming a State-machine. It works to realize juridical order (although never fully), but not to create it; and it operates the *Rechtsverwirklichung* [actualization of the Juridical Idea] on the basis of a modern "compulsion for form" that it never calls into question. The State takes charge of the necessity of political order; but at the same time, it assumes the impossibility of reaching a perfectly pacified and self-sufficient organization. As such, the State also takes on the necessity according to which political form, in order to subsist effectively, must recognize its originary and insuperable deformity.

Insofar as the task of the State is sovereignty, Schmitt argues, its task is clear: it must deal with an aporia—the noncoincidence of politics and juridical order—which is at one and the same time also the point of departure for a radical critique of the Modern (given that the Modern aims at a politics that is fully self-justified, and theorizes the full connection between politics and juridical order). This disconnect is the nonrational immediacy at the origin of the State's rational mediation. Schmitt is thus critical not only of liberalism (which thinks the State as rational mediation whose center and origin is the individual) but also of juridical positivism (which dissolves juridical order into the State). When, in *Der Wert des Staates*, Schmitt affirms the notion that every State is based on the "rule of law" [*Stato di diritto*],[10] his formulation may then seem Kelsenian, but it is in fact directed against Kelsen. With this formulation, Schmitt means not so much that the State must coincide with juridical order, but only that the State presupposes the Juridical Idea, and that, because of the disconnection of that Idea from reality, it uses decision and political praxis to realize that Idea into positive juridical order. This is what differentiates Schmitt's dynamic concept of decision from Kelsen's statual concept of norm: in the former, the juridical order's lack of foundation is posed as a problem, whereas in the latter the question of the origin of juridical order is consciously renounced.[11]

2.3 Schmitt's polemic against Kelsen is also clear in his 1922 *Political Theology*,[12] the text that reveals the true significance of the disconnect between Juridical Order and Politics, and of the role of the State in dealing with it. In this study, Schmitt identifies the State not with sovereignty that orders but with sovereignty that decides. What produces order here is not rational and institutional mediation but the "sovereign decision," and the origin of this order is not law but disorder—the disconnect between Law and Politics—which here takes the name of the "exceptional case," the originary "remnant," the shadowy zone of modern political conceptuality in which mediation cannot be distinguished from immediacy. Schmitt's critique of the State in this book is also openly deconstructive: a political order cannot be founded on stability (or staticity) but only on openness to disorder. It is necessary, but never possible, to exit the state of nature. The State is functional only if it is capable of creating and negating its own system of norms; it is a crystal marked by a constitutive crack, the exception and the decision, which destabilize it while also making it functional.[13] Politico-juridical order is *wirklich* [actual] only if it "remembers" its own origin in crisis, only if it opens itself to crisis instead of closing itself off. This is a principle of political incompleteness and indeterminacy; it contains both the originary compulsion for form, and the co-implication and the disconnection between order and disorder. Politico-juridical order, necessarily, obtains legitimacy not because of its formal completeness, but only thanks to its imperfection, and this is visible precisely in the decision, which is a wound, an opening on the Void of disorder.

Schmitt's position does not imply the triumph of *Macht* over *Recht*. The order Schmitt discusses always remains juridical, as in *Der Wert des Staates und die Bedeutung des Einzelnen*. The difference is that in *Political Theology* the Juridical Idea, which preexists the State, is even more clearly deprived of content and reduced to a "compulsion for form" that orients the State around the task of producing a unitary and juridified political form. Against Kelsen's thesis of the self-sufficiency of the norm, Schmitt perfects his thesis of decisionism and exceptionalism: with the decision on the state of exception, the State (understood as sovereignty) creates juridical order (understood as positive law) without needing juridical order (a fundamental norm) or natural law, but only on the basis of the compulsion for order that manifests itself in the State and is characteristic of the modern age. For Schmitt, as for Kelsen, juridical order is unfounded. For Kelsen, however, its lack of foundations makes it "pure" and objectively analyzable, whereas for Schmitt, that same lack "stains" juridical order with politics, makes it impure, and positions it against an enemy. Despite their opposition, which has become paradigmatic in the history of juridical thought, Schmitt nevertheless shares with Kelsen a certain intellectual radicalism, as well as a commitment to scientific procedure based on strong theoretical hypostatization, which is lacking from the authors to whom Schmitt is usually compared (such as Rudolf Smend and Hermann Heller, who, like Schmitt, pursue juridical order in its concreteness but who, unlike him, ignore its tragicity).

In *Political Theology* as well as in Schmitt's 1929 essay "Das Zeitalter der Neutralisierungen und Entpolitisierungen" (The Age of Neutralizations and Depoliticizations),[14] Schmitt emphasizes the genealogy of the State, its epochal dimension, and the logics of its transformations. The analogies between God and State already were present in Schmitt's 1914 *Der Wert des Staates*: studying them at the same time as Kelsen, Schmitt reclaimed these analogies from Jacques-Bénigne Boussuet, the Catholic counterrevolutionaries, and Mikhail Bakunin.[15]

In Schmitt's works of the 1920s, meanwhile, these analogies acquired a double significance. From a structural point of view, the analogy between God and State is a theory of modernity as secularization. Against the claims of modern political theory, the State is not the product of a human reason that burns its bridges with the past and with premodern tradition; it's instead the transposition into politics of the traditional idea of God as the foundation of the order. The analogy between tradition and the Modern points therefore to the permanence of an ordering impulse as a constant factor of Western civilization. The State, on this read, is the interpretation that modern politics gives of this impulse. At the same time, however, there is also a deep chasm between modernity (and the State in particular) and the premodern tradition of *auctoritas*. This chasm derives from the fact that, while tradition presents God as the substance and foundation of politics, modernity is incapable of thinking either substance or foundation except in individualistic forms that are destined to fail. In this sense, the State is analogous to God, but only from the formal viewpoint of a compulsion for order. From a substantial point of view, however, the State positions itself in the most radical and immediate absence of order and foundations—which is to say, in the tragic disconnect, in principle, between the Juridical Idea and its political realization. With this, Schmitt overturns Hegel's theory of secularization, which foresees the permanence of substance coexisting with the discontinuity of its apprehension by thought. The notion of the originary incompleteness of the modern State[16]—which is thematized and "urbanized" by Ernst-Wolfgang Böckenförde, who reads it to say that historical substances are antecedent to the State-form—has its source in this theory of secularization.[17]

From the dynamic point of view, then, Schmitt grasps a sliding movement from State-forms that are conscious of their origin toward forms that are ever less conscious of that origin, in parallel progression with the transformation of the central "focal points" (Zentralgebieten) of modern metaphysics (such as the theistic personal God, the deistic impersonal divinity, pantheism, and atheism). From this perspective, modern political history is the history of a State-God who cannot but turn into a State-machine, in the same way that technics, throughout the centuries, replaces the God of metaphysics as the central reference-point of reality. The various forms of the modern State, one after the other, all attempt to resolve politics and its immanent tragedy in an order that is neutralized, depoliticized, pacified, rational, and immanent. During modernity, the compulsion for order affirms itself in a unilateral manner, unaware of its own structural aporia. As a mediation that's unaware of the immediacy originarily connected to it, it is, therefore, an immediate mediation.

This is, for Schmitt, the key for explaining the vicissitudes of the modern State. The progressive oblivion of the State's complex origin explains its compulsion for form; it also explains the simultaneous co-implication and disconnection between politics and juridical order, and the coexistence—necessary but unharmonic and nonpacified—between order and disorder, between form and conflict. Schmitt does not, however, read modernity as nothing more than derivation, decadence, and neutralization. To the contrary, both compulsion for form and its impossibility, both juridical order and political energy, both norm and exception, both politics and the energetic and originary forms Schmitt calls "the political"—all belong structurally to the modern State. It is typical of Schmitt's thought to interpret the historical moments in which the exception manifests itself, and reveals its energy, not only as constituent, revolutionary, and creative moments, but also as dangerous events. It is also typical for Schmitt to attempt to bring the instances of this energy from society (where it manifests itself) into the State, so that the State becomes the direct carrier of the "political" instead of trying to neutralize it (the very attempt at which risks overwhelming the State). In short, even though Schmitt's concept of the "political" does not coincide with the State, it is nevertheless inseparable from it. The fact that the "political" makes its appearance in parties is the problem, not the solution; in fact, it is precisely this that explains the active yet incomplete neutralization employed by a decisionistic statuality.

In light of this complex evaluation, Schmitt interprets modernity by subdividing it into three phases. The first is the classic epoch, in which the State demonstrated political capacity because—on the basis of decision—it was able to perform active neutralizations of religious civil war. The second is the phase of hyperpolitical revolution in which the force of the constituent power manifests itself as the people's sovereignty. The third is the liberal and legalistic phase (the State of law, even where it does not coincide completely with the liberal State). This phase is even more depoliticized, as the State has attempted to consign itself to an even more integral and passive depoliticization of its own origin, and to radically expel disorder from its space. The twentieth century, meanwhile, recognizes the centrality of economy and technics—or better, the centrality of the issues posed by these two forms of social life—which implies that the State must be able "to understand and direct economic relations."[18] Faced with this new task of the State, liberalism made a pretense of solving the "political" through discussions—through *logos* understood as an exchange of individual opinions (not unlike the Romantic "eternal conversation" that Schmitt already had criticized in his 1919 *Political Romanticism*).[19] With this, however, liberalism infused itself with the ideology and the practice of the modern State, organizing the State as nothing more than an institutional system that believes it has the power to resolve society's concreteness and conflictuality (by parliamentary representation, the production of a universal and abstract law, the separation and balance of powers, and by differentiating between

State and society). For Schmitt, liberalism—whose subjectivism he considers to be the mirror double of juridical positivism's norms—is the passive face of modernity. It is the reduction of modernity to nothing more than the compulsion for form, to a neutralization that ignores the tragic side of modern politics.[20]

Schmitt criticizes liberalism in the first place for its idea that politics (understood, in this case, as the public) consists in the private singularity of individuals. He then underlines the contradiction according to which individualism coexists with the universalism of the law, disparaging liberalism's pretense that politics (as foundation and as subjectivist destination) consists only and exclusively in the State (which somehow remains separate from society, even though it is produced by it and remains at its beck and call). Schmitt also criticizes liberalism's assumption that the powers of the sovereign must be separated, so that their neutral balance may form an order that is both juridified and effective. Because of these originary and structural contradictions, Schmitt argues, not only does nineteenth-century liberalism fail to establish political objectivity; it also fails to establish and preserve the separation between State and society, and to preserve and emphasize the singular subject within the universal form of the law. Along with the final component of the State's depoliticizing trajectory—technics—these circumstances together allow for the birth of the nineteenth-century administrative State (the fourth phase of the modern state). This is a form of the State that is postliberal in fact even as it remains infused by liberal ideology, and that operates within the abstract framework defined by universalistic law and the separation of powers, even as that framework continues to be progressively threatened. In the concrete, this State operates through the "measure" [*Massnahme*], holding fast to the belief that society, which is by now indistinguishable from the State, can be governed through rational logics centered on knowledge of objects. These logics also pertain to knowledge of subjects, which the administrative State understands as a special class of objects, as one among many "things," as an entity whose needs can and should be neutralized by means of technics or satisfied by means of bureaucracy. In Schmitt's view, however, technics cannot substitute for politics, and in fact only ends up underscoring the need for politics. This, in fact, is one of the central theses of Schmitt's thought: it is impossible for a political order to be completely neutral and at the same time to be effective. In its iteration as the administrative

State, the State now finds itself incapable of politics, unable to respond to the nineteenth-century forms of disorder that overwhelm the liberal State and the liberal subject alike—both of which discover that they are powerless to confront the problems of technics, pluralism, and democracy, and to find new ways of actively neutralizing them.

2.4 The peak of Schmitt's work as a political thinker is his 1927 *The Concept of the Political*.[21] This book draws the conclusions of a thought that takes the disconnect between Juridical Idea and reality as the origin of politics. In this work, Schmitt gives this disconnect the name of the "political," whose content—the relationship between friend and enemy—is not just hostility but also and at the same time the principle of association. The "political" is the extreme form of the nonpacified coexistence of order and disorder. It's the origin of politics understood as an always unbalanced coexistence of form and exception, Idea and contingency, peace and conflict, revolution and constituent power.[22] This is the principle of disequilibrium—a cornerstone of Schmitt's political theory.

Schmitt's "political" does not imply that politics consists only of conflict, revolution, and civil war; nor does it imply that conflict is completely foreign to the institutions of the State. If modern politics tends to be, according to its own self-interpretation, nothing more than mediation, then Schmitt's politics is not just immediacy; it's the tragic coexistence of mediation and immediacy, that does not admit any dialectical resolution. It's an order that's traversed by a lack of foundations, by an absolute risk, and it is exposed to the most radical contingency, to conflict, the Void, and death. The "political" pertains both to public space and to the possibility of killing and being killed, both to order and to disorder. Here too, in other words, Schmitt sees the State as an institution that is not originary, and that instead has its origin in the "political." The opening declaration of *The Concept of the Political*—"the concept of the state presupposes the concept of the political"[23]—says just that. With this assertion, Schmitt means that the State cannot realize a closed order, that the State cannot fill with its positive law the lack of sense and substance that characterize it from its origin. The State instead always should be aware of its constitutive instability and contingency, as well as of the existence of the politicity [*politicità*] that's also outside of it (in society and the population). For Schmitt, this is the political problem par excellence.

This overturns the formulation proposed by one of the masters of juridical positivism, Georg Jellinek, who in his 1900 *Allgemeine Staatslehre* argued that the "political means statal [*staatlich*]. When one thinks the concept of the political, one thinks of the concept of the State."[24] Schmitt transforms Jellinek's theory of a coincidence between State and "political" into a decisionist theorization of a disassociation between the same, both in fact and in principle. What follows from this, of course, is that the State is only one of many possible institutions that can act as a carrier of the "political." In the wake of its technical-neutral development over the course of the nineteenth century, the State is no longer an effective institution; it's now deprived of the capacity to recognize and deal with the "political," which now lies outside of State institutions. This implies the circulation within society of a disorder and violence that determine the end of the State; but these same forces also imply the beginning of a new efficacy for political form. The "political," according to Schmitt, may still be thought vis-à-vis the State, so long as one can openly admit that the season of the liberal and positivistic State has come to an end, and can instead imagine institutions of the State that assume a shape that is less formal and normative, less defensive. Grounded on the distinction between State and society, these new State institutions also would have to be more aggressive and effective, precisely because they would have to be able to openly face the contingency and conflict circulating within society, and to neutralize them in a manner that is active, not passive.

3. The State in Schmitt's Political Experience

The notion of the State provides us with the interpretative key to understand Schmitt as a "politologist" and "historian," as an analyst of the German State during the first half of the twentieth century. It also helps us understand Schmitt's view of the Second Reich, which he saw as a political form that derived from a compromise, since it was never able to decide on the polemical relationship between society and State (understood as a conflict born from the evaluation of the war between Bismarck and the Prussian parliament, between 1862 and 1866).[25]

Schmitt's principle of indeterminacy—which is to say, of originary co-implication and disconnection between order and disorder—along with his principle of disequilibrium, constitute the core of his political theory. Taken together, these two principles indicate the impossibility that the State could ever become a rational universal order. From a politological perspective, meanwhile, the principle of indeterminacy becomes a principle of legitimacy—a principle designating the need for the political order to have its origin in a content that is particular, determined, concrete, and above all, conflictual (from whence legitimacy actually proceeds). To function in this manner, it needs to rest its efficacy on the "memory" of its partial and polemical origin, and to reserve, in a necessarily indeterminate way, the power of deciding on the exclusion of the foreigner. In other words, Schmitt proposes to overcome the idea of the State as the legal guarantor of equality, and instead assigns it the role of posing, interpreting, and excluding difference, so as to become the conscious carrier of the "political" (which is to say, the capacity for internal hostility). With this, Schmitt undoes (or at least begins to undo) the two cornerstones of modern statuality: the distinction between internal and external (to which he will still refer soon after the war), and the distinction between State and society (or, put differently, between the space of juridified politics and that of the politically neutralized competition).

In practice, Schmitt's political program consists in recognizing the obsolescence of the liberal State, and in seeing in the advance of illiberal democracy the possible origin for a new political form for the State—one in which the deforming energy of the "political" (of which the people are here the carriers) precedes and exceeds the State's institutions, but never exists apart from them. It should be added that democracy, for Schmitt, has a number of different characteristics: it includes mass democracy as much as the polemical and constituent power of the people understood in nationalist terms; it covers Marxist social conflict as well as Bonapartistic plebiscitarism; it contains both Jacobinism and Leninism. The concrete face of democracy, in Schmitt's understanding, is the emergence of the problem of the economy. The economy is the new central reality of society, and it poses an ineluctable challenge to which one must respond, since its invasive and overflowing character calls forth conflict and power dynamics that are intrinsically political. In Schmitt's view, the State cannot back away from these new dynamics, as the liberal State would have attempted to do, proposing to represent them in parliament and hence to deal with them through the formal instrument of the law. It instead must realize a new synthesis of administration and direct political government.

3.1 The first brilliant and extreme formulation of this program is Schmitt's 1923 essay *Die Geistesgeschichtliche Lage Des Heutigen Parlamentarismus* (The spiritual-historical condition of today's parliamentarism).[26] In this text, Schmitt reconstructs the politico-practical side of the same nexus of thinking that finds its theoretical center in *Political Theology*. The aim of Schmitt's polemic here is liberal trust in the discursive reproduction of the political universal (namely, the State). The parliament is the institution that, more than anything, mirrors this trust, since it rests on the supposition that private opinions, with their relativism, can turn themselves into universal laws thanks to dialogue and discussion. Schmitt opposes this ideology, which is unaware of the origin of politics and never had any factual enforcement (except perhaps during the brief period between 1830 and 1840 in France). The German jurist also opposes the dialectical thinking of both the Hegelian and Marxian sort, which is prisoner to faith in the power of *logos* in a different, even more tenacious way. Against both of these traditions, Schmitt argues that in the twentieth century it is no longer possible for politics to be fully juridified and enclosed in a scheme of institutionalized representation. Politics draws its energy and novelty instead from the irruption of democracy, understood as the presence and identity of the people, into the lifeless arena of parliament. Subtracted from mediation in terms of representation and *logos*, the democratic people remain the object of a series of identifications (which, in practice, is of course constructed, since neither identity nor political unity are a given). From Jacobinism to Leninism, these identifications are nothing but dictatorial gestures, products of decision and of the exclusion of the nonidentical, aimed at the annihilation of those who are not homogenous and who thus could qualify as an internal enemy.

In the twentieth century the forms of violence implicit in modern politics pave the way for the possibility of a politics that is not founded on reason and in which the mediation of the *logos* is substituted by direct action, by the power of a political myth. This transformation, emblematized by the general strike of the revolutionary trade-unionism and of anarchism, is a concrete Absolute, which is to say, the conceptual and practical opposite of the mix of relativism, individualism, and universalism realized by liberalism. It carries with it both a destructive conflict and a new need for order, which is not neutral but polemical and oriented against an enemy. If myth is the historical form of the exception, then its objects are the mass parties (which Max Weber, in his 1918 text "Parliament and Government in Germany," defined as the carriers of "a particular *Weltanschauung*"),[27] and the political form that's adequate to it is democracy, which Schmitt sees as the opposite of liberalism but not of dictatorship. Whereas liberalism interprets politics by reducing it to the State, to the institutional frame that guarantees the formal juridical equality of the citizens, democracy is based on a type of equality that implies inequality, which is to say the homogeneity of a people built through conflict and exclusion. In its democratic form, the State can acquire political significance only if it allows itself to be traversed by the power of democratic political logics—only if, once again, unity passes through division, and is nurtured by disorder.

The presence of incompletely legalized and neutralized political violence within the State, in other words, is inevitable, and it deeply modifies the State's liberal form. Schmitt already had underlined this situation in his 1921 book *Dictatorship*.[28] In this text, Schmitt reconstructs the way the formation of the modern State depends crucially on a centralization of power that assumes the form of commissarial dictatorship (which is arranged by the king's attendants) and sovereign dictatorship (which reveals itself in revolutionary moments from Cromwell to the Jacobins, and which is the historical side of the decision). Schmitt conducts his study with an eye to the "proletarian class struggle," which is to say the Russian revolution, and offers a reinterpretation of the State that seeks to carry the same high-level energy that Bolshevism expresses—a reinterpretation of public law, in short, in light of Lenin. From this perspective, keeping in mind the centrality Schmitt gives to myth in his 1923 *Die Geistesgeschichtliche Lage Des Heutigen Parlamentarismus*, it's clear that in the early 1920s Schmitt's inspiration was Georges Sorel. Schmitt understands that it's not possible to think the State without democracy and without revolution (in fact, he soon will begin thinking the economy). Even so, it should be noted that Schmitt's refusal of rational-representational mediation as the origin of political forms does not mean that he advocates immediacy pure and simple. Dictatorship has the same aim; the production of political forms through exclusion takes the place of forms produced by means of the parliament.

3.2 The mode in which the "political" manifests itself within the State is thus clear: it appears through democracy, understood as a political energy that produces orderly forms by means of conflict and exclusion. The juridical name of the "political," meanwhile, is the "constituent power" that forms the pivot point of Schmitt's 1928 treatise *Constitutional Theory*, and that Schmitt in fact introduces into twentieth-century German jurisprudence. For Schmitt, the concept of "constitution"[29] does not refer either to the ensemble of constitutional laws (the *Konstitution*) or to the way juridical institutions function. It designates the concrete *Verfassung*,[30] which is to say, the complex but unitary juridical structure that a people (who are always in excess of the State) gives to itself through an originary decision. In practice, this decision comes into being through a revolution or a constituent assembly that realizes a caesura between systems of order, which is exactly how constituent power—the capacity to constitute the fundamental legitimacy of a political order—is exercised by the people. Openly taken by Schmitt from Emmanuel-Joseph Sieyès and from the French revolutionary experience, constituent power—as distinct from the liberal individual and the contract—is the engine of any effective political order: it is the energy of the people understood as an active totality (and hence not as a totality that is given once and for all) that is able to sovereignly decide on its own political form, thus creating constituted powers without also relinquishing the ability to transcend them.

Schmitt's 1927 *Volksentscheid und Volksbegehren* (Plebiscite and referendum)[31] also presents a systematic opposition between the presence of the people who decide by way of acclamation, on the one hand, and representative institutions that seek to realize mediation, on the other. Actually, however, the strength of Schmitt's thought lies not in his reevaluation of a direct democracy that pits its full immanence against State mediation, but in his conception of the necessity of form (in this case, of juridified institutions) together with the power of presence of the people—or, in other words, his grasp of the tension between form and immediacy. Schmitt understood State institutions to be permanently crossed and disquieted by constituent power, by the originary presence of the people. Schmitt thinks the assumption of form and unity by the people not in terms of votes for parliament but with reference to the plebiscitary acclamation evoked by some Caesarian leader in whom the power of the people is concentrated and expressed (and, of course, connected together by means of the persecution of dissidents). In other circumstances, Schmitt understands democracy (and not liberalism, the two always being opposed in his thought) as a constituent power that never neutralizes itself either in constituted powers or in acclamation, and that consists instead in the continuous formation of the unity of the people, in an uninterrupted dynamic of inclusion and exclusion. In all cases, constituent power, for Schmitt, starts from a legitimacy (expressed in the originary political will of the people) that is different from, greater than, and prior to legality (understood as the organization of laws both constitutional and ordinary).

Schmitt emphasizes legitimacy (which is, for him, never rational) vis-à-vis legality in order to underline the fact that the State never will be able to resolve itself in an equilibrium of constituted powers and in the universal neutrality of the law. Its political energy resides instead precisely in the always active disequilibrium between constituent power and State powers, indeed between legitimacy and legality. Although politics thus passes through institutions and through the State, it's nevertheless not completely contained or neutralized in or by that passage. Institutions and their will (which is to say, laws) aren't neutral; they're oriented by the originary act of constituent power that both establishes and disquiets them. In Schmitt's theory of the constitution, we thus witness the concretization of Schmitt's other fundamental principle: the principle of indeterminacy. In fact, in Schmitt's formulation, the constitution is an open system in which originary political energy still circulates; it is, consequently, an order born from a concrete conflict, and that derives its political energy from its ability to contain an indeterminacy—a general political surplus value, i.e., legitimacy—that, in turn, allows for institutions to be bent to exclude those who, from time to time, are chosen as the enemies of the constitution. It should be noticed, though, that even though constituent power contains the principle of indeterminacy, it also determines politico-institutional forms, conferring on them an orientation that is originarily polemical (whether in the direction of inclusion or exclusion). Without recourse to another analogous originary political energy, therefore, constituent power—substantial legitimacy—is also a factor for the conservation of values and contents: understood as Verfassung, the constitution cannot be abrogated or substantially modified by a law of parliament, or even by a legal majority.

It's not then the case, as Schmitt expressly states,[32] that he dedicated his major juridical work not to the State but just to the constitution, understood primarily as a nonneutral politico-juridical order (able to hold value because it recalls effectively its origin), and as the constituent act of the people who decide to establish that order.[33] Even so, Schmitt's thought here clearly continues to move at the margin of the Modern: his concept of the constitution, in fact, preserves some key principles of the deep syntax of modern politics (such as the need for political unity and the importance of the constituent subjectivity), even as it clears these principles from institutionalist rationalism and from the pretense that politics be built as a system that balances powers.

3.3 From a practical viewpoint, Schmitt's analysis—which turns democracy into a totality that carries the "political," and that expresses the need to recognize and put form to the politico-polemical potential of the social—may imply, operatively, that a constitution be preceded by general principles or general clauses. This is a need that proved essential during the constituent process that took place in the aftermath of World War II (in Italy, for instance, where the republican constitution was strongly influenced by the jurist Costantino Mortati, a careful interpreter of Schmitt's thought). Schmitt's analysis of democracy, however, also may imply an authoritarian turn that sees the safety and regeneration of the State being promoted by the appropriation, interpretation, and polemical use of the origin—which is to say, of the legitimacy of the constituent power used against constitutional legality. For Schmitt, in other words, there is in practice an inescapable short-circuit between *the power of the origin of politics* (which is Schmitt's theoretical discovery) and *the power of the politics of origin* (which is the practical aspect of Schmitt's thought, the authoritarian reassertion of a legitimacy beyond formal legality).

The defense of the State through the deformation of its crystalline and rational structure is, in fact, Schmitt's position in the late twenties and early thirties, during the final crisis of the Weimar Republic. In the analysis of the problem of the State set forth in his 1931 *Der Hüter der Verfassung* (The guardian of the constitution) and his 1932 *Legality and Legitimacy*, Schmitt employs all of his historical, political, and intellectual analyses to declare the death of the liberal form of the Weimar Republic, and to try to keep alive the notion of a substantial and democratic legitimacy[34]—to preserve the spirit against the letter, the constitution against the constitutional law.

In one section of "The Guardian of the Constitution," a political science treatise, Schmitt reconstructs the various stages of the State, from the medieval "jurisdictional State"[35] to the early modern "governmental

State," to the liberal "State of laws" (including juridical positivism), to the twentieth-century "administrative State." Schmitt's thesis is that neither acts of government nor concrete forms of jurisdiction (such as martial law) are conceivable within the liberal form of the Weimar Republic. The latter's architecture—its construction according to the separation of powers, their balance, the principle of parliamentary representation, and the principle of legality—is inadequate to deal with the new condition of politics, which is to say, "polycracy" (a term Schmitt borrows from Johannes Popitz). The challenges of the present—consisting, essentially, in the collapse of the distinctions between State and society, and between politics and economy, that together with individualism constitute the axiom of liberal politics, but that have not been valid for a long time—require new solutions. Thanks to the power of the economy, the State enters society, and society enters the State. This means that the public scene is characterized by a pluralism of parties and interest groups, which is to say, by social dynamics that have an immediately political valence, and are destructive of unity.[36]

From the disappearance of the boundaries between State and society, the total State is born. With this term, derived from Ernst Jünger's "total mobilization," but bent to an almost opposite meaning (for Jünger, total mobilization is in itself morphogenetic,[37] whereas for Schmitt it is a challenge that needs to be shaped by politics), Schmitt points to the new political reality of the twentieth century, which can present itself in two modalities. The first is *the total State of weakness*, in which the liberal State turns itself into an administrative State that pursues ever-new questions produced by various states of affairs, and that—even though it sacrifices universal "law" for "particular" measures—remains passively traversed by economic conflicts that together form a plurality of power centers, thus rendering the State incapable of preserving the political unity of the people. The second mode hypothesized by Schmitt is *the total State of intensity*, which is to say, a political order that's able to enact an active neutralization of social conflict, and that emerges when the State, having renounced the axioms of liberalism, allows itself to commingle with society and with its economic and technical powers in order to dominate and govern them.[38] The aim of this State is to arrive to an openly political neutralization founded on a decision and supported by an "ethics of the State" (which, to be clear, is not a call for an "ethical State," but only indicates a *Pflicht zum Staat* [a "duty toward the State"], a duty to realize a concrete order, a compulsion for form).[39] This situation implies a State that acts through measures with a legal value (even though these measures differ from law, since they are particular and not universal), and that founds those measures on the reactivation of originary legitimacy, which is to say, on the plebiscitary presence of the people,[40] which is not entirely crystallized in institutions but is instead a reservoir of energy available to whomever is able to use it politically.

What this means is that Schmitt grasps the new exigencies of governance that are born from the dynamics of the economy and of the mingling of society and State (thus disrupting the balance of liberal politics). It also means that Schmitt doesn't entrust his response to these new exigencies to the legislative power of parliamentary representation (which is paralyzed by "negative majorities," by the inert mirroring of the divisions within society). He entrusts it instead to a power that's at once personalized and superlegitimate, a power able to conjoin the power of technics (in the form of the "measure") and direct access to constitutional legitimacy (or better, its constant reinterpretation). Schmitt uses the second part of the Weimar Constitution (the "social" and democratic side) against the first one (the "liberal" side), and within the first, he opposes the "reserve constitution" contained in Article 48 of the Weimar Constitution to the parliamentary principle. In so doing, he proposes that the president of the *Reich*, who is elected by the people and hence plebiscitarily legitimized by the originary source of power, be the custodian of the constitution (and it's worth remembering that the Weimar Constitution was an originary decision of the German people against the Bolsheviks). This implies that the president should govern society and its new economic forms, and should defend the republic from its enemies (in whose category Schmitt placed both the Communists and the Nazis), as well as from their attempts to acquire a legal majority in parliament that would allow them to modify the substantial legitimacy of the constitution.[41]

Thus it is that Schmitt, while aiming at saving the Weimar Republic from itself and against itself, arrives at the hypothesis of a presidial State, of an authoritarian and protected democracy, characterized by a supremacy of the executive, and especially of the president, over the legislature.[42] It is in fact the president, through systematic recourse to the extraordinary powers granted to him by Article 48, who deals with the short-circuit between the technical measure (or concrete decision) and democratic-plebiscitary legitimization (the memory of the constituent power and of its polemical and foundational energy) that constitutes the new link between particular and originary, and that overcomes the liberal political mediation assured by the rational universality of the law. The president of the republic is a personal institution that is capable of concrete decisions—decisions that are not completely formalized and that hence are able to deal with conflicts with an eye toward their active neutralization, that are oriented to the defense of the originary values of the constitution, and that exclude the enemies of the republic (although it must be said that Schmitt did not elaborate upon the penal offense of the "criminal party," as did the Nazi jurist Otto Koellreutter).

Schmitt's interpretation of democracy as the active presence of people, as totality, is never free from the moment of the representation of order, or at least of orientation to order. Nor is it free from the authority of the command that establishes democracy itself, and that de facto reduces the people to the passive role of a mass who unanimously acclaims the extralegal (but legitimate) decisions that come down from the summit of political power. What from the theoretical viewpoint is the discovery of the origin of politics thus becomes in practice a concrete "politics of the origin," which is to say an authoritarian political use of originary legitimacy that's able to undo the determinations of all political life and to reject disorder (but only at the cost of a constant reinterpretation of the reasons for order). Only if the State agrees to shake off its liberal and rational architecture, only if it is able to make itself total, can the State remain vital and able both to defend the constitution and to bring order to the new social world of the twentieth century. This is the reason why, between the very late twenties and the very early thirties, Schmitt draws closer to Italian Fascism: although it posed a great emphasis on the State, Italian Fascism overcame its liberal form, and above all openly took charge of the problem of economy (even if Schmitt judged the corporativist solution still too economistic and insufficiently political).[43]

It's worth noting that Schmitt was a committed enemy of the social State, if by this we mean a polycratic democracy that constitutes itself as an equilibrium of conflicting interests. His interest lay instead in the search for new ways to stabilize society, which in this phase also took the shape of a "direct grip" by the State on society itself and on its different articulations (thus losing the separation between State and society). Thus, to affirm that Schmitt's stance is only conservative and pro-monopoly, only antisocialist and antisyndicalist,[44] misses the fact that Schmitt didn't retreat when faced with the challenge of the mingling between State and society. What Schmitt had in mind was precisely an authoritarian and nonpluralistic version of the social State, since for him the good to preserve was not so much the freedom of the capitalists (which constituted only a by-product of his reasoning), but the unity of the State, its capacity to command.

3.4 The failure of the Weimar Republic before its Nazi enemies in 1933 pushed Schmitt to put an end to his own attempt to revitalize the republican State on the basis of a plebiscitarian-technico-authoritarian interpretation of its constitution (which in fact totally upset that State), and also an end, in a certain sense, to his attempt to revitalize the State-form in general. From this point on, Schmitt no longer tried to save the political force of the State by deforming its form; he now openly tried to overcome it from the direction of "concrete order." It's as if he thought that the deformations of the architecture of the State now had gone beyond any possibility of conferring on it a political capacity, and hence had reached a point of rupture. From the viewpoint of Schmitt's relationship with the State, this is the significance of Schmitt's deplorable Nazi phase, especially in his writings of the first year of Nazi rule (namely, his 1933 book *State, Movement, People: The Triadic Structure of the Political Unity*).[45] In his Nazi period, Schmitt completely dissociated the already precarious decisionistic relationship he had established in his earlier works between State and active politics, between order and energy, between institutions and constituent powers, in order to locate political energy instead totally inside the movement (the Nazi party). Here "the people" are no longer figured as a constituent revolutionary nation; they are simply the biological substance—precious but passive—of politics. The State, meanwhile, is now only the formal framework for bureaucratic order, and as such is incapable of active politics. In *State, Movement, People*, Schmitt not only declares the death of Hegel's functionary State; he also takes leave from the "total State of energy," which is to say his late-Weimar proposal (and, in any case, the Third Reich very soon abolished the political category of "total State" anyway).[46] To his authoritarian interpretation of totality, Schmitt thus adds an interpretation that is now precisely totalitarian: the exigency of politically governing society and economy, of bringing concreteness into politics, is now satisfied by the concentration of political energy in the movement-party and in the racial homogeneity of the people (or, to be precise, *Gleichartigkeit* ["substantial homogeneity" or "racial homogeneity"] as opposed to *Artgleichheit* [formal homogeneity]). Racial homogeneity, in Schmitt's view, is able to assure that the automatic dynamics of the market and of technics don't take destructive forms. Within a political syntax dominated by the programmatic substitution of the stability, universality, and formality of the State by the mobility and partiality of the party and the substantiality of the people, the relationship between movement and people allows Schmitt to distance himself (at least in public) from Italian Fascism, whose solution of the problem of the relationship between politics and economy pivots on the link between State and corporation.

In this context, Schmitt entrusts the exigency of stability and political order to the racial dimension, which implies a remarkable limitation of the political role of the State. Similarly, Schmitt overcomes decisionism—rightly seen as an extreme deformation of the normativistic formalism, and hence still categorically dependent on statuality—in favor of the juridical concept of "concrete order," which is to say, of the juridical institutions and particular concepts typical of a people and its history, bonded by a peculiarity that excludes any attempt toward formalization and universalization.

This distancing from the State and its categories did not save Schmitt from criticism by the orthodox supporters of the regime. These critics understood that the passive role of the people, which in this phase of Schmitt's thought is evident despite his denials, demonstrated how far Schmitt was from *völkisch* ideology. They also recognized the traces of his previous intellectual and political framing of dictatorship and of the sovereign decision (and in fact, even if Schmitt did declare this previous phase officially overcome, it's not by chance that in 1934 he ordered the reprinting of *Political Theology*, as we shall see in chapter 2). Last but not least, these orthodox Nazis recognized that Schmitt's conception of institutions reveals his thought on concrete order to be indebted, as well, to his early work on political form (which is of Catholic origin, and which is hence hated by the Nazis).

3.5 After 1936, having been attacked by the Schutzstaffel (SS), Schmitt no longer dealt with internal politics, directing his attention instead to the reflections on international politics that would occupy him until his death. Even from this viewpoint, Schmitt's position clearly leans toward the overcoming of the State, the recognition of its political obsolescence, and the historicization of its trajectory and of its efficacy. Until 1944, Schmitt pursued the overcoming of the State with enthusiasm through his theory of the *Reich* and the *Grossraum*, the Empire and the "Great Space" that took the place of the State and of sovereignty, both internally (by overcoming the formalism of the citizenship, determined by the bond with the "blood and soil") and externally (by upsetting the balance between States, by creating hierarchies among peoples, and by constructing an international order structured by oppositions between enclosed great spaces).[47] In the aftermath of World War II, Schmitt's conservative phase followed on his early, decisionistic, and totalitarian phases. In fact, in his 1950 *The Nomos of the Earth in the International Law of the Jus Publicum Europæum*,[48] the most important of Schmitt's works of the second half of the twentieth century, his diagnosis of the death of the modern State remains part of an elegant analysis of its genealogy and crisis (which is nevertheless schematic and in many ways ideological, as I will show in chapter 5). However, Schmitt's general approach toward the State now assumes the form of a lament for its lost capacity to let order and political energy coexist. It's not by chance that, in his 1950 *Ex Captivitate Salus*, he defines himself as the last representative of the *jus publicum europæum*, which is to say, as the last jurist able to employ the concepts of the State with full consciousness of its beginning and end.[49]

Schmitt had always explained the State through nonstatual categories (such as exception, decision, constituent power, "political," and people). He now began to interpret it in light of the category of *nomos*, which is to say of an order oriented by an originary decision. *Nomos* is the cut that divides the earth and that allows its partition and oriented ordering. It's a concept that summarizes the fruit of Schmitt's thought: far from neutral, all political order incorporates within itself an originary disequilibrium and a scission that paradoxically also constitute the condition for its balance. From the viewpoint of the international law this means that for Schmitt the modern State is the product of a specific and contingent balance of disequilibria, of a particular arrangement of world divisions, and is therefore the result of a particular *nomos*, which in turn cannot become universal or carry any universality within itself. This *nomos*—the *nomos* of international modern juridical order—is a concentric ensemble composed of the differences between earth and sea, between the continent and England (as Schmitt says in his 1942 *Land and Sea*),[50] between Europe and the rest of the world, and finally between the various sovereign continental states. The modern progress of rationalism (the neutralization of the internal war and the limitation of the external war) does not involve stages of civilization moving toward Enlightenment universality; it is made possible precisely because of its particularity, because it concerns a differentiated space, Europe, and because it applies only there. The whole of modern political conceptuality—citizenship, sovereignty, the distinction between friend and criminal—pivots around the State. The State, in turn, is explained by those differences, by their division of world space: there are no extra-European states, and when they start to exist—the United States, above all, here looms large for Schmitt—the *jus publicum europæum* begins its end. This trajectory is accelerated by the transformation of the world space caused by universalistic powers—economy and technics—that are born precisely within the State. These forces bind the State and all its legal power to the dynamics of industrial progress, which are the only legitimizing ones and which transform the State into an instrument of the various ideologies that contend for the dubious privilege of bringing to completion the grip that technico-industrial forces have on the world.[51] Taken together, these tendencies carry the State to its death, along with the categories of modern politics (which can only find their place in the space of the State).

In the smooth space of the unity of the world, politics itself doesn't die; only modern politics does. The latter sees its classic concepts become confused where before they were clear. Schmitt recognizes that the modern State, in some of its guises, had constituted a principle of political form (however unstable) and as such had contained the drift of technical automatism and the logic of absolute conflict (both of which are quite at home in modernity); but Schmitt also recognized that today the State is no longer able to perform this task. Faced with the resulting chaos, Schmitt affirmed the exigency of a new *nomos* of the earth—the need for a juridical order that is newly oriented, and for a new poststatual and postmodern order, made possible through new partitions of the planet (in practice, through the pluralism of new "Great Spaces" that would replace States and that like them would relate to each other according to Westphalian modalities). New partitions such as these would allow forms of hostility that would be concrete and real, not absolute and discriminatory like those born from the humanitarian, universalist, and Marxist ideologies (as Schmitt argues in his 1963 *Theory of the Partisan*).[52] They also would allow for the emergence of a new conceptuality capable of expressing those hostilities. Schmitt thus affirmed, in short, the need for a new *katechon*—a *katechon* that in some aspects (especially internationally) would function in the same way that the plurality of sovereign centers functioned during the epoch of the State.

4. Schmitt's Intellectual Sources

Among the intellectual positions that helped Schmitt develop his attitude toward the State, which consists at once of detachment and deep involvement, there is, in the first place, the field of counterrevolutionary Catholicism. Beginning with the earliest years of his intellectual career, in fact, it is possible to notice the influence of the classical thinkers of traditionalism such as Louis de Bonald, Joseph de Maistre, and Juan Donoso Cortés (who is actually almost something of a discovery for Schmitt, which is why Schmitt places him side by side with Tocqueville and Marx),[53] as much as of thinkers and polemists such as Léon Bloy and Charles Maurras (whose thought is characterized by an aggressive antibourgeois Catholicism), and the anti-Romantic Paul Valéry. These extreme forms of political Catholicism—which certainly are antiliberal, but which have not yet realized antiliberalism's full potential—allow Schmitt to criticize modern rational mediation, and to subtract himself from the pathos of the great Protestant narrative of productive secularization. Whereas the latter view of secularization sees the State as the new form of divine substance, Schmitt interprets secularization and the State in formal continuity with tradition yet also in substantial discontinuity with it (quite contrary to the Hegelian-Protestant paradigm, in other words). From these thinkers, however, Schmitt does not take a theory of the theological foundation of politics. What he takes is a criticism of the foundational pretenses of modern political rationalism and of liberalism, which he interprets and develops (in the mature phase of his thought, at least) in a manner less Catholic than decisionistic, less social-organicistic than politico-sovereign, and that actually verges on nihilism.

The fact that Schmitt was interested not only in the reactionary aspect of the Catholic thinkers but also in their polemical side is proven by his very strong debt to revolutionary thought. From Oliver Cromwell to Mikhail Bakunin, from Emmanuel Joseph Sieyès to Georges Sorel (of whom Schmitt is one of the first exegetes in Germany), from Vladimir Lenin to Walter Benjamin, and obviously going through Marx, what interested Schmitt was the decisive moment of political violence, the catastrophic rupture of order, of constituent political energy brought to the extreme[54]—indeed to the incandescent point at which politics becomes the "political." This was also a way to criticize modern rational mediation, and precisely because of this Schmitt rejects the element of *Aufhebung*—the attempt to mediate the relation between immediacy and mediation—which he detects in Marx and official Marxism.

Paradoxically, Schmitt drew important reasons for his critique of rational mediation even from the tradition of political rationalism itself— yet another sign that while Schmitt did indeed criticize the State, he did so from the margins of its horizon, returning to the very origin of the Modern in order to understand the crisis of the nineteenth century.[55] This relationship between criticism and crisis has as its main protagonist Hobbes more than Bodin. Hobbes allowed Schmitt to investigate the problem of the State and to succeed in his critique of juridical positivism, for Hobbes was the first thinker to fully rationalize politics and to consider the State the only source of political order. At the same time, Hobbes also provided Schmitt with the interpretative key for reading this rationalization and positivization in a nonpacified way, for Hobbes is also the inventor of technicized politics, of the artificial State, and Schmitt deems him capable of identifying and thinking the origin of juridified political form in the sovereign decision much more than in the contract. For Schmitt, Hobbes is also able to show the shrewd reader how much nonrationality the origin of the modern State contains (nonrationality is in the form of the myth, of the decision, or also, in the 1965 essay on Hobbes, in the opening to Transcendence). Whether decisionist or Christian philosopher—the two extremes between which Schmitt's interpretation oscillates—Hobbes was, for Schmitt, the only one who was able to think the State as concrete political unity, to demonstrate the nonrational origin of political reason, even if Hobbes was also at the same time the very initiator of that technicization and formalization, of the very political neutralization that in the twentieth century will bring the State to its death. In his ambivalence between concreteness and abstraction, decision and contract, immediacy and mediation, Hobbes was, for Schmitt, the epitome of modern politics.

Schmitt also received an important stimulus from modernity's dialectical side (even if, as always, in a manner at once selective, unilateral, and extreme). In his reading of Hegel, especially, Schmitt emphasized not so much the dialectical and the conservative element of Hegel's *Aufhebung* (his philosophy of history and Spirit) as the concreteness and the realism with which Hegel thought politics. Even as Schmitt owes a debt to Hegel for his criticism of contractualism (namely, his argument that the rational mediation of the State does not originate from the mediation among single individuals but from the relationship between Idea and contingency), he thus also diverged from Hegel's interpretation of secularization. Whereas for Schmitt the Modern stands both in formal continuity and in substantial discontinuity vis-à-vis tradition, for Hegel modernity understands even more fully than tradition itself the very same spiritual substance that weaves together the fabric of history, thus giving history a philosophical rather than a religious form.[56]

Schmitt's convergence with the style and problematics of negative thought is also worth noting. Despite his Catholicism, Schmitt's contribution to the field of negative thought is major. In the background, Schmitt keeps Nietzsche's great deconstruction of the modern rational mediation, which he openly criticizes without ceasing to see that deconstruction as the "truth" of the originary nihilism of the Modern.[57] Schmitt both continues and radicalizes (with his "Catholic" attention for the juridical objectivity of structures) the relativization of the State and the problematization of Western rationalism already begun by Weber (with a "Protestant" emphasis on the originarity of individual action of an economic type). Schmitt furthermore deepens Weber's interpretation of the Modern as secularization, of politics as conflict, of the centrality of power, as well as Weber's intuition into the polytheism of values.[58] Yet not only did Schmitt intend to reach beyond Weber and beyond Weber's disenchanted nationalistic and Protestant adhesion to a modern statuality revitalized by charisma (in Schmitt, neither the deciding sovereign nor the custodian of the constitution are charismatic leaders in a properly Weberian sense); he also presented himself as independent from Weber on the basis of his methodology (which focuses on juridical order more than on sociology and economy) and his argumentative style. Overall, then, Schmitt was much more than a simple epigone of Weber. The distance between them is the same distance that runs between the disquiet of Wilhelmine academic science, on the one hand, and the tragic agony of Weimar Germany and the "promise" of Hitler's New Order, on the other.

While at first glance there appears to be a connection between Schmitt's *Entscheidung* [decision] and Martin Heidegger's *Entschlossenheit* ["decidedness" or "resoluteness"]—a demonstration of a spontaneous convergence of philosophy and of political thought toward concreteness, alongside a parallel criticism of rational mediation—in truth Schmitt always paid greater attention to Ernst Jünger, especially because of Jünger's capacity to interpret the signs of the times (in particular the mobilizing and destabilizing role of technique vis-à-vis the formal order of the State). Nevertheless, there remains an undeniable distance between Jünger and Schmitt, above all because Schmitt saw in the advance of technics, and in the dynamics that bring modernity to a point of collapse, real challenges to be met with the invention of a new conceptuality (even if, in the end, he himself was not up to the task). Jünger, by contrast, read these same events more optimistically, as a stage in the self-movement of some extrahuman Substance, to whose development he entrusts the overcoming of the crisis of modernity. Similar differences emerge in other common themes that both Schmitt and Jünger discuss, such as the relation between East and West, the irregular figures of the rebel and the partisan, and the world State.[59]

Last but not least, although this shall not detain us here, it goes without saying that there is great relevance in Schmitt's relation to French jurists (from Maurice Hauriou's institutionalism to Carré de Malberg's analyses of revolutionary constitutions), as well as their German colleagues (not only Jellinek but also Gerhard Anschütz, Rudolf Smend, Hermann Heller, and antagonistically, Hans Kelsen).

5. *Conclusions*

In conclusion, it's necessary to underline that Schmitt's significance consists in his deconstruction of the juridico-political structure of the State—his ability to see conflict behind juridical order, scission behind unity, decision behind neutralization, and energy behind form. Schmitt's deconstruction is, however, very different from the decentering of the State effected by Michel Foucault. Schmitt inverts the relationship between power and juridical order: instead of deconstructing State power into a microphysics,[60] Schmitt overturns it with a *macrophysics*. Schmitt's ambiguous dependence on the State reveals itself precisely here: he does not, in the end, break out beyond the threshold of the categorial horizon of modernity, but simply identifies a mode of legitimacy for the State that differs from juridico-rational legitimacy.

Schmitt's strong grasp of the exhaustion of the classic categories of modernity goes hand in hand with a theoretical move that, however nonrecuperative it may be, nevertheless remains paradoxically unitary. Schmitt places his discovery of scission at the service of his attempt at a new construction of the One—a One that is, however fragmented, never overcome as a horizon in Schmitt's thought. In Schmitt's modernity, plurality and pluralism are always evil insofar as they are inside the State, but always good outside of the State. Schmitt is the self-aware epigone of a juridical and political civilization that is contradictory and that cannot be reformed; he is able to think the crisis of this civilization because he is internal to that crisis (instead of safely outside of it). For this same reason, Schmitt is able to present an exceptional genealogical reconstruction of modernity and of its fundamental historico-political product, the State, at the moment of its decline. The crisis of modernity's classic paradigms—the increasing confusion of modern concepts that once were clear and distinct—is precisely also what enables Schmitt's own intellectual force, as well as his own status as a "classic."

Beyond the nexus Schmitt's thought articulates between criticism and crisis, however, and quite despite his efforts to free his gaze from statuality, from a theoretical viewpoint Schmitt in the end remained incapable of seeing beyond the boundaries of modernity. Exactly this, in fact—that Schmitt's thought remained internal to limits of modernity, deforming its form from within—is what allowed for some of his political proposals to acquire validity after the Second World War, even if in this context those proposals were much less radical than when Schmitt first formulated them (under conditions that were first authoritarian and then totalitarian). As far as internal politics is concerned, there is no doubt that the social State of the second half of the twentieth century is characterized precisely by the failing ("politically" orchestrated, certainly) of the boundaries between State and society, between politics and economy, which Schmitt interpreted as the end of the liberal statuality.

There's also no doubt that the social State faced the new relationship between State and society with political instruments that greatly pressured the classic architecture of the State: the triumph of the executive over the legislature, the use of decrees, the parties' occupation of various institutions (parliament above all). Finally, there's also no question that in indirect ways and in less radical formulations, Schmitt's thought influenced some of the framers of the Italian constitution, the French Fifth Republic, and the German *Grundgesetz* [basic law], especially regarding the issues of the defense of constitutional legitimacy and the construction of the welfare State as the proper form of democracy.

All of these mingling and stabilizations, however, took place under the sign of liberal humanism and democratic pluralism—not of authoritarianism or totalitarianism, as Schmitt proposed. Political energy was absorbed not by the State but instead by individuals, and their real social groupings (parties) were recognized as the real and ultimate source of this energy. In the years following 1945, after all, the individual has not been seen as a private entity, and parties have not been seen as enemies of political unity: both instead have proved to be carriers of properly political dynamics and spatiality (the crisis of the individual, of civil society, and of parties, which today is evident, happened much later, as a moment in the epochal crisis of modernity, in which the State is involved with the same amount of radicalism).

Meanwhile, the postwar State turned out to lack sovereignty's external dimension (understood as *jus ad bellum* [the "right to wage war"]), which now devolved to the two superpowers that partitioned the world. In the chaos of globalization that followed the fall of Communism and the bipolar order, it sometimes seems as though there is a possibility for a return of the efficacy of the principle of statuality through the regular use of the state of exception. This return has taken place, however, in a new context—a new political space, that of the global[61]—that radically calls into question the efficacy of sovereignty (even in its decisionistic mode) and of any "concrete order." Schmitt is too close to the Westphalian model of the State, despite his reinterpretation and revision in a tragic key, to feel at ease in the global age. The political decline of the State and its transformation have followed a path of which Schmitt's political theory—the theory of a specific crisis of the State, a crisis that belongs to the past, even if to us it, in part, still feels present—only caught a glimpse. Faced with this turn of events, Schmitt was not able to support the realism of his analysis with theoretical propositional force; nor was he able to identify a concrete political praxis.[62]

Today, therefore, we're obliged to go beyond the ambiguous relationship—almost a *nec tecum nec sine te* [I can't live with you or without you][63]—with statuality entertained by the jurist who was, by his own account, "open to the joys of the spirit." To grasp globalization, and to generate perspectives that help solve the political problems that confront us, our thinking must begin where Schmitt's reflections end.

....

CHAPTER 2

SCHMITT'S POLITICAL THEOLOGIES

Many believe that the term "political theology" (*politische Theologie*) is Schmitt's invention.[1] This, however, is not true in the strict sense. In fact, we may owe the coinage of the term to the young Marx,[2] whose text (a short fragment) was not yet known in 1922, the year in which Schmitt published his work on the topic.[3] But even if Schmitt did not actually invent the term, he did reinvent it in practice, perhaps influenced by the reading of Bakunin who, for his part, used it polemically with reference to Mazzini,[4] or perhaps also because of the term's assonance with the "moral theology" that was a well-known discipline in the realm of ecclesiastic formation. As such, we owe to Schmitt the first impulse to the wide circulation of the term, which has developed in a direction heavily critical of Schmitt himself.[5]

Schmitt wrote two works dedicated to "political theology," which were published almost half a century apart; he also thought about composing a third.[6] The theme thus registered a presence for a long period in Schmittian intellectual productivity. This chapter discusses the structure of such works, their significance in the wider scope of the development of Schmitt's thought, their role in the debate on the relationship between the sacred and power, and on secularization.[7] Our inquiry will allow for the emergence of the wide range of meanings that the notion of "political theology" assumes in the long development of Schmitt's reflection, while at the same time taking into account how it always indicates the inescapable relationship of politics with the theological sphere, and as such how it constantly expresses the most bitter polemics against the liberal pretense to actuate a full neutralization of political theology through the so-called "grand modern separation" between the theological and the political (grounded in the liberal and the rational). In the most disparate historical and intellectual conditions, Schmitt gives this concept and term the task of deciphering the epistemological and practical status of politics, and the directions toward praxis that descend from such diagnosis. In this way, it's possible to affirm that "political theology" is Schmitt's "political philosophy," in the nonprescriptive mode in which he interprets "philosophy," which is to say, as "genealogy."[8]

1. Decision, Norm, Representation, Secularization

The Schmitt who publishes his first *Political Theology* is a young, brilliant, and successful jurist of Catholic formation who, from his radical approach to the judicial theme of sovereignty, arrives at his first grand deconstruction of the political categories of modernity. In *Political Theology*, in fact, what already had emerged in *Political Romanticism* and in *Dictatorship* is still evident (namely, that Schmitt's Catholicism continues to be the source of intellectual inspiration in his profession of legal theorist),[9] but also that it has now ceased to constitute the foundation of an attitude of frontal opposition against modernity (an attitude that, until that moment, Schmitt had nurtured with a bit of posturing). Although with some hesitations, as we see in his coeval *Roman Catholicism and Political Form* (which in some respects constitutes the opposite of *Political Theology*),[10] Schmitt's Catholicism instead becomes the point of view, external to the self-understanding of the Modern, from which it is possible for Schmitt to interpret the structures and dynamics of modernity, and to recognize its necessity without posing it as a value—and, above all, without entering into its fundamental principle, subjectivism.

Political Theology, on the contrary, achieves its general consideration of the Modern through the specific path of a reflection on the juridical question of sovereignty, which Schmitt treats through three oppositional couplets: exception and norm, authority and power, and tradition and modernity. These problematic pairs govern the argument of, respectively, the first, second, and third (together with the fourth) chapters of his book.

1.1 The first chapter is the foundational text of Schmittian decisionism. Here Schmitt expresses the antipositivistic thesis that sovereignty is not the necessary effect of closure of the juridified statual order, the highest power that functions as logical completion of the whole order. Sovereignty is instead the decision in so far as it makes that order come into being by opening it up to contingency, to the exception that traverses it in an originary manner. Sovereignty is not then deducible from the order it calls into being, and the order in turn cannot be deduced from it. As a concept of the "outermost sphere,"[11] sovereignty as a decision on the exception is the point of crisis of modern rational mediation—which is to say, of the link between juridical order and politics, as well as between the individual and the totality. According to Schmitt's text, the project of modern rationalism—which is Lockean, enlightened, and positivist, and which tries to make politics revolve around the individual subject, to turn political command into an impersonal and legal function, and to exercise politics in transparency and in continuity with subjective rationality—was a complete failure. To obtain a rational and impersonal ordering that's normatively valid, there must be a personal command that's prelegal and prerational, that founds that order beginning from that normative Void that is decision.[12] Schmitt is, of course, not a nihilist, if by this term we mean complacent or unwitting consent to the dynamics of the Modern. Nevertheless, Schmitt cannot avoid facing modernity's nihilism, its absence of foundations, in which (well before Martin Heidegger's 1927 *Sein und Zeit*) he recognizes that the only possible concreteness of which the Modern is capable is provided by consciousness of nihilism and hence too by opposing its formalistic concealment (which is to say, the merely formal determination, abstract and pacified, of the political order).[13] From a philosophical perspective, Schmitt clarifies the "concrete" role of decision over Nothingness with the long citation of Kierkegaard that closes his first chapter.[14] From a historico-political perspective, meanwhile, it appears evident that the *Ausnahmezustand* to which Schmitt makes reference is an extreme radicalization of the *Notzustand* contained in Article 48 of the "Reserve Constitution" of the Weimar Republic, which is presidential and not parliamentary, which should be activated only in case of emergency, and which Schmitt interprets as a concrete and originary right of the State to self-preservation, to maintain itself as order by going beyond the law.[15]

The exception, which precedes the norm logically and epistemologically, is the conflict that, as irremediable contingency, is absolute beginning, the origin of the politico-juridical form, of the regular and efficacious norm.[16] The decision on the exception thus constitutes the sovereignty that's also the origin of political order. Whether the sovereign decides on the exception, in the sense that he recognizes it as being in action in the political order (in which case sovereign is he who defends threatened order) or whether he creates the exception (in which case the sovereign is the subversive revolutionary who destroys an old order to create a new one), decisionistic sovereignty in each case inverts the modern relationship between "inside" and "outside": if the modern State determines itself as an order that pacifies and neutralizes its interior, an order that pushes conflict away from its borders, instead in the case of decisionistic sovereignty, the only condition on which such an order can be created, preserved, and revolutionized is the sovereign recourse to a disorder that is internal, never completely neutralized.

In this way, Schmitt radically negates *both* the modern thesis according to which the State is produced by the rational activity of the subject (through the contract) *and* that of the full rationality of the functioning of the State and of its juridical order (the neutrality of the rule of Law). We encounter here a theorem of indeterminacy that prescribes not only that the sovereign remain undetermined (he does not hold specific personal qualities, even if he has to be a "person": the sovereign can be anyone who decides effectively on the exceptional case) but also that order itself subsist only at the cost of always hosting within itself the exception, the conflict—which is to say, its own negation. The determination of a politico-juridical order, in short, is given only by its indeterminacy, while the concreteness of the norm is given by the decisionistic opening to the nonnormal situation. Order, it follows, is not completely rational, neutral, and indifferent: even when it remains a political order, it is always "oriented" toward a concrete original case (such that "all law is 'situational law' [*Situationsrecht*]"). In other words, public law is an order that remembers the emergence, the contingency from which it was born; the sovereign, meanwhile, is the one who activates this memory.[17]

This theory of sovereignty—as the creation, preservation, and destructuration of order through disorder—signifies, more generally, that just as the juridical norm is generated by the exception, so too is political order generated and explained by revolution. For Schmitt, the origin is an energy that is never fully constituted (and that yet can even take on the name of "constituent power," a term he does not cite in *Political The-*

ology but that's already present in *Dictatorship* and then is amply thematized in *Constitutional Theory*).[18] In this way, Schmitt is able to think what the modern jurists (and politicians) wanted to neutralize: the creative power of action that's at the same time concrete and nihilistic, deprived of foundation. Sovereignty is, therefore, not so much "perpetual" as something that never ceases, so long as it is effective, to transcend constituted power (which is to say, institutions and formal juridical order as they are normatively intended).[19]

This disjunction between exception and norm, between sociology and juridical order, between order and its negation, does not actually entail their complete separation, as if they were two wholly different genres. It simply means that the "normal" order and its relationship with sovereignty cannot be thought in terms of self-referential juridical function. According to Schmitt, there is indeed a relationship between decision and norm, not a nonrelationship: both are in fact "within the framework of the juristic."[20] However, this relationship is not constituted by modern mediation (which is rational, constructive, and deductive, and which seeks to mediate between particular and universal, the empirical and reason, subject and world, citizen and State). It is a co-implication, a relation in which the decision breaks through modern mediation's transitivity and discursiveness: in the face of exception, a thought that is solely rationalistic remains speechless, resulting in a blockage of the narrative and ordinative function of the modern *logos*.[21] The point at which juridical order and the absence of juridical order turn out to belong to one another is also the point at which reason and nonreason show themselves to be originally united. In *Political Theology*, we might then say, Schmitt thinks the *dead center* of reason, the point at which juridical order and its absence, law and contingency, originarily touch one another. He thinks the aporetic passage, the broken route between the nothing-of-norm and the juridico-political form. "Decision" is the name he gives to this route.

The decision on the exception is, in sum, a decision for an order, a form—a key term of the second chapter of *Political Theology*—that cannot but find itself hanging over a void. It is, in other words, emptied of ontological consistency. This form is a represented form (a "baroque" form, the later Schmitt will say),[22] and the decision is, properly speaking, "decision for the sake of representation." The two inseparable principles of political form that Schmitt discusses in *Constitutional*

Theory[23]—identity and representation—are the political projection of the inseparability of exception and norm, of decision and order, of energy and construction that Schmitt identified in *Political Theology*. In *Constitutional Theory*, however, the exceptional decision is not the decision of the single sovereign; it is the constituent power of the people that wills itself as political unity, and that realizes this will through representation, only without exhausting it in itself. This analogy between the theoretical and the political profile of Schmitt's thought constitutes its intrinsic systematicity, the fundamental unity that lies in the originarity of its energy and in its originary inscription in the horizon of the order.

All of this certainly does involve a paradoxical relationship between reason and nonreason, between idea and contingency, that pushes to an extreme the logics of modernity, challenging and reversing them. We are, nevertheless, always faced with a relationship. Schmitt does not, in fact, theorize politics without juridical order or without reason, brute power deprived of norms. Even his deciding sovereignty is destined to make itself into institutional power, albeit one that originates not in reason but in the decision that always exceeds reason. That the decision is, despite everything, a juridical concept is what makes Schmitt a tragic thinker: he knows that order is both necessary and at the same time, in its modern configuration, impossible. The State, in Schmittian thought, continues to live beyond the State, as a demand for order that can never be made perfectly rational.

1.2 The affirmation we find in the first chapter of *Political Theology*, according to which "authority proves that to produce juridical order it need not be based on juridical order,"[24] opens the space for the book's second chapter. Here, against Hans Kelsen and his student Hugo Krabbe, Schmitt restates the intimate juridicity [*giuridicità*] of his own thought, which is fully ascribable to the theme of *Rechtsverwirklichung*, the "actualization of juridical order." He reaches his aim by rediscovering the difference between *auctoritas* and *potestas*, drawing it not from the Catholic world, in which the concept of authority is central, but from Hobbes, and in particular from a passage in chapter 26 of the *Leviathan*: *auctoritas, non veritas, facit legem* [authority, not truth, produces law].[25]

What Schmitt refers to here, as a point of contrast to the simple legal power of the norm, is thus a nontranscendental authority, a concept he takes not from an antimodern text, but from Hobbes, who opens the

Modern. The authority to which he refers functions neither by founding the norm on an objective Truth (as with the "Authority" of tradition), nor on the rational device of the construction of a pact. Modern order, on this view, is indeed artificial, but it is not rational-individualistic in its origin (Schmitt considers Hobbes's political reason a Blitz: a decision, not a contract).[26] Schmitt thus interprets Hobbes's authority as sovereignty, as decision for a form of representation that is both personal and punctual, positioned between the juridical Idea and the concrete event (without also, of course, mediating between them), in a way that makes the former "leap" into the latter. For Schmitt, in other words, "authority" is neither a modern rational mediation between subject and object (played out in complete immanence), nor the traditional pontifical mediation between Heaven and Earth, between Truth and History. "Authority" is, as decision, precisely the "leap" that makes clear the impossibility of a linear path between idea and reality, between juridical order and politics. It is also a "break": not only does the juridical idea not apply itself to reality, but the order it founds is no more automatic than the law it issues is "natural."[27]

From this perspective, the origin of the concrete juridical order does not inhere in the discursive mediation of a juridical Idea. It needs the work of the nonrational if it is to become an effective "form" (and not, contrary to the notion of "form" proposed by Weber and by the neo-Kantians, an assumption of the "rationality of the real" or the potential to become technically rational). The *Rechtsverwirklichung* Schmitt thinks, and that implies decisionistic sovereignty, is consequently the representation of the *absence* of a juridical Idea.[28] It follows that Schmitt does not accept the self-affirmation of Modernity, its ideological pretense to sustain itself on its own, to found itself in and through subjective reason, contract, and legality. What does not follow, however, is that Schmitt's concept of "authority" is simply a matter of the "politics" that founds juridical order and that remains distinct and distant from it: we should be wary of believing that, simply because the irrationality of decision lies at the origin of the rationality of order, authority somehow remains different and separated from it. Although authority is for Schmitt the "last instance" that explains the norm without also deriving from it, Schmitt also in this second chapter attempts to think the absence of any juridico-rational origin for juridical order precisely as a juridical problem[29]—a problem that is not external to, but situated within, jurisprudence. For Schmitt, in fact, to stop at the formal and normative level is equivalent to remaining "in the antechamber of jurisprudence." Jurisprudence must instead recognize (and this is the core of decisionism) that juridico-political form is indeed unfounded, but only in the sense that the decision that founds it "emanates from nothingness," and not in the sense that it is free from the problem of foundation. Authority, decision, is exactly this foundation of juridical order on the juridical Void, on the Void-of-Order, on the aphasic lacuna, on the existential concreteness of exception and of conflict. Throughout *Political Theology*, Schmitt disquiets and critiques rational mediation (liberal political form), but in general remains within the modern compulsion toward form: juridical order remains the horizon within which Schmitt moves.[30]

For Schmitt, the leap—the disconnection of principle between Idea and reality, the nonnormative origin of form and order—is a juridical problem. The absence of foundation acts upon the juridical order: the disconnection between idea and contingency is also, at the same time, their necessary co-implication. In this labor of the Void-of-Order, in this presence and in this power that absence holds on transcendence, which is subterranean and internal to the order, lies the difference between Schmitt and Kelsen. For Kelsen, the nonjuridical origin of juridical order is a sociological fact, and not, as it is for Schmitt, a juridical fact. It is, therefore, a fact that does not belong to juridical order. In Kelsen we find a "pacified" absence of foundations that produces an effect of disenchantment and makes possible the formalistic method with which he thinks the system of norms. Kelsen reacts to the lack of foundations of juridical order by accepting it, and also by negating in a Kantian manner as "nonscientific" every attempt to return to a prejuridical instance (such as God or sovereignty)[31] that might explain the existence or "being-there" of juridical order. Juridical reason is, in this account, nothing more and nothing less than the analysis of that "phenomenon" which is ordering. It is oriented not to the decision but to the impersonal *Grundnorm* that is capable of establishing the competent instance for the application of any norm. Schmitt, by contrast, thinks a different modulation of the disenchanted recognition of the unfoundedness of juridical order. For him, "science" consists not in erasing but in including within the discipline of jurisprudence the rational unfoundability of juridical order, its being decided by a person whose competence is unpredictable. And this is why, as Schmitt already affirmed in the first chapter of *Political Theology*, it is oriented toward decision as an authentic "point of ascription."[32]

There is, of course, an opposition between Kelsen's unfounded formalism and Schmitt's unfounded decisionism, as well as between Kelsen's impersonal law and Schmitt's personal authority. Nevertheless, both start from the same horizon of the crisis of modern mediation that attempted to hold together, without contradictions, subject and order. But whereas Kelsen privileges the latter, Schmitt privileges the former (not of course as subject in the liberal sense or as person in the Catholic sense, but as authority in the sense of a concrete instance, a formative decision, that is capable of founding the juridical order). "The problem of juridical form," Schmitt thus argues, lies in "the contrast between the subject and the content of a decision and in the proper meaning of the subject."[33] What's more, it's worth noting, Schmitt's refusal of the self-justification of the finished—of order's own self-positioning—excludes from its horizon not only the simple and linear rationalism of modernity, but also traditional foundationalism, and lastly romantic and vitalistic irrationalism.[34] There is, in Schmitt, a sui generis acceptance of the Modern: on the one hand, he acknowledges that it is impossible to be elsewhere than in the space and time of the foundation on the Void, which is precisely in decision; on the other hand, he maintains that it is impossible to ignore that the Void within modernity is a problem, one that ends up dismantling the foundations of modernity's ideological pretenses of self-sufficiency.

In short, the first two chapters of *Political Theology* disclose that the essence of modern political existence is, according to Schmitt, *to be decided* and *to be represented*. The critic of modern juridical (and political) reason as an ideology of self-foundation here arrives at the discovery of the authentic coordinates of modern political existence, understood as existence concretely determined by the absence of ontological foundations and by the insufficiency of rational mediations to fully found the Modern. The Modern is, on this view, structurally unfounded, exposed to the power of the absence of transcendence. Schmitt modulates this absence as decision during the twenties, as full biological and *völkisch* immanence during his Nazi period, and as an "opening to transcendence" (albeit an always absent one) during his postwar period. It is, in fact, the red thread of Schmitt's thought, even if he did pose it in very different ways over the course of his long life.

1.3 Before analyzing the third and fourth chapters of *Political Theology*, in which the notion of political theology reveals its developmental (diagnostic and prognostic) aspect, it's important to grasp the specific mode in which Schmitt turns from a discourse on sovereignty to a discourse on modernity. Schmitt's theory of *Rechtsverwircklichung*, remember, is also a theory—a genealogy—of modernity as secularization. It is what Schmitt will call a "sociology of juristic concepts": a specific theory of the genesis of modern juridico-political concepts, programmatically understood as a result of the secularization of theological concepts—a secularization that, precisely, makes these concepts political.[35]

The key to the interpretative problem of *Political Theology* consists in understanding what Schmitt means by "secularization." To this end, it will be helpful to point to the general frame of theoretical reflection within which Schmitt places himself. Among its many possible meanings, "secularization" means, in this framework, that Modernity derives in some way from the sphere of theoretical and institutional elaborations of the sacred in its Christian form.[36] Modernity is not then autonomous, as claimed by the Enlightenment and by the discourse of the Modern in general. Not a new beginning, Modernity needs a history behind its back if it's to exist, and this history always presents a remnant with regard to Modernity's pretense of self-sufficiency. This is, in various guises, the translation (*Übersetzung*) and reoccupation (*Umbesetzung*) of traditional theological apparatuses.

All of this—whether it be Schmitt's struggle against the self-sufficiency of the Modern, intended as self-creation and completeness, but also as separation and neutralization of politics and religion; his struggle against the exhaustiveness of its categories and of its game of mirrors between particular and universal, between subject and State—can be modulated according to very different logics and arguments. In Hobbes's transcendental-formal system, for example, which operates on divine transcendence according to public logics of emptying and of private interiorization of the sacred,[37] God is the keystone and the guarantor of obedience to the sovereign. In the Catholic-foundational system of the counterrevolutionaries, meanwhile, God is the substance that alone gives meaning and consistency to the political order.[38] And in the logic of the Protestant-Hegelian system—in Hegel's mature texts, but also in his earlier theological writings[39]—we find an opposition between Catholicism (which logically separates the finite and the infinite only to then reunite them in a surreptitious way) and Protestantism (which separates them in order to reconcile them). In section 270 of The Philosophy of Right, Hegel maintains that for Catholics, divine infinity is nothing else but the weakness of a contingent that relates to an external Absolute, conceived as a force on which to lean; whereas for liberals, infinity consists not in the divine but in another foundational claim (such as the humanities or science). In this reading, both liberalism and the Church (despite their enmity) see in the State only the moment of necessity, while the Absolute lies elsewhere. In Hegel's view, by contrast, the Absolute dialectically enters into history with the French Revolution, and ever since then it has been the State that stands for the Universal, whereas the Church stands for the particular. In fact, the State knows the relationship between the Absolute and history (that is, the Absolute as something that was elaborated during the phases of human self-consciousness), while the Church continues to know the Absolute only as external fact, as an "objective" God, as authority and in the form of sentiment. In section 552 of the Encyclopedia, Hegel affirms that the relationship between religion and politics cannot be assimilated to the relationships between subject and object (i.e., it cannot be treated through modern rationalism). Instead, philosophy's introduction of the divine spirit into reality enables both the State and philosophy to realize the substantial content of religion in more appropriate forms. This happens through Protestant conscience and its capacity to separate finite and infinite while at the same time realizing the conciliation between the interiority of the subject and the world. Thus, taking for granted the criticism that Hegel directs to Catholic fundamentalism, the liberal and modern separation between the various spheres, between politics and religion, is also for Hegel "a monstrous error," against which he opposes the speculative knowledge of ethics, which is to say, the knowledge of the free nature of the spirit that realizes itself in the mundane and immanent, self-justified, sphere, and that is at odds against Catholicism, the religion of servitude.[40] Different still are both the Weberian individualistic political theology (which reads modernity as the elabora-

tion of a subjective rational action that derives its power of disenchantment from the Protestant religious tradition)[41] and Nietzsche's rebel-
lion against every political theology and all mediation.[42]

Schmitt, an enemy of the "Grand" liberal-modern separation between
religion and politics, assumes that the Modern is the secularization of
the Christian theological tradition, although in a specific sense. For
him, it is not possible to imagine the Modern, as does Hegel, as the progressive evolution of the same substance (the Spirit) that takes on new
forms (philosophy and the State) in the wake of the old ones (Christian
religion). There is, on this point, a chasm between the Lutheran philosopher and the Catholic jurist. In Schmitt's view, it is also not possible to
imagine the Modern as self-sufficient reason: for Schmitt the Modern is,
if anything, permanent revolution. To Protestant dialectical conciliation
(the return from the separation of religion and politics), Schmitt opposes neither the neutralizing self-interpretation of modernity (the separation in nonproblematic form) nor a Catholic fundamentalism, but
rather a tragic vision of discontinuity and disconnection. For Schmitt,
in other words, there is a relationship between tradition and modernity,
between theological concepts (or metaphysics) and political concepts,
and this relationship is, moreover, essential for any understanding of
the Modern. Neither progressive nor regressive, this relationship consists in categorical and conceptual permanence and transformation, in
formal continuity and substantial discontinuity. Schmitt indeed defines
it as a relationship of "analogy," although not in the Thomistic sense of
analogia entis (understood as the order of a created world that is wanted
and guaranteed by the Maker), but of an analogy that atones for the absence, in the political concepts of modernity, of a foundational Being.[43]

The interpretative key to Schmitt's thesis is the analogy between
sovereignty as decision on the exceptional case and the miracle in the
traditional sense. In *Political Theology*, the decision is indeed a secularization of the miracle (both suspend the laws of normality). As it is more
clearly stated in *Dictatorship*, modern constituent power—which is to
say, sovereign dictatorship, which amounts to the extreme version of
decision, the mode that does not limit itself to exceptionally defending
an existing order but that destroys it to create a new one—no longer has
a fixed point of reference in God, in transcendence that also functions
as foundational substance whose order (or orders) the political power
must respect (execute), and whose person the political power must rep-

resent. Modern constituent power is power that is absolute and free, that is itself analogous to God,[44] now secularized by way of "emptying." What's central in Schmitt, much more than the banal direct analogy of counterrevolutionary origin between modern political theories and theologico-metaphysical concepts (absolutism as theism, liberalism as deism, etc.),[45] is thus the chiasmus that came to institute itself between tradition and modernity. On the one hand, the Modern is *radically discontinuous* with respect to the presence of traditional foundational substance (which is absent in the Modern,[46] albeit in a very "active" way, as we have already seen). On the other hand, however, tradition and modernity remain linked by a *strong continuity*: even though each has the capacity to destroy order, they both obey the necessity of reconstituting new orders. Their continuity, in short, consists in their compulsion to create orders whose form is "monocentric."

This is political theology in its proper sense: not the deduction of politics from theology, but the theory according to which modern politics—its concepts and institutions—preserves something of religion, emptying religion of its theological concepts without also overcoming those concepts (especially when it comes to the unity of order and its sovereign creation). It follows from this that the relationship between modern politics and theological tradition is twofold. On the one hand, modern politics is structured by the absence of foundational divine substance, and is therefore contrary to theology. On the other hand, modern politics reproduces theology's monistic ordering function, even if only in a formal-rational way. This twofold and contradictory relationship is Schmitt's version of Europe's "Christian roots."

The absence of an order that lies at the origin of the need for *Rechtsverwircklichung*, the need to realize the juridical order through representation, is determined by the absence of theological foundation with which modern political theory functions. From both viewpoints, that absence is operative: it has an intrinsic power that determines the characteristics and epochality of modern political space. If, in other words, in the previous chapters of *Political Theology*, the doctrine of sovereignty as "political theology" was a juridical theory oriented toward the practical and the operative, in the third chapter it reveals itself to be a discourse on— and not internal to—the philosophy of history. It is here, that is to say, a method of interpreting modernity as secularization, a genealogical hermeneutics of political modernity that reinterprets the secular pretense of the full emancipation of politics from religious tradition (the pretense to the self-justification of the finite) by reading the Modern as an epoch in which the exception—conflict, the absence of a substantial foundational order—has become normal (or, in other words, the side of *discontinuity* with respect to tradition, which necessarily turns politics into the space for exception) and, at the same time, as an epoch in which precisely the absence of substance makes politics destructive, while also obliging it to exhibit an even stronger tendency to the construction of a monistic formal order (or, in other words, the side of *continuity* with respect to tradition, in which the compulsion toward order that governs the whole political and intellectual experience of the Western world manifests itself in traditionally substantial forms and in modernly exceptional forms—or, in other words, in the constructivist and nonsubstantialist metaphysics of the Modern).

"Political theology" also embraces secularization. Along with Bakunin's open atheism, and Alberico Gentili's *silete theologi!* (to say nothing of the historico-philological correctness of Schmitt's interpretation), Schmitt sings the tune of modern political theology.[47] Political theology, consequently, is not a theory of the theological foundation of politics, but of the historical and categorical context of the origin of the Modern and of the compulsions that dominate it. It is the horizon of the absence of transcendence in which modernity is given; and to the extent that it's able to allow for the emergence of the foundation of absence—the Void-of-Order—that is the unsaid and unthought of the Modern, it is a figure, or even the main figure, of "concreteness" and of genealogy.

In the third chapter, in fact, Schmitt shows that to interpret modernity as secularization means to exist in the Modern without accepting its ideological self-interpretation, whether evolutionary and progressive or rationalistic and constructive. Instead, Schmitt's interpretation of modern politics is genealogical, a discourse on the origin of the Modern identified both in its lack of substance and in the permanence of its compulsion toward order. Because it keeps together (without synthesis) both exception and juridical form, the deciding sovereignty that Schmitt discussed in the first two chapters is, if not "necessary" (in modernity there is indeed no "necessity," only contingency), then certainly "indispensable" in an epochal dimension that turns the Modern into the epoch of exception. Only decisionistic and representative sovereignty is adequate to politically inhabit modernity, to continuously evoke the immense energy necessary for order to come into being, to battle against any drift toward an "automatic" concept of politics.

Schmitt's position, accordingly, does not coincide with those who (like Löwith, Voegelin, and Strauss) interpret the Modern as a compact of religion, philosophy, and politics that realizes, in immanence, the fullness of substance that Christianity proposed as *eschaton* or as openness of conscience, and also as a natural and objective foundation of human experience.[48] Albeit getting close to such theses, Schmitt's thought is more categorical than ideological (or critical of ideology) in its reasoning and scope, thus exposing his spare decisionism to the paradoxical risk of legitimating any political form (except liberalism, of course), including the most "substantial" ones (although we do need to remember that, in his attempt to "truly" be a Nazi, Schmitt had to abandon decisionism).

From the viewpoint of the relationship between theology and juridical order, Kelsen—champion of the most disenchanted scientific knowledge of modernity—also vouches for discontinuity, excluding any possible relation between traditional theological explanation and scientific explanation of juridical facts. Kelsen's emphasis on discontinuity nevertheless implies that every political, psychological, theological concept of substance be translated, in modern science, as "function."[49] Schmitt, by contrast, does not believe that "function" is appropriate for thinking juridical categories, which in his view need instead to be thought starting from theological categories and from the peculiar secularization (indeed, the political theology) those categories undergo.[50]

Political theology is, as we have seen, an interpretation of the Modern that is at the same time tragic and formative: the Schmittian sovereign's exposure to the Void can be certainly interpreted—as Benjamin did in memorable pages[51]—as the melancholic exposition, at the peak of Baroque glory, of the creaturely nullity, of the character of "tragic drama" (*Trauerspiel*) of the Modern. Nullity of this sort implicitly makes possible the fulminous irruption of the time that saves, of the contracted time of the great decision, of the *Jetztzeit*.[52] But if the telos of Benjamin's Jewish political theology, according to his materialist philosophy, is redemption, as a Catholic jurist, Schmitt's own political theology is order and form. Whereas for Benjamin religion acts as a utopian unbinding with respect to political order, Schmitt's intent is constructive (despite the deconstructionism running throughout his theory of sovereignty, as revealed in his polemics against Benjamin on the theme of Hamlet's inde-cision).[53] Going against Benjamin's thesis, Schmitt refuses the notion that Hamlet's indecision is Christian, imputable to the roots of modern politics. It instead remains lateral to modern politics, as it were: English, not continental. Modern politics, although "founded on the Void" and although forced to exhibit its original Void in the sovereign decision, is not tragic drama but the actual Tragödie of formed statuality—which is illuminated but not explained by Hamlet's barbaric story (since form is, of course, foreign to Hamlet).

Even if decision is indispensable to the State, it thus precedes the State, for the Void-of-Order is the environment and the horizon of the Modern and of its political form. This is the meaning of Schmitt's Politi-cal Theology, the highly radical theorem of incompleteness that employs the theological not to found politics but to highlight its unfoundedness and the compulsion toward order that constitutively pertains to it.

It is worth noting that, duly domesticated, Schmitt's position mi-grated into the reflections of Ernst-Wolfgang Böckenförde, for whom the fact that "the liberal State relies on presuppositions it cannot guar-antee"[54] means that the separation between the public and the private sphere (in which there is also room for religion) is not born only from the modern State and its secular ideology, but also develops and brings to conclusion something that precedes it. Secularization, for Böcken-förde, is not simply the "emptying" of religion (as it is, say, in a Hobbes-ian perspective); it translates, into political forms, petitions for liberty that previously existed in a different form. Formal modern juridical order has its genesis in historico-political concreteness, without also being epiphenomenal to that concreteness.[55] The Schmittian power of the absence of transcendence—a power that can be only treated with decision—here turns into a humanistic awareness of the unity of history and destiny of European culture, into a refusal of the self-interpretation of the Modern as an absolutely new beginning.

1.4 Thanks to the theoretical apparatus Schmitt offers in Political The-ology, once we reach the "twofold" origin of the Modern (the disconnec-tion and the co-implication in principle between idea and contingency, and at the same time the compulsion toward represented order), we can also return to identify the double face of modernity—on the one hand, the concrete, deciding, and ordering face, and, on the other hand, the abstract-formal one, the side that assigns order through the mere automatisms of reason and technics (and, of course, the juridical). These two faces belong to one another, as Schmitt already has intuited in his analysis of modernity's possible dynamics and drifts.[56] Modern reason encounters extreme difficulty in staying open toward its origin in crisis, to pursue necessary order without falling into the temptation to enclose it, found it, and emphasize it, or to turn order into a machinery that pretends to be at the disposal of the individual (but that, in reality, turns out to be a machinery that dominates the individual).

Accordingly, Schmitt's concept of "political theology" is neither only practico-operative (the deciding and representing sovereignty) nor only genealogical (the twofold origin of modernity, of exceptional crisis and ordering coercion); it is also diagnostic-interpretative. It allows Schmitt a sort of skeletal philosophy of history: from this point of view, political modernity seems to Schmitt to be signed as much as by the decisionistic concreteness of the first great modern author (who is, for him, not Machiavelli, but Hobbes, who is able to hold on both to the awareness of the disorder of the world and the need to rationally order it) as by an evolution (which is progressively oblivious to the tragic origin of the Modern, to the unresolved tension between decision and order that leads decisionism to liberalism and to juridical positivism, and, finally, to formalism).[57] This process—the turn from one Zentralgebiet [area of focus] to another—follows a trajectory characterized by an ever more radical unawareness of the original structure of the Modern, by an ever wider pretense to build on the origin a technico-rational order in defense of the individual and that substitutes sovereignty in its function as origin of the order. This process is furthermore characterized by an ever stronger impotence of this neutralized technical form, which is not oriented toward the concrete event and the defense of the subject (which is instead destroyed) and not inclined to grasp itself efficaciously and to form living substance (which, in Schmitt, is neither exactly substance nor Life in the irrationalistic sense, but is instead concrete exception, conflict). From this third viewpoint, "political theology" is, besides a diagnosis, also a prognosis and a proposal of therapy for the nonordering tendencies of the Modern, of the individualism and technicism that produce and at the same time negate it. For Schmitt, when the State (the modern order) ceases to be a duty and instead becomes an instrument of the individual (according to a logic already implicit in Hobbes), it also ceases to be order, because it forgets its origin in the concrete exception and the compulsion toward form.[58]

In order to contain those technical and automatic drifts that lead to loss of both subject and concrete order, Schmitt does not attempt a foundationalist escape (which would bring him back to political Catholicism). Instead, he takes as an example his doctrinaire discovery, Donoso Cortés, the Spanish counterrevolutionary who recognizes that modernity has reached the end of any legitimacy (any foundation of power on transcendence). Against the structural illegitimacy of the Modern, Schmitt reacts from within, with decisionistic dictatorship.[59] It's from this viewpoint, which is certainly disputable from the historico-political side, that, in the fourth chapter of Political Theology, Schmitt brings in the Catholic counterrevolutionaries, whose legitimistic and antimodern foundationalism he interprets as not dogmatikós but agonikós—bent toward an ultramodern decisionism. The heavily ideological tool to which Schmitt here resorts in order to critically confront the Modern, in other words, he uses while also negating: despite the authors he cites, from the point of view of the ultimate significance of his intellectual work, Schmitt is not a reactionary Catholic.[60]

The heart of his first Political Theology lies in decisionism, that is to say, in the concrete existential exposure of politics to the normative nothingness (an exposure determined by the power of absence of transcendence). The same is true for the texts connected to it, which are still animated by the trust that in the evolution of modernity both the subjectivistic and the technico-automatic can be interrupted and won by the formative decision, the decision that creates order precisely by opening itself to the exception (which is to say, to the "political").

2. Interpretations and Self-Interpretations

Although interpreters of Political Theology have easily perceived its clear antiliberal content,[61] the same is not true of its structural and epochal significance as a critique of modern ideology and as a discovery of the aporetic origin of modernity. Also on account of the Catholic path Schmitt took to achieve his deconstruction, this text appeared to many as nothing more than a brilliant exercise in antimodernity, if not also a recuperation of foundationalistic and simply "analogic" themes of counterrevolutionary thought, focused on the simple and direct, almost mechanical *analogia entis* between theology and politics. But at this point in his intellectual career, Catholicism is for Schmitt merely a "path," a cultural means to subtract himself from the self-valorization of the Modern, from the Protestant ideology of "productive secularization." It certainly is not, in other words, a religious or political "end."

2.1 *Political Theology* was interpreted—both positively, by authors close to the Nazi regime (such as Alfred de Quervain, Emanuel Hirsch, and Wilhelm Stapel), and negatively (Erik Peterson)—as a theory of the presence of God in politics, that is to say, either as a repoliticization of religion, or as a sacralization of power (two convergent hypotheses). It furthermore was read (by Friedrich Gogarten, also a collaborationist) as a theory of secularization in terms of the absence of God, as a distance between the divine and the world, destined to be filled by ethical claims. In 1934, Schmitt's book was reprinted in an almost identical version, only now with the addition of a foreword in which a complacent Schmitt took note of the success of the term [political theology] amid religious and political debates on secularization and on the existential nexus of theology and politics.[62] The content of this first self-interpretation shows how interested Schmitt was in underlining *Political Theology*'s antiliberal side, and in negating once and for all the (neutralizing) modern-bourgeois thesis that turns religion into something other than politics. However, having ascertained that there exists a relationship between the two dimensions, and furthermore that it is an unchangeable modality of human experience, Schmitt did not explain in detail the meaning, from this point of view, of *Political Theology* (a text that was, by the way, published for the first time well before Nazism).

Instead, Schmitt's 1934 text demonstrated that he realized that decisionism, which is the obligatory corollary of his political theology, is, quite beyond any ideological opposition, nothing but reversed liberalism. Or better, he understood that liberalism and positivistic normativism are precisely a degeneration of decisionism (although each theorizes the impersonality of law and the absence of exception, whereas decisionism conceives in the exceptional case the command of one only). After having reinterpreted Maurice Hauriou's institutionalism as a "theory of concrete orders," Schmitt found in Hauriou, who conjugates the concreteness pursued by decisionism with the superpersonality [*sovrapersonalità*] of the law, the new horizon of juridical order.

Hauriou was also important to Schmitt because Nazism was hostile to decisionism and dictatorship and favored an organic—*völkisch*—interpretation of politics.

2.2 The theory of concrete orders is Schmitt's reply—drenched in ideology—to the theoretical and historical defeat inflicted on decisionism, and to the perspectives offered by *Political Theology*, by the final crisis of the Weimar Republic (which could not be healed by the defensive and plebiscitarian use of Article 48 of the "Reserve Constitution" of the Weimar Republic, as Schmitt had proposed). To the even more catastrophic defeat of Nazism, Schmitt reacted with a new interpretation of political theology, which, starting from what he wrote beginning in 1937–38, in connection to his research on international law and culminating in *Nomos of the Earth*, he developed ever more clearly as a theory of *katechon*.[63]

With this Pauline term, indicating the historico-political force that restrains "man from sin"—the "mystery of iniquity"[64]—Schmitt indicates an ability to build relatively stable political forms, a capacity that first pertained to the Church and then to the origin of the modern State. As usual, Schmitt relates the modern State to Hobbesian thought, which he reinterprets in 1965 in a less decisionistic way than he had in his analysis of 1938.[65] In this new interpretation, Schmitt now underlines that even though the modern State cannot exhibit any substantial foundation, due to its "modern" origin in crisis, Hobbes's State is nonetheless still a "Christian State" (which is also the title of the third part of the *Leviathan*). According to Schmitt, the same crisis from which the State is born can act as a "restraint" to the drifts of modern automatism, if political form, which is made necessary by the crisis, opens up to transcendence, if it renounces the ideological pretense of rationalistic completeness, the self-foundational effort that characterizes it after Hobbes, starting already with liberalism, and that reaches its peak with technics.[66]

In the context of Schmitt's conservative turn in the aftermath of World War II (following his early juridical and Catholic phase, the decisionistic phase of his maturity, and his Nazi-totalitarian phase), "political theology" continues to refer to the inescapable relationship between politics and the theological sphere. It continues to be a theory of secularization, and continues to locate the central characteristic of modernity in the absence of traditional theological foundation, and the condition of concreteness of modern political forms in the "memory" of that absence of foundational transcendence. Now, however, Schmitt no longer interprets the decision for order as a formal, empty, arbitrary gesture; he is aware that an effective sovereign neutralization can take place only starting from a concrete response to concrete conflict ("Jesus is the Christ" is a suitable answer to civil wars of religion). Decision lies in history, and not in its unfoundedness (as he argued in *Political Theology*). It's clear that the enemy, for Schmitt, is always the oblivion of the origin, of the power of the absence of transcendence. It is the pretense—born from the great separation between religion and politics—of automatic order, of a full foundation for modern politics (liberal humanism) or of its full unfoundedness (formalism or technics). Now it appears to Schmitt that such "memory" lies not so much in sovereign decision as in an "opening" of order toward transcendence, an opening that is not a neofoundationalism, but rather a new reaffirmation of Schmitt's earlier theorem of incompleteness. It's as if the modern State, in order to be stable, should renounce its attempt to be self-sufficient in its enclosed rationality, and should instead always be aware of its Christian roots and even exhibit them, even when they are no longer true roots any more, but only a trace of the connection of the State's structures to theological matters. It's as if it were indispensable, for Schmitt, that modern civilization refer continuously to the great Christian framework of which, despite everything, it is still a part. In this phase, concreteness lies neither in decision nor in institutions; it lies in the "restraint" of its own drifts that politics may deploy, of course in an aporetic way, as long as it remembers the religious context in which the Modern is established, interpreting the Modern as secularization, that is to say, as operating absence of the Christian religious tradition.

Along the same lines, Schmitt now sees Hobbes as the one who brings the Reformation to completion, in the double sense that he appropriates its attack on the Church's indirect political role, and that he tries to terminate, indeed to restrain, the destabilizing effects of the reformers, namely, the risks of perpetual disorder lying in their theology, which were strongly based on individualism (even if Lutheran individualism is different from the Calvinist one). Hobbes, in other words, tries to restrain the dangers of revolutionary disorder in the immediate present and, as a response to it, the dangers of the technical and automatic order that should preserve the life of the individual. Revolution and technics lie in the same epochal framework as two opposed problems that have in common the same oblivion of transcendence. In his construction of the modern State according to Schmitt, Hobbes is driven by a "Christian" awareness of the existence of a theological problem, one that now, however, has become political (because of the civil wars of religion) and that needs a political solution in light of the awareness of its theological origin (as distinct from awareness of a simple need for peace that can be solved through merely technical means). The State can provide the "restraint" to modern disorder (technical or revolutionary) only if it is a Christian state and if it is sufficiently self-aware to be able to position itself within an ever-open theological question: the question of the absence of God (which is to say, of the modern multiplication of the images of God). This absence does not admit either to response or to repair, but it does continue to weigh, and it cannot be resolved with a hurried self-founded secularism. While Schmitt in his first "political theology" was worried about the "scientific" blindness of juridical formalism, he is now preoccupied with the automatic blindness of technical progress. In this new version Schmitt's attention is focused less on the power of decision than on a compulsion toward order that is concrete but neither automatic nor formalistic.

2.3 Hans Blumenberg interpreted the modern debt to theology—Schmitt's persistence in indicating the legitimacy of the Modern in its relationship with theological tradition, even if not in a foundational way—as a delegitimization of the Modern that, for Blumenberg, is generally implicit in the concept of secularization, a concept that Blumenberg wanted to substitute instead with "reoccupation" (Umbesetzung).[67] For Blumenberg, completely autonomous modern political concepts are self-founded and legitimized precisely by their conscious constitution as rupture vis-à-vis tradition and as "new beginning." On Blumenberg's reading, modern political concepts do not derive from theology but take the place of certain theological concepts. In this way, Blumenberg proposes a functional equivalence that Schmitt also seems to accept,[68] letting Blumenberg (who initially had criticized Schmitt for being too Christian and, in the end, for being a legitimist) conclude that Schmitt's political theology was not political theology in any proper sense, but only in the sense of "political metaphysics." This was an acute evaluation, but in some ways it was also limiting. The definitive predicate of "political theology" is indeed that modern metaphysics—undoubtedly the object of Schmitt's analysis, which indicates its origin, logics, dynamics, and aporias—structures itself in relation, although one of absence, with theology.

2.4 The core of *Political Theology II*, Schmitt's final self-interpretation, is a reply to Peterson that arrives more than thirty years later than the publication of the text with which the Protestant theologian, converted to Catholicism, "liquidated" any political theology as a "pagan" remnant. The criticisms coming from Blumenberg, a phenomenological philosopher, and from Peterson, a theologian with a strong ethical background, are two opposed ways to refuse the combination of theology and politics prepared by Schmitt. Besides being politically suspect, this mix is for both "impure," and it furthermore does not actually give reasons for what it claims to explain: modernity and the position of religion with respect to politics.[69]

For Peterson, the essence of Christianity, Trinitarism, and the radical transcendence and alterity of Heaven to Earth is betrayed by the "monotheistic" layout of the relationship (of foundation or mirroring) between God and Power. This structuring was first elaborated by Eusebius, theologian of the era of Constantine, and was essentially resumed by Schmitt. The contingent political preoccupations behind the distinction between politics and religion proposed by Peterson are clear: the need never to legitimize Nazism, especially through a "theological" argument. Peterson in truth interprets Schmitt's political theology as something he never intended it to be, namely, the deduction of specific political contents and directions from theology and religion.[70] (This is the position, however, of "new" political theologists like Johann Baptist Metz, Jürgen Moltmann, Rudolf Karl Bultmann, and Dorothee Sölle, who derive the legitimization for revolution from Christian eschatology.)[71]

It is easy for Schmitt to reply that it is precisely the radical separation between theology and politics, as invoked by Peterson, that would make it impossible to theologically "liquidate" political theology. Furthermore, in comparison to the usual arguments, all belonging to the realm of a political theology understood as the permanence within politics of the formal structures of religion, here it emerges that, for Schmitt, "political theology" indicates not only the entry of religion into politics, but also the entry of politics into religion. Besides the history of the Catholic Church in its historico-political existence, besides crucifixion, even the dogma of the Trinity is exposed to the power of the "political" (also the Trinity is generated from *stasis*, from the conflict of the One against itself).[72] In Schmitt's view, this separation is also confuted by the whole of human history, from the very beginning of civilization. Everywhere, not only in monarchy or in Eusebius, there is "political theology," a relationship—whichever way it is structured—between religion and politics. This relationship in fact grows stronger the more politics focuses, in a modern manner, on democracy and revolution, absolute powers that reproduce on earth, often unwittingly, divine omnipotence.[73] Compared by Peterson to Eusebius with a strongly critical aim, Schmitt intends to employ his ordinative political theology—here reinterpreted in a conservative sense—as a *katechon* for political theologies of conflict, for political Augustinism (which he understands as a teleology of history) and its revolutionary results, and lastly for ancient and modern *gnoses*.[74]

But in the 1970s, political theology was threatened, and made obsolete, precisely by the automatisms of technics, which Schmitt believed he could master with decision or restrain with a *katechon*. Now, following typical patterns of the post–World War II conservative criticism of civilization, Schmitt instead recognizes that the age of technics can do completely without political theology (understood as a relationship with transcendence) and that it can neither be understood nor managed according to theologico-political diagnoses and prognoses. It's not only a matter of reinterpreting technics as self-divinization of man, and to reproach Prometheism and its reversal into slavery; it's also a matter of realizing that the modern theologico-political origin of technics has turned into a "process-progress" that nurtures itself incessantly and self-legitimizes itself as "new." Deprived of history, resistant to genealogy and sovereign decision, technics is today what acts in place of man, enhancing and devaluing him. Technics is, really, immanence gone out of control.[75]

Thus it is that Schmitt's final published words on political theology amount to a death certificate.[76] Neither as decision, nor as a modern *katechon* of modern dynamics, is political theology able to overcome technics and its mobilizing power—a power that destroys the concrete stability of the State and every possible value and sense that once accrued to the concepts of authority, legitimacy, transcendence, form, relationship with tradition (and also, it would seem, to the concepts of "political" and of "politics"). The triumph of the logics of modernity, uncontrolled in their automatism, signals the end of political theology and of the very possibility of political thinking, as Schmitt understands it. He admits that his categories do not give him the power to understand the age of technics, that is to say, the age of automatism and, at the same time, of disorder. Not even the extreme theology that emerges within the global era, and that jeopardizes once and for all the supposedly great separation between the theological and the political, can be accurately deciphered through Schmittian categories[77]—unless, of course, those categories are dilated well beyond their historical reach. Even so, by allowing us a radical interpretation of the modern age and its destiny, Schmitt's thought already had achieved its objective.

....

CHAPTER 3

SCHMITT AND MACHIAVELLI

Even if an unpublished piece on Machiavelli were found in Schmitt's *Nachlass* (which is kept in Düsseldorf in the Hauptstaatsarchiv of Nordrhein-Westfalen), the scholarly interest of that piece would in the end be only a small tile in the already polychromous and changing mosaic formed by the many citations of Machiavelli in known Schmittian texts. The latter already are sufficient to delineate the profile of Schmitt's unstable relationship with Machiavelli, which is composed alternately of biographical and intellectual identifications, attempts to distance himself from the Florentine author, as well as misunderstandings, self-pitying commiserations, and farewells.

Schmitt's explicit position on Machiavelli, whose thought he accessed directly and without linguistic difficulty in the original Italian, must be presented in an adequately periodized form. Although the *Discourses* also were known to him, the German jurist privileged *The Prince*. Some clear points emerge from the critical analysis of Schmitt's attempts to understand Machiavelli. First, despite the persistence of his approach, Schmitt thinks Machiavelli only in an extemporaneous and external way: the Florentine does not have the same central presence in Schmitt's thought as does Hobbes or Donoso Cortés. Second, Schmitt gives a conventional reading of Machiavelli, while also using him in a dubious way, deploying Machiavelli to make sense of problematics and polemics that belong entirely to the twentieth century (which, frankly, also holds true for Schmitt's more central authors, whom he reads innovatively but controversially). Third, the key to understanding the gap between Schmitt and Machiavelli, which remains wide open despite

Schmitt's efforts, lies in the different theoretical stances they establish, both implicitly and explicitly, with the epochal logics of modernity.

1. Machiavelli: Lie and Technics

"Nothing is to me more intelligible and more sympathetic than Machiavelli's opinion: if all men in the world were good, it would be wickedness to lie and to cheat. If, however, all are obviously just mob and rabble, then it would be stupidity to be noble and decent."[1] With this June 26, 1914, diary entry, to which he would return in his later years, the young Carl Schmitt began his personal identification with the Florentine, applying not only to Machiavelli but also to himself a reflection—that Machiavelli's theory "speaks only of a good but disappointed man, of the indignation of a noble mind"[2]—that offered a self-justification for his existential attitude (which was not always consistent). This also marked the start of Schmitt's "facile" relationship with Machiavelli, in which he interpreted Machiavelli according to the most vulgar anti-Machiavellian commonplaces, even as he held a quite different value judgment about the Florentine. Facile, but also ambiguous: in addition to Machiavelli's attitude toward lying, of which Schmitt approved on a psychological level, Schmitt focused on another theoretical and practical attitude, according to which politics should be considered not according to its essence but according to a superficial technical dissimulation (as we will see, Schmitt considers this attitude absolutely negative). It's as if by practicing the lie, Machiavelli just ended up fooling himself. The psychological affinity with Machiavelli revealed in Schmitt's diary entry thus coexists with Schmitt's categorical and conceptual distance from the Italian thinker—a contradiction that, as we shall see, says something about Schmitt's difficult relationship with Machiavelli. In his later work, Schmitt would arrive at a position in which he would no longer oppose the two faces of the Florentine to one another, but instead would understand, beginning with his emphasis on Machiavelli's completely "political" concreteness, that the lie should not be evaluated psychologically, and that technics is not itself one face of the lie. In Schmitt's later thinking, indeed, both technics and the lie are outcomes of the ruthless law of political necessity, which it is the merit of Machiavelli to have discovered and accepted.

Before reaching this mature interpretation, however, Schmitt's first true critical formulation on Machiavelli was marked by a *Stimmung* (a disposition) that was openly hostile to modernity and rationalism. This mood, so typical of Schmitt's early work, was derived from French reactionary Catholicism (and in particular from Maistre and Bonald, and from Maurras and Bloy). From this standpoint, Schmitt saw Machiavelli as one of the main thinkers responsible for modernity's self-justification of politics as a completely immanent activity. In this phase, Schmitt did not reject the traditional themes of Catholic anti-Machiavellianism (such as the accusation that Machiavelli carried out a blasphemous inversion of value and of the hierarchical arrangement of traditional morality and politics). Nevertheless, since Schmitt's Catholicism did not function as neofundamentalism, but rather as a viewpoint partially foreign to modernity—a viewpoint that allowed him to notice some of modernity's more salient negative traits—Schmitt turned these accusations into psychological acceptance and a corresponding political refusal, which situates Schmitt's evaluation of Machiavelli within the twentieth-century debate on technics and instrumental reason. For the young Schmitt as well as for the Schmitt of early maturity, therefore, Machiavelli is, even if not entirely within the mainstream of modern politics, one of the originary accomplices responsible for modernity's true stigma and fundamental defect: the transformation of politics into technics, a process that would be complete by the twentieth century. Schmitt, however, held fast to the belief that the drift of the Modern did not imply the death of politics, but was only the sign of the exhaustion of modernity's "ordering" forces.[3] The impossibility of a complete technical neutralization of politics—this, instead, is the basic thesis that moves Schmitt toward the constant effort to find, in the contradictions of the Modern, the emergence of an authentic politics subtracted from technics. Because Schmitt, at least in his early phase, regarded technics to be the central point of Machiavelli's thought—to be, in particular, the "demonic" outcome of the power with which politics sought to justify itself, a power that was even willing to enter "evil" if necessary—he regarded the Florentine to be part of the problem, not the solution.

This position is explicit in Schmitt's 1921 *Dictatorship*, where he attributes to Machiavelli the characteristic—common to the whole Renaissance—of being dominated by the "technical" problem of "how" to do a certain thing.[4] Machiavelli's anthropological pessimism is, for Schmitt, very different from that of Luther, Hobbes, Bossuet, Maistre, and Stahl (for whom pessimism is the indispensable axiom for bringing absolutism into being). On the contrary, in Machiavelli's pessimism, from Schmitt's point of view, there is only a technicity [tecnicità] that's indifferent to any higher finality, so much so that Machiavelli will vouch for any political result whatsoever—to the benefit of either the Prince or the people indifferently, depending simply on where the circumstances indicate the greatest possibility of success (or the virtues), in the former or the latter. Machiavelli's theoretical system is hence even less "political" than is that of the modern State, to whose absolute or governing variant Schmitt assigns, and still will for a long time, a political capacity (which, according to Schmitt, was later lost in the technicity of the "State of laws," in both its positivistic and liberal declensions).[5] Well before the State-form appeared in its full bloom, in other words, technics had already manifested itself in Machiavelli as the radical cipher of modernity, as the form of a rationality oriented to an end and not to value.

Schmitt conveyed a similar attitude toward Machiavelli in his 1923 *Roman Catholicism and Political Form*, where he claimed that "the Machiavellian conception . . . makes of politics a mere technique in that it isolates a single, extrinsic factor of political life."[6] This claim, which reveals the extent to which Schmitt anticipated the technicism of both the capitalists and the Bolsheviks, also reveals how Schmitt counteracted Machiavelli with recourse to the Catholic Church. It's not by chance, after all, that Schmitt turns Machiavelli into an emblem of the drifts immanent to the Modern, arguing that Machiavelli does not consider politics in its entirety but only its organization, its "mechanics." The Catholic Church, by contrast, encased within the shell of the "bachelors' bureaucracy" it uses to confront modernity, was able to keep the Idea alive and to nurture the awareness that "there is no politics without authority" (where "authority" has the sense that Schmitt typically gives to it, where it is opposed to "power").

To characterize Machiavelli in terms of "technics" is, if not a serious misunderstanding, then certainly a very partial interpretation (however influential it may be within anti-Machiavellianism). It means that Schmitt saw in Machiavelli the main negative trait of the Modern, which is to say the loss of any bond with transcendence, which is essential for effective politics. One should also characterize along these same lines what Schmitt writes about Machiavelli in his 1919 *Political Romanticism*. Along with the doctrine of rational natural law, Schmitt here considers

Machiavelli to be one of the sources of Spinoza's political philosophy. Schmitt interprets Spinoza's philosophy as contractualistic,[7] and as such distant from the "emanationist" scheme of Spinoza's metaphysics, which exhibits Machiavelli's "technical" influence. In reality, Schmitt came close to a factual connection between Spinoza and Machiavelli—a relation that is not, however, in the realm of technical and contractual rationalism, but in that of "power" (and hence in continuity with Spinoza's theoretical philosophy). In his later comparison of Machiavelli to Hobbes, Schmitt would realize Machiavelli's value as an alternative to the technico-rationalistic vicissitudes of modern statuality. In this way, Schmitt would also recognize clearly the insurmountable differences between Machiavelli and Hobbes. But it appears, in fact, that Schmitt never pronounced himself on the true affinities between the Florentine and Spinoza.[8] In any case, Schmitt's early references to Machiavelli, which overall are misleading, show that at this stage Schmitt thinks that Machiavelli exercises his negative influence on the whole spectrum of the Modern (even though, according to Schmitt, he remains exterior to the absolute State).

Lastly, it is important to underline that Machiavelli's absences from Schmitt's thought are just as significant as the presences, as in the case of the decisive first text of Schmitt's mature phase, his 1922 Political Theology. In this book, Schmitt paradoxically revitalizes modernity and makes it once again a producer of order precisely by overturning rational mediation (which is the fundamental contribution of Schmitt's thought). This overturning, which privileges the concrete and exceptional case over the abstract and universal norm, allows Schmitt to distort the categorial axis of the Modern from within, to draw from the dramatic existential concreteness of politics, and to think politics as a contingent "answer to a challenge"—an order that incorporates disorder without also neutralizing it.

2. Machiavelli and the "Political"

Schmitt's initial image of Machiavelli construed him, on the one hand, as only obliquely "modern," yet also, on the other, as fully carrying the negative drifts of modernity (such as technics with its oblivion of politics and its subsequent inefficacy). Later on, in his full maturity, Schmitt would elaborate a second view of Machiavelli. This time it would be a positive image, which would reveal and attempt an identification with Machiavelli based on more than just psychological grounds. From about the midtwenties until the midforties, Schmitt saw Machiavelli as a thinker whose conceptuality was able to invert the Modern's trend toward technics (which by now had almost completely occupied the sphere of the State) and who was capable of a type of political concreteness contrary to the abstract rationalism that gave birth to technics. In this reconsideration, Machiavelli obviously remains within modernity and continues to appear unassimilable within the central current of modern politics (which is to say, the rational State based on individuality and legality whose destiny is technics). Precisely because he is not a thinker of the rational and legal State, Machiavelli is, in Schmitt's view, also not "technical" but capable of "concreteness." As a consequence, Schmitt deemed him able to adequately grasp the "political."

Despite this transformation in Schmitt's evaluation of Machiavelli, however, Machiavelli nevertheless remained essentially outside Schmitt's thought, used only by Schmitt to corroborate certain positions reached through a path along which Machiavelli certainly was not central. Furthermore, Schmitt's positive interpretation during this phase was entirely focused—with the exception of Schmitt's 1928 *Constitutional Theory*—on Machiavelli's negative anthropology, which Schmitt saw as a sign of "concreteness." Here, as before, Schmitt's reading of Machiavelli remained very conventional. One could even say that Schmitt's most favorable remarks on Machiavelli seem to proceed from a need to demonstrate that he is an acute but not extravagant intellectual with ambitions for a political role. In this way, Schmitt could appreciate Machiavelli as a carrier of political concreteness and as a precursor for Schmitt himself, whose intellectual plan during this phase indeed was to shelter the Weimar Republic, by exceptional means, from a deadly crisis. Schmitt uses the real significance of the imperfect similarity between Machiavelli and the State-form, as well as the claim that Machiavelli discovered the "political," to legitimize his own strategy to return political energy to the State, thus reenabling it—once it passed beyond an exclusively technical sense—to resist the disruptive pushes of modern society.

2.1 In Schmitt's indirect citations of Machiavelli, one can find linguistic clues of the newly positive role he now attributed to the Florentine. In his 1929 essay "The Age of Neutralizations and Depoliticizations,"[9] for instance, Schmitt's citation of a "ritornar al principio" [return to the beginning], which he quotes in Italian in the original German text, is a clear reference to Machiavelli's *Discourses on Livy* 3.1, where Machiavelli proposes to "ritirare al principio" [to draw back toward its beginning] all corrupted republics.[10] This reference describes the radicalism of those political movements that, by opposing the age of technics and its negative neutralization of politics, aim indeed to draw politics to the beginning—to go back to its ideas and to the struggle for their own affirmation. One could also adduce Schmitt's 1931 foreword to *The Guardian to the Constitution*,[11] which ends with a quotation from Dido's welcoming speech to the Trojans in Virgil's *Aeneid*: "res dura et regni novitas me talia cogunt moliri."[12] This may be an implicit reference to Machiavelli, who cites the same passage in chapter 17 of *The Prince*, "Of Cruelty and Pity; and Whether It Is Better to Be Loved Than Feared, or the Contrary."[13] The meaning of this excerpt is that politics is forced to confront exceptions and contingencies, and that politics' real raison d' être consists in its ability to face this concrete "novelty." Schmitt might have wanted to associate Machiavelli with this strategy.

2.2 As far as direct statements go, the crucial text revealing how Schmitt came to reevaluate Machiavelli is a 1927 article, "Machiavelli," that appeared in the *Kölnische Volkszeitung*,[14] written on the occasion of the fourth centenary of the Florentine's death, in which Schmitt groups together all the themes involved in his relation with Machiavelli.

In this text, Schmitt expresses with some reservations his most favorable evaluation of Machiavelli. The leitmotiv of the argument is that Machiavelli was able to fully grasp the indestructible strength of the "political." A brief reconstruction of Machiavelli's significance in this light brings Schmitt to recall that the Florentine's thought in the seventeenth century was accompanied by the rise of princely absolutism, and that, at the end of the eighteenth century—the century that tried to moralize politics—Hegel and Fichte rediscovered Machiavelli in light of German nationalism, preparing him to be the herald of Germany's national *Machtpolitik*. Schmitt also points out that, in 1924, an enemy of liberalism like Benito Mussolini wrote his dissertation thesis on Machiavelli, and that in 1927 a Catholic like Herman Hefele edited an anthology on Machiavelli, in which he contrasted the "political" to the economic.

Schmitt went on to affirm that Machiavelli's immense fame—larger than any other political writer—stands in contrast to the fact that Machiavelli was neither a great politician nor a great thinker, and that he was always wrong in his personal political stances (he was a democrat and as such was defeated in 1513). Machiavelli was, in short, a poor devil ("ein armer Teufel"). The Prince, in Schmitt's estimation, doesn't have what it takes to make a great political work—neither depth nor elegance, neither political nor philosophical novelty. Even Machiavelli's immoralism has nothing of the enthusiastic or of the prophetic, unlike Nietzsche (whose excess the Catholic and "formal" Schmitt didn't appreciate, since his deconstructive force had a different origin and scope).[15] Here, however, we see Schmitt free himself from Catholic polemics against Machiavelli's immoralism: for Schmitt, in fact, Machiavelli's immoralism is now nothing more than the discovery of the "political."

On Schmitt's reading, Machiavelli's political immoralism consisted in the recognition that a new prince cannot govern in the same manner as the old dynasty he replaced (which, in practice, means that the prince must govern without a legitimizing tradition and even without traditional morality). Machiavelli's immoralism, Schmitt argued, is certainly banal if compared to the immoralism of a Bolshevik (and in this way Schmitt explicitly corrects the idea of the technical continuity between Machiavelli and the outcomes of the Modern, which he had supported in Roman Catholicism and Political Form). Schmitt maintains that even if non-European cultures (such as India) could conceive an immoral form of politics without having read Machiavelli, Machiavelli's thought was still important for a western European because of its adhesion to human nature. This naturalism—together with Machiavelli's linguistic naturalness—was not only of classical origin but also conveyed an unfailing interest for the matter of the "political." It emerged from a solely political point of view in which neither moralism nor the ostentations of immoralism had any part. In Machiavelli, humanity has not yet turned into sentimentality; it manifested itself instead as the capacity to make concrete experiences (and hence too to experience the "political").

Machiavelli derived his understanding of the field (Gebiet) of the "political" through humanistic uses of historical examples that were bent completely to contemporary historical-political interests. However alien to twentieth-century culture this strategy may have been, Schmitt considered it to be superior to the generalizations of sociology (in 1927, the year of the first edition of The Concept of the Political, Schmitt was still at the Gebietskonzeption of the "political" seen as one "field" among others, and had not yet arrived at the Intensitätskonzeption of 1932, in which the "political" was an especially "intense" polarity that both appears in and ruptures all fields). The "political," as Machiavelli grasps it, implies the knowledge that private virtues do not apply to the State and that the political man should only pretend to possess them. Because of this anthropological pessimism that brings Machiavelli to positions that are at once natural and human, concrete and objective, Schmitt understood Machiavelli to be aware that the "political" was an unavoidable part of human nature—that it was, indeed, a force that could not but be the origin and the essence of the State.

For Schmitt, in other words, Machiavelli's greatness was precisely that he was not a "Machiavellian": Machiavelli didn't hypocritically dress up his political discoveries with ideals, and he couldn't be exploited either by anonymous and invisible powers or by the mass psycho-apparatuses of propaganda. What was really Machiavellian, in Schmitt's view, was the intellectual strategy of Western powers during World War I, in which the latter masked their desire for power with humanitarian ideals all while polemicizing against Germany's presumed Machiavellianism (understood as a "politics of power").

In this article, Schmitt wanted to give the "political" a meaning that was anthropological, human, concrete, and objective, and that focused on the theme of force as the origin of the State. But he also wanted to trace the "political" back to an illustrious ancestor like Machiavelli—a move that doesn't completely coincide with the true origin and substance of Schmitt's thought, which resides in modern juridical doctrine (or, better, in its crisis and its epochal reinterpretation). Schmitt's article concludes, understandably, with a paraphrase of a passage from The Prince: "my ideas would be evil if men were good; but men are not."[16] In this we can hear resonances of a theme—the necessity of the lie—that fascinated the young Schmitt, and that the mature Schmitt now had carried from a psychological level to that of the political.

2.3 Above and beyond this novel appreciation, which is based only in anthropology, Schmitt's 1928 Constitutional Theory offers, almost in passing, a more insightful interpretation of the essence of Machiavelli's thought. Although Schmitt's reading does, admittedly, contain some rather infelicitous claims (pertaining, for example, to Machiavelli's presumed preference for political forms in their purity, or to the notion that with Machiavelli "the word 'republic' often only negatively involves an opposition to monarchy as state form"),[17] these always appear alongside more precise observations (such as Schmitt's note that for Machiavelli, as distinct from Thomas Aquinas, political virtue does not lie with the aristocrats but in democracy).[18] Reprising a theme he'd previously mentioned in a 1927 newspaper article, Schmitt here interprets *The Prince* as a treatise on the difficulties that the "Principe nuovo" must face in order to govern during an "illegitimate" situation, after having broken up the continuity of the monarchical tradition.[19] In this evaluation, Schmitt demonstrates a good understanding of Machiavelli's epochal significance, which—quite beyond any anthropology—consists in Machiavelli's recognition of the impracticability of traditional legitimacy. In 1928, therefore, Schmitt begins to see in Machiavelli a thinker who has grasped (though only partially) the epochal crisis from which modernity originates, and which turns all power into necessarily illegitimate power.

In this way, Machiavelli confirms what had become clear to Schmitt through another path, that of the critique of secularization he took in *Political Theology*, and before that in *Der Wert des Staates und die Bedeutung des Einzelnen*. In these works, Schmitt argued that modernity in its entirety is inscribed in this perception of illegitimacy, in this irreversible discontinuity from tradition, without also being necessarily discredited by it. But from the type and quality of the use Schmitt makes of Machiavelli in *Constitutional Theory* (which, in truth, is modest), it clearly emerges that Machiavelli and Schmitt think this general illegitimacy very differently: for the former it can be faced with "virtue" and energy, whereas for the latter it can be faced only with a decision for political form.

2.4 In *The Concept of the Political*, negative anthropology clearly remains the leitmotiv for Schmitt's positive interpretation of Machiavelli.[20] Given the palimpsestic structure of this text, one should draw a distinction between Machiavelli's presence in the 1932 third edition and his place in the parts Schmitt added in 1963. The fundamental turning-point is again in the 1932 text. In fact, here Schmitt affirms that negative and pessimistic anthropology (the claim that man is "evil" by nature) is essential for "every political theory in the proper sense."[21] In this phase of his thought, Schmitt gathers together a group of authors whom he sees as "political thinkers in a specific sense" because they practice a similar anthropology. To this group—which already includes Hobbes, Bossuet, Fichte, and, with some reservations, Hegel, and which even reaches into the thought of the Catholic counterrevolutionaries, for whom pessimism was a theory of sin—Schmitt now adds Machiavelli. Schmitt interprets pessimism in an objective sense—as man's instinctual evil—and not just in a psychological sense, as a tendency toward evil (which is Wilhelm Dilthey's position).[22] It's precisely this pessimism, Schmitt maintains, that allows Machiavelli to think the relation between friend and enemy in the concrete.[23] Machiavelli's negative anthropology is thus no longer merely "technical"; it is now "political."

For Schmitt, remember, technics is an ensemble of rules and devices, of tricks aimed at gaining power, which can all be put to any end whatsoever. He now credits the reduction of politics into technics not to Machiavelli, but to that degeneration and betrayal of the Florentine's thinking that instead goes under the name of "Machiavellianism," a figure of the detested *potestas indirecta* [indirect power]. On Schmitt's reading, Machiavelli is not Machiavellian (i.e., a hypocritical moralist) but a concrete political thinker: when Machiavelli writes for and about Italy, he has in mind a real enemy, the foreign princes. In a 1963 note, Schmitt adds that were Machiavelli a Machiavellian instead of a theoretician of the *potestas directa* (which is the responsibility born from a concrete confrontation with the "political"), then Machiavelli would have written an *Anti-Machiavelli*.[24] The "existential" value of Machiavelli would be demonstrated by the fact that also the German philosophers who have rehabilitated him, such as Fichte and Hegel, had the concrete problem of defending Germany from the Crisis of the Holy Roman Empire and from Napoleon.

Schmitt grounds his identification with Machiavelli on their common attempt to inject political energy into modernity through anthropological pessimism, and on their shared conception of politics on the basis of the friend/enemy relation. Schmitt does not, however, insist on this identification—either in 1932 (in his "good times") or in the aftermath of World War II (during his "bad times"). Following the war, Schmitt certainly will compare himself to Machiavelli, seeing a common destiny of scapegoating; he also will perceive a connection in the fact that both he and Machiavelli received moralistic criticism for the courage with which they thought the radical abyssal dimension of politics. But this comparison will remain just a remark: in the end, their attitudes and apparatuses of thought are too different for Schmitt not to notice, and Schmitt does not derive the lexical invention of the "political" as the friend/enemy relation from Machiavelli, but from a Spanish Baroque thinker, Alamo de Barrientos.[25]

2.5 Schmitt's mature identification with Machiavelli would also become an instrumentalization. During the first phase of his Nazi period (1933–36), Schmitt referred positively to the Florentine based on a new harmony in ideas between Italy and Germany. Schmitt was a jurist with great ambitions, and he had been for a long time an admirer of Italian Fascism, although his admiration was not completely reciprocated.[26] He was certainly aware of Machiavelli's success during Fascism, a success fostered by Mussolini himself. The Fascist interpretations appreciated Machiavelli as the supporter of a strong State led by a heroic personality, and Schmitt—more or less in good faith—played along. Schmitt's overt embrace of Machiavelli's thought for political reasons is noticeable in his *L'era della politica integrale* (The age of total politics), a text he delivered at a conference in Rome in 1936. This article is based on the assumption that of all the European nations, only Germany and Italy had found the political form proper to the twentieth century: totalitarianism. Thanks to Fascism, the German jurist asserted, Italy was able to recognize the new State, a recognition that manifests the same clarity of the Italian spirit with which Machiavelli grasped, with infallible objectivity, the decisive political figure of the new Prince, and with which he elaborated the idea of the modern State.[27]

For Schmitt, Machiavelli is the bearer of a way of thinking the State that is more energetic and originary than the legal-rational interpretation of the State form. Schmitt bends this reading of Machiavelli to support Italian Fascism, whose strong affirmation of the State he appreciated. Interpreted by Schmitt as the least formalistic among the thinkers of the modern State, Machiavelli is at this point an element—external, marginal, ornamental, but prestigious—of Schmitt's cultural and political strategy, which in those years, combined an acceptance of the totalitarian overcoming of the State form with an attempt to preserve a vestige of modern statuality. It was precisely this statualism (on top of his Catholicism) that made Schmitt into the object of Nazi criticism, and that would cost him his public appointments.[28]

3. Machiavelli the "All Too Human"

After his relationship with the Nazi regime was put into question in 1936, Schmitt quit his appointments in internal politics and also ceased to refer directly to Machiavelli. In his subsequent works, one can nevertheless still find some judgments of the Florentine, which give a sense not only of Schmitt's attempts to distance himself from Machiavelli, but also of yet another attempt by Schmitt to identify himself with the Italian thinker, and lastly to establish a relationship with him that is more objective.

3.1 With his 1938 book on Hobbes, Schmitt took his leave from constitutional law and internal politics, while also reconstructing international politics in terms of the relationship between earth and sea. In this phase, Schmitt attributes modern statuality completely to Hobbes, whom he sees as the origin of both juridico-positivistic technicism, and its opposite, decision. For Schmitt the development of the State-machine and of its juridical rationalism—of which he is becoming increasingly critical during these years—is still the main characteristic of the Modern. Referring to the pathetic conclusion of *The Prince*, Schmitt rules out Machiavelli from this process, precisely because he is, in Schmitt's view, "humane."[29] Schmitt also absolves Machiavelli from the accusations produced by his negative myth, starting with his posthumous responsibility for St. Bartholomew's night.[30] This recognition happens at the same time as the positive evaluation (following a secular condemnation) of the fascist "myth of Machiavelli," seen as the symbol of the heroic objectivity of politics, at war against the moralistic lie. Schmitt employs the image of Machiavelli as a "poor devil" not just to characterize his infelicitous political choices, but also to negate the efficacy of his political thought. During this phase, Schmitt sees Machiavelli's thought only as a helpless and vain defense of the "political." The Evil of modern politics does not go through Machiavelli, but through the machine, which is to say through the technical and juridico-positivistic Leviathan. In this way, Schmitt overturns the ideas of his first phase, in which he highlighted the "technical" aspects in Machiavelli's thought. Furthermore, he changes the focus that characterized his second phase, in which he saw Machiavelli as fully and effectively political. At this point, in 1938, Schmitt has taken the first step toward the post–World War II interpretations of Machiavelli: the Machiavelli "too human."

3.2 After 1945, Schmitt tried to appropriate Machiavelli's humanity, implicitly turning the Florentine into his own mirror. Schmitt saw Machiavelli as "the conquered who writes history,"[31] and also as the scapegoat first of Nazi power, and then of the power of Western democracies, which even after World War II Schmitt continued to associate with moralistic liberalism.[32]

In later years, Schmitt acknowledged his existential identification with Machiavelli with a spectacular gesture, when he gave the name "San Casciano"[33] to the villa in Plettenberg where he retired in 1947,[34] following his incarceration and interrogation in connection with the Nuremberg trial, which culminated in a "Berufsverbot" (employment ban) that was never revoked. Actually, the two exiles did not look alike at all. There is nothing beyond the mere empirical claim that, just like Machiavelli, Schmitt was not a great practical politician. Similarly to Machiavelli, and despite all his efforts, Schmitt was often (but, unfortunately for him, not always) "out of place" regarding the real configurations of power. Schmitt's outdatedness [inattualità] was caused neither by his intellectual coherence nor in the bad political wagers to which he, like Machiavelli, could have been brought by inexhaustible political passion. The actual causes lie in his inclination for ideological and doctrinarian provocations, borne by intellectual dissatisfaction and by his parvenu resentment. This attitude detached him from both the Second Reich and the Weimar Republic, but also from Nazism, which he joined not out of conviction but out of opportunism (as the Nazis themselves noticed). His provocations also separated him from postwar democracy and, since the twenties, from the Catholic Church. In the end, the real significance of the name "San Casciano" lies beyond Machiavelli. Its esoteric meaning refers to Schmitt's identification with Cassian of Imola, a martyr from the Diocletian era who was stabbed to death by his own disciples.[35] This sort of unexpected revelation—at once smug, erudite, and polemical, at once self-pitying and proudly conservative and Catholic—is, of course, quite typical of Schmitt.

It's not then a surprise that Machiavelli is completely absent from Ex Captivitate Salus, the work of "the wisdom of the jail" that Schmitt wrote during the years 1946 and 1947. This is a key book for Schmitt's self-understanding: it's the site where he tries to rehabilitate his human and intellectual image, which he then in turn would try to sustain throughout the postwar years. Well, as it turns out, Machiavelli does not contribute to the eponymous "salvation" (salus) of this book—which is to say, to the full, if belated, understanding of the antihuman mechanisms of modern power. As icons of his defeat, Schmitt will therefore prefer Benito Cereno or Epimetheus.[36]

3.3 In Schmitt's view, Machiavelli did not, in the end, fully understand the mechanisms of modern political power and of the State. Helped as he was by Hobbes, however, Schmitt achieved just this understanding in his *Glossarium*, a sort of diary from the years 1947–51 that Schmitt was preparing for posthumous publication, and in which Hobbes is the most cited source (together with Jünger, Däubler, and Hitler).

In this text, Schmitt openly compares Machiavelli and Hobbes and discovers that the former completely missed the fully modern equation between power, on the one hand, and the protection from death, on the other (not to mention the premodern equation between power and correction of sins). For Schmitt, the modern form of "power" (*Macht*)—which is to say, dominion (*Herrschaft*, which also could be translated as "sovereignty")—is but a "façade in the face of death." The same could be said about the "life" that that modern power guarantees. The thinker who was aware of the essence of the State as a "façade," Schmitt claims, was not Machiavelli but Hobbes. In fact, Hobbes is an authentic Baroque thinker, as shown by the "mysterious drapes that appear on the front cover of the *Leviathan*"[37]—the same drapes that, in Schmitt's view, later will be destroyed by the critical efforts of liberal interiority when it spills outward.

Schmitt accuses Machiavelli of two related issues in these important pages. First, that Machiavelli did not fully enter the biopolitical dimension of modern power and hence didn't grasp—with his view of politics as vital energy—a nexus that is essential for comprehending modern politics and the State: the link between sovereignty and the individual's life and death, between disorder and protection from disorder. Schmitt's second accusation is that Machiavelli, whose discourse naturalizes power, falls short of grasping modern political theology, not to mention the link between decision and representation, that Baroque representation and artificial objectivity which is indispensable (even if, like all appearances, it is intrinsically nihilistic) to the construction of politics as form. From the eighteenth century on, Schmitt argues, the individualistic critique would have corroded Baroque representation, resulting in the liberation of an antihuman nucleus of power, one that was earlier concealed and restrained by the State (and here, reworking an established counterrevolutionary position, Schmitt outlines a pathogenesis according to which totalitarianism originates in the Enlightenment desire to illuminate and reveal the *arcana imperii*).

For Schmitt, therefore, Machiavelli was a thinker—"all too human"—of open, natural, immediate power, and for precisely this reason could not understand that modern political power is essentially a mystery (in its Baroque form, but also in the traps and twists of totalitarian power). Machiavelli's discourse on power, as one finds it for example in *The Prince*, is in Schmitt's view naïve and vain chatter; it is "misery" (*das Miserable*). Every theorization of "the will to power," meanwhile, amounts to what Schmitt calls "the peak of essential stupidity and of the most miserable bad taste."[38]

Beyond the confrontational attitude that Schmitt usually reserves for Nietzsche, we also find something else implicit in this passage: the subtle nexus that links Nietzsche and Machiavelli (whom Schmitt earlier saw as opposed thinkers). At this point, the focal point of Schmitt's theorization is Machiavelli's humanity: when Machiavelli proposes a substantiated politics of a power that is rooted in life itself (and not just a representation of life), that focuses on energy instead of on sovereignty's theatrico-representative construction or its power of control over life and death, his humanity is lacking in political and intellectual efficacy. With this reflection, Schmitt really captures Machiavelli's essence: Machiavelli's modernity does not include technics, the legal-rational State, or deeper logics (such as modern nihilism and the categories of representations whose limits define not only Hobbes and the Baroque but also Schmitt). Schmitt grasps Machiavelli even, especially, as he detaches himself from him. It's as if Schmitt captures the essence of Machiavelli's thought precisely because he was never able to master him, despite having struggled with him for years, and because, at the very moment he grasped him, Schmitt realized how foreign Machiavelli was to the essence of his own thought and development. It's not for nothing, after all, that Machiavelli is absent from Schmitt's most significant postwar works.[39]

4. Conclusions

Before giving a comprehensive evaluation of Schmitt's interpretation of Machiavelli, I'll first gloss its position vis-à-vis twentieth-century Machiavelli scholarship in Germany.

4.1 Interpreted with the latter horizon, Schmitt's reading is not innovative but marginal. This is true both when he underlines Machiavelli's "technical" side (a reading that's indebted to Catholic tradition) and when he reads Machiavelli as the thinker of power and force as the origin of the State, of its intrinsic morality and of its historical necessity, along the same lines of Fichte and Hegel (and with a negative anthropology that Wilhelm Dilthey would develop in the same statualistic dimension). This line of continuity nevertheless did not prevent Schmitt from detaching himself from Dilthey, who transformed Hobbes into a minor disciple of Machiavelli.[40] Schmitt also would be openly polemical of Meinecke in his review of Meinecke's most famous book,[41] which situated Machiavelli at the origin of the modern Reason of State (in which *kratos* was supposed to be in continuous polarity with *ethos*). Schmitt contested this interpretation for two reasons. In the first place, Schmitt was hostile to Meinecke both on the basis of his (Romantic) dualism—which constituted a sort of pendulum theory of the relationship between ethics and politics—and because of his individualistico-moralistic choice in favor of *ethos*. What's more, in Schmitt's view the State underwent many changes during the modern age; Meinecke, by contrast, wrongly took the State as an invariant, based on the Reason of State, and then connected it to Machiavelli. In 1926, Schmitt maintained, it was no longer possible to talk about either *Ratio* or *Status*, even if it did remain possible to recuperate Machiavelli and to use him in the moment of the full technicization of the State as the thinker of the political energy that could return force back to the State.

The political use that Schmitt made of his interpretation of Machiavelli, as traditional as it was personal, in turn influenced the reception of both Machiavelli and Schmitt in Gerhard Ritter's seminal and tormented 1948 book *Die Dæmonie der Macht*.[42] Ritter construed the Machiavellian "demonic" in light of the Schmittian "political," which is to say as an inescapable tendency toward power that manifests itself not just outside but also within the space of internal politics.

4.2 We can clarify the overall significance of the relation between Schmitt and Machiavelli through the analysis of specific keywords.[43] To the extent that we understand Schmitt as the thinker of the genealogy of politics, then Machiavelli is not part of Schmitt's genealogical itinerary: Schmitt, in fact, reaches his genealogical understanding of politics on the basis of other authors. At the same time, however, if only because of the resonance of Machiavelli's name, Schmitt will often refer to Machiavelli in order to legitimize his own theses. We are thus led to conclude that Schmitt uses Machiavelli instrumentally: although Schmitt rarely kept his distance from the Florentine, he did just that whenever he approached the inner nature of Machiavelli's political thought.

The crucial point is this: Machiavelli's conceptualization of the origin of the modern State as "force" or "virtue" does not coincide—although Schmitt at times says the opposite—with Schmitt's conceptualization of the origin as "political," which is to say as the inescapable presence, within order, of the relation between friend and enemy. Schmitt's accomplishment was to have genealogically dismantled European public law (despite belonging to its horizon, i.e., the modern sovereign power that tried to create order by separating internal space from external space).[44] He understood the origin of politics—that is, the "political"—through the crisis of the legal-rational State of Hobbesian derivation. What this means, however, is that Machiavelli, with his naturalistic paganism (about which both Dilthey and Meinecke agreed), was also distant from another key concept in Schmitt's thought: political theology. Through the concept of political theology, Schmitt grappled with the issue of the juridico-political form of the modern epoch, and grasped the radical novelty of modern politics (not to mention its "illegitimacy"). Political theology was the concept that allowed Schmitt to recognize, within political modernity, the secularization of traditional theological concepts: even as the Modern stands in a position of substantial discontinuity vis-à-vis traditional theological concepts (because the Modern lacks any foundation), the two are also linked by elements of continuity (because of the Modern's compulsion toward clear form, and its monocentric theoretical schemas of *potestas*—such as, for example, sovereignty as secularization of the miracle).[45] Machiavelli interprets the new politics, totally deprived of traditional foundations, as "energy" (or "virtue")—which is to say, as the armed people of the "tumultuary republic" described in the *Discourses*, and as the armed prince (who in turn arms the people) described in *The Prince*. Schmitt, by contrast, is preoccupied with the possibility that the Modern, although "illegitimate," exhibits a "form"—a concern he owes essentially to Hobbes (which he interprets, anyway, in a decisionistic and not rationalistic mode).

It's true that Schmitt later grasped the substantial illegitimacy of modern politics in terms of "energy," which is to say as constituent power. But he derived this conceptualization from Sieyès and Rousseau, not from Machiavelli: Schmitt's democracy aims at a political unity of the people, which is organized according to exclusionary processes of identification, with a strong monistic value.[46] Schmitt also grasped the Modern's compulsion toward formal and single-centered political order through the decision. But he built this concept starting from Hobbes, going through Hegel (his theory of "monarchic power" in particular) and Kierkegaard—and, again, not through Machiavelli. For Schmitt, the decision was a spasm of sovereignty that at once creates and negates juridico-political form; he didn't relate this concept either to the free play of power or to Machiavelli's civil passion. The fact of the matter is that Machiavelli was not a part either of Schmitt's "political" or his concept of political theology, and that Schmitt owed none of his crucial concepts to Machiavelli (from the early concepts of decision and *Verfassung* to the late concept of *nomos*). This in turn explains the difference between Machiavelli's and Schmitt's concepts of concreteness. It's certainly true that politics is, for both authors, intrinsically exceptional and contingent, and that it cannot be treated merely according to "norms" (the precepts of traditional morals for Machiavelli, the laws of the State for Schmitt). But the reason for this is that, for Machiavelli, politics is constituted of natural and human substance—passions and matter, energy and conflict—whereas for Schmitt politics is constituted of a "crack in the crystal"—by the polemical orientation that generates formal order, the scar that shoots through it and opens it up in the face of its original contingency. Schmitt's concreteness, in other words, partakes in the nihilism of the Modern, in a politics marked by death (determined as an escape from *summum malum*, the highest evil) and in the State understood in Hobbesian terms as a "great representation" (which is precisely what Machiavelli doesn't grasp). Whereas Machiavelli's concreteness is marked by *immediacy*, Schmitt's concreteness is thus characterized by *failed mediation*.

The same could be said for conflict. The Schmittian formula describing the "political" in terms of friend/enemy certainly did establish a continuity between war and politics. But even if Machiavelli often affirmed the coincidence of "good laws and good weapons," and thus too an originary relation between war (or better, conflict) and politics, it doesn't follow that Schmitt and Machiavelli thought of politics in the same way. Actually, they stand on two different sides of the antithesis between order and conflict. Schmitt was a thinker of conflict as failed order, from the viewpoint of a sovereignty that brings order precisely because of its capacity to reach the extreme point of its decisionistic spasm. Machiavelli, meanwhile, accepts conflicts as constitutive of politics understood as a collective human matter. Schmitt actually fears conflict, in other words, while Machiavelli does not. For Schmitt, conflict is the origin of politics, as well as its tragic destiny; for Machiavelli, it is an end in itself (so long as the conflict is glorious and not provoked by greed). This structural distance dismantles the presumption of a consonance between Schmitt and Machiavelli, and even more their identification as the two teachers of what is usually called "political realism" (a thought suspended between the recognition of the role of violence in politics and the search for the "laws" of order).

A closer look, in fact, reveals that the categories and the political applications of their thought appear much more distant than expected. Machiavelli's "tumultuary republic" is not the excluding Jacobin democracy, the prince is not the deciding sovereign, and power is not the same thing as decision. In the end, then, Machiavelli and Schmitt are separated by the way they belong to the Modern, as well as by the way they relate to the liberal-rational State, to which neither ever fully subscribed. Machiavelli is part of a mode of modernity that constitutes an alternative to modern rationalism (namely, politics as energy). Schmitt, meanwhile, may have been a strong opponent to modern rationalism, but his critique ultimately stayed at its extreme border: he may have refused the self-legitimizing narration of the Modern, its discursive mediations, but he didn't refuse its categorial horizon (sovereignty).[47] Even though neither Machiavelli nor Schmitt can be assimilated to the rationalistic thought of a politics that coincides with the contract and the norm, their differences from this thought thus derive from different, even opposed, sides.

That Schmitt frequently attempted to interact with the essence of Machiavelli's thought, that he misunderstood it, that he used it instrumentally, that he did not include it in his reflection even when he did grasp it—all of this shows that it's impossible, in the end, to identify Machiavelli's politics and Schmitt's "political." More to the point, it shows that Machiavelli achieved alterity and freedom from rationalistic modernity, whereas Schmitt remained both its revealing critic and its prisoner.

....

CHAPTER 4

SCHMITT, STRAUSS, AND SPINOZA

Carl Schmitt's confrontation with Leo Strauss passes, above all, through Hobbes and the concept of the "political." It is through these interconnected domains that the two authors attempt to understand whether or not liberalism and modernity, taken together, can exhibit what Schmitt calls "concreteness" (which he locates in the sovereign decision on the state of exception) and what Strauss calls "criticality" [*criticità*] (which is to say, the practice of philosophy and its relation to transcendence that forbids modern reason to withdraw within itself, and to saturate the political space).

Schmitt discovers concreteness in Hobbes's use of the biblical figure "Leviathan" as a political symbol, even though the Hobbesian State runs many risks and suffers from many contradictions.[1] In his 1938 book *The Leviathan in the State Theory of Thomas Hobbes*, Schmitt regards Hobbes's "Leviathan" as a polymorphous being (which is at one and the same time man, God, monster, and machine). In 1965, meanwhile, Schmitt understands concreteness as a multidimensional political theology, a coexistence (or "integrity") of reason and faith (transcendence, in Schmitt's late reading of Hobbes, is not lost). For Schmitt, therefore, Hobbes is the author who most fully demonstrates the precarious possibility, within the modern State, that political order created by the sovereign decision could coexist with the disorder that very same decision calls into being. For Strauss, by contrast, Hobbes is the atheist philosopher who opposes Christian faith on the basis of a modern faith, the faith in the instruments of natural science, and whose understanding of politics as mere self-preservation amounts to little more than a "base" caricature of traditional politics and its "elevated" objectives.[2] According to Schmitt, Hobbes's thought indicates the possibility of a political theology that is capable of actively neutralizing the crisis of Christianity (namely, its religious civil wars) and that represents the origin of the modern State, both in its abstract and concrete components. According to Strauss, meanwhile, political theology persists in Hobbes, but only as a passive instrument employed to exclude conflict, and consequently too in a form that overthrows traditional forms of political theology. For Strauss, therefore, modern political theology demonstrates an originary vocation for catastrophe: as would become all too clear in Nietzsche, the impotence of its will to power cannot but result in the impossibility of history, science, and ethics.[3]

This difference explains Strauss's interpretation of Schmitt. For Strauss, Schmitt is that nonliberal who, writing in a liberal age, understood that it was Hobbes who, writing during a nonliberal age, gave life to modern liberalism. Nonetheless, Strauss observes, even if Schmitt's concept of the "political" was indeed able to reach the nonliberal roots of liberalism—or, better, the nonrational origin of modern political reason—after all, the aim of Schmitt's thought remained "science" in the modern sense of the word, and this prevented Schmitt from attaining the "concreteness" and "integrity" to which he aspired. Strauss thus wanted to go beyond Schmitt's deconstruction of liberalism, which was, in his view, interested only in identifying the original nexus of reason and nonreason in the sovereign decision (or, in other words, the presence of the state of nature in the political state). For Strauss, Schmitt's limitation is that he wanted to give a scientific analysis of the irrationality and unfoundedness of modern reason (or of the "political," that is to say, of the state of nature). Because Schmitt attempted to describe these phenomena in a nonpolemical manner, Strauss argues, he accepts them as the horizon of his thought.[4]

The relation that Strauss and Schmitt adopt toward Spinoza is determined by (and is a consequence of) their relation to Hobbes. For Strauss, Spinoza aligns with Hobbes's adherence to modern atheism, but he differs from him—in a manner that, for Strauss, is implicitly positive—because his rationalism shows signs of disquiet when it comes before Law and Revelation. Schmitt's interpretation of Spinoza, by contrast, is manifestly negative. For Schmitt, Spinoza exists in a marked discontinuity with Hobbes: he insinuates himself into a weak spot in Hobbes's philosophical-political system in order to destroy its concreteness and to drive the modern State toward the development of individualistic liberalism and its pernicious abstractions.

Enigma, on the one hand, refusal, on the other—these are the ciphers of Spinoza's presence in the thought of Strauss and Schmitt.[5] Clearly, if we are to understand how Strauss and Schmitt converge and diverge, and to figure out which aspects of Spinoza's thought they exclude, and why, we need to submit their own interpretations to interpretation.

1. Strauss's Spinoza

Spinoza is the object of Strauss's earliest studies and of his first great book, Spinoza's Critique of Religion (1930).[6] In this text, which represents part of the return of the theologico-political question of German Judaism in the first decades of the century, Strauss wants to clear Spinoza from the accusation—made by in 1915 by Hermann Cohen, a liberal assimilationist Jew—that Spinoza wrote a sacrilegious book, and betrayed Judaism by declaring it incompatible with modern rationalism.

Cohen, Strauss argues, aims at the wrong target. Although Spinoza's philosophic discourse is consistent with the logical syntax of Descartes and, above all, Hobbes (who concedes to religion only an instrumental role, and who is therefore more radically atheist and immanentist than Descartes), Strauss observes that Spinoza does not disprove Revelation and orthodoxy per se. At most, Strauss argues, Spinoza offers a merely philosophical critique of Scholastic philosophy. In fact, according to Strauss, the very core of the Spinozian project—the demonstration of the nondemonstrability of miracles—can succeed only on account of Spinoza's preliminary decision to place himself within the territory of reason. Interpreted in this manner, Spinoza reveals that his own exercise of reason is ungrounded—that it is itself an act of faith.

As distinct from Hobbes, therefore, Spinoza's atheist and immanentist rationalism is not simply an instrumental ablation of transcendence. It is instead the absolute self-affirmation of reality. For this same reason, however, Spinoza does not find a way to exit metaphysics, and indeed the new political reason he proposes is also itself metaphysical.[7] Implicit in Hobbes's conception of God as a transcendental, formal function of any political order, Strauss recognizes, is the fact that Hobbes faces and resolves the theological question before posing any political question. Spinoza, by contrast, brings the rational critique of theology inside politics from the very beginning, situating it within the concrete union of men, and thus conceives of substance as self-movement.[8] From the political point of view, however, this does not mean that Spinoza knows how to philosophically draw from the unexhausted power of multitudes. Quite the opposite. Strauss interprets Spinoza as if he introduced a very dubious separation, an abyss, between the sage (the contemplative philosopher who is able to criticize religion) and the political mass of the people (who are the intended audience of the teachings of rationalized religion). On Strauss's reading, in other words, the modern philosopher, very much like the ancient philosopher, separates himself from the city. This permits Strauss to discern two contradictions in Spinoza's concept of political reason. It first of all fails to establish a rational ground, and therefore too a justification for itself in the face of faith, except through an originary decision in favor of reason. What's more, it cannot cover the totality of experience—for, indeed, it excludes politics itself.

Strauss's second and third texts on Spinoza,[9] written in 1948 and 1965, respectively, deepen and in part correct this image of the philosopher (or more precisely of the meaning of Spinoza's philosophy, of his contradictions and of his failure to actuate a full rationalization of the real). Particularly in his 1948 work, Strauss maintains that Spinoza can be understood only if we follow him to the letter without also adhering to his own self-interpretation.[10] Strauss presupposes, in other words, that there is operative in Spinoza's thought a strategy of reticence, which must in turn be submitted to hermeneutics. On this basis, Strauss argues that Spinoza is more an atheist than a believer, but one who, instead of entirely eliminating Revelation through philosophy, leaves open a contradiction between philosophy and theology. Even though he negates miracles, Spinoza seems to remain uncertain regarding the value of prophecy (which is to say, the political use of religion), which he accepts so long as it steers clear of the intolerance of theologians and rabbis (for Spinoza, the Bible is more tolerant than theology, and hence too more rational than theology). For Strauss, this position—Spinoza's moral acceptance of the political use of religion— is undoubtedly exoteric. The purpose of Spinoza's proposal of a tolerant deism, on Strauss's reading, is to protect the philosopher from the persecution of the city. Spinoza's real position—his esoteric teaching—is, by contrast, the radical criticism of revealed religion. His real position, in other words, is that of philosophy, whose outcome is rational atheism and, in political terms, perfectly immanent liberal democracy. On this read, the value of the Bible is, for Spinoza, not cognitive but moral, and this is why it is less rational than philosophy. This, in sum, is Spinoza's esoteric teaching. If we look at what he openly sustains—a deistic tolerance that is connected with the moral duty of living according to Revelation and to the faith in God's justice—Spinoza is a son of his time. But if we look at what he denies and criticizes—at his rational attack against revealed religion as superstition—Spinoza is a follower of the "philosophia perennis."[11]

On Strauss's reading, then, Spinoza wants to lead the reader—and the Christian reader above all—away from the Bible and closer to philosophy.[12] But Spinoza's main polemical target, for Strauss, is less Revelation than theology, and most of all political theology (which is to say, the dogmatic and intolerant use of the Bible to govern the minds of citizens). In Strauss's view, in other words, Spinoza dismantles Jewish political theology, but morally appreciates the Bible—while at the same time trying to bring the Christian, now converted into a philosopher, to rationally criticize it.

In this way, Strauss delineates in Spinoza's work a plurality of levels of experience, a triangulation between Revelation (or Law), Reason (critical philosophy), and Politics (the sources of obedience and of the social bond). Strauss's final thesis seems to be that Spinoza, despite everything, does not fall into the trap of unifying these levels. In Spinoza's thought, Reason keeps itself apart, in the contemplative solitude of the philosopher, and its primary function is to keep the Law from turning directly into Politics. To be sure, Strauss's 1965 text on Spinoza is itself a sort of Straussian intellectual autobiography, one that Strauss writes about himself by way of Spinoza. In it, Strauss credits Spinoza not only with the will to restore philosophy as contemplation but also with the modern schema (much more idealistic than rationalistic) of a substance that, understood as an immanent process/progress, continuously enriches itself (a process that is indeed much richer than the God of tradition), and that entails a republicanism that foreshadows the full humanistic immanence of liberal democracy.[13] Spinoza is thus, for Strauss, Machiavelli lifted to "theological heights"[14]—he is, in other words, a philosopher who is able to comprehend that, if humanism is to be realized, traditional theology must be overthrown, and not simply set aside. It follows from this that Spinoza is, for Strauss, the advocate of a neutralized and rational liberal society that is governed by the authority of a Bible rendered newly tolerant for having been cleansed of everything senseless. As a liberal atheist, Strauss's Spinoza is characterized by reticence and by purposeful contradictoriness; he is not moved by hatred for Judaism. Instead, quite contrary to Cohen, Strauss considers him the father of assimilationism.[15]

Yet for Strauss, Spinoza's negative (modern) traits go together with some implicitly positive determinations. Indeed, in Strauss's view, Spinoza aims not only at defeating the rabbinate but also at converting Christians to the true philosophy: criticism. This conversion liberates Christians from their political theology—both from the dogmatism of the theologians and from its apparent opposite, modern secularization (which, with its hostility for traditional theology, simply turns theology upside down without being able to exit it). All in all, Spinoza—who does not, and cannot, hold Judaic Law as such as his main polemical target—offers an alternative both to dogmatic rationalism (which wants to saturate the entire space of experience) and to any and every allegiance between religion and political form. For Strauss, Spinoza is more than just the esoteric philosopher who, in a prudent and concealed way, wants to substitute vertical mediation (Religion and Law, inasmuch as they get corrupted into theo-logy and theo-politics) with rational mediation (Enlightened, deistic mediation). He is also more than simply the exoteric philosopher who accepts a political role of tradition for the people, so that tradition thereby becomes less intolerant and less irrational (which is to say, neither Christian nor Judaic). Strauss's two later texts on Spinoza suggest something more: for Strauss, Spinoza is a philosopher who, despite his immanentism, does not side with modern rationalism. This is because Spinoza's critical and philosophical reason is certainly atheistic, but in a way that is higher and more aware than Enlightenment atheism, while, on an exoteric level, it has a non-Orthodox but nevertheless complex relationship with the Law. For Strauss, who now understands Spinoza only by following all of his contradictions, Spinozian atheism, which is born from intellectual probity, and deprived of the harshness of the Enlightenment and of the equivocal reverences of Romanticism, implies (at once hiding and revealing it) a negative relationship with the Law.[16] This atheism is constituted neither by indifference nor by simple reversal; it is constituted instead by silence, as if the Law were the Shadow of Reason, the limit that escapes it, the sign of an absent transcendence whose power consists entirely in the capability to impede and to deconstruct, with its mere being, the domination of modern reason (which, after all, always remains theologico-political).

In Spinoza's thought, far more than in Hobbes, the plenitude of immanence is not only magnificent but also anxious, and it is the presence of the Law—in the mode of its immediate absence, of its untranslatability into Order—that allows the reason of the philosopher to criticize the bad rationality of modern rationalism. The Shadow of the Law allows light to be shed on the originary dialectic of the Enlightenment, which is still internal to the purpose of domination, namely, the reduction of experience to a single dimension (a rationalistic dimension, within modernity, or a dogmatic and religious one within other experiences). It is this Shadow that allows philosophy to be critical rather than apologetic, to open itself up to contemplation and not merely to speculation (the mere mirroring of the real), to become perennial philosophy and not merely captured by its own time. Perennial philosophy is philosophy as *eros*, as opening. This is not limited to the attainment of an Object (God, World, or whatever the case might be); it is the negation of consent to *idola fori* [gods of the marketplace] in order to draw closer to an ever-elusive truth. But precisely because such a philosophical notion of Truth coincides, for Strauss, with the death of every political order, Strauss's radical attitude comes to an end: he retreats in the face of this anomic event. This is why he reads in Spinoza, and proposes in his own name, the detachment between the critical destiny of the philosopher and that of the people, who are unable to linger in the dangerous critical tension that philosophy opens up.

Certainly, Strauss wants to situate himself in the tradition of openness to transcendence that characterizes the thought of Plato, Abū Nasr al-Fārābi, and Moses Maimonides.[17] This tradition marries the juridical foundation of philosophy to the philosophical foundation of the law, so that perfection unquestionably resides within philosophy. But even though it possesses clear logical primacy,[18] philosophy has no chronological and practical primacy. Because philosophy is itself made possible by the existence and operation of the social order, it is therefore obliged to respect that same order and to avoid radical criticisms of it. At the same time, however, Strauss situates Spinoza within another tradition, which believes in the absolute primacy of reason, which runs from Aristotle through Thomas, and which is overturned (but not, in Strauss's view, surpassed) by Hobbes and modernity. Strauss sees Spinoza as a true member of this tradition but at the same time as a true philosopher because the critical and atheist power of his philosophy drives him further from the representation of Truth as a knowable Object, and makes him instead perceive it as Norm—which is to say, as a Law whose Revelation consists in the impossibility of its being contained within a theological and theo-political cage. Thus it is that both Spinoza and Strauss come to rest in a place in between the insufficiency of Enlightenment, the impossibility of Orthodoxy, and the consciousness of the limits of philosophy.[19]

2. Schmitt's Spinoza

Although Schmitt's references to Spinoza are not infrequent, they are, with a few exceptions, not essential either, and critics consequently have not given them much attention.[20] Among the more meaningful of these references, we may single out those contained in two works of Schmitt's early maturity: *Political Romanticism* (1919) and *Die Diktatur* (1921). In *Political Romanticism*, Schmitt discerns in Spinoza a remarkable difference between the theoretical and the political side of his thought.[21] Whereas Spinoza's theoretical thinking is atheistic, pantheistic, and emanationist (going beyond the difference between thought and being in an immanentism that would even involve Malebranche and Schelling), Spinoza's political thinking is mainly rationalistic. This interpretation, which already was quite dated at the time, became more complex in *Die Diktatur*.[22] In this book, Schmitt connects Spinoza's political thinking to the internal system of modern rationalism and to the Hobbesian tradition, while also arguing that Spinoza cannot be understood as a simply rationalistic and mechanistic thinker. Because, as Schmitt points out, Spinoza's theoretical account of the relation between *natura naturans* and *natura naturata* is similar, from a political standpoint, to the relation Emmanuel Joseph Sieyès establishes between the constituting power of the nation and its constituted political form, the possible political cipher of Spinoza's thought resides more in *excess* than in *contract* (as is also the case, of course, in Schmitt's own *Constitutional Theory*).[23]

In these early texts, in other words, Schmitt discerns in Spinoza the theme of a political energy that cannot be contained in or by political institutions; he also sees in Spinoza the hermeneutical instruments for understanding how politics is not reducible to the contractual or conflictual nexus between individual and State. He does not, however, foresee the relation between *multitudo* and *potentia*; nor does he develop this interpretative thread along the certainly very different path that would disclose in Spinoza a self-aware political theology. Although there is, of course, a political theology present in Spinoza (as we learn plainly enough from Schmitt's later writings), it is a sort of political theology that is completely immanent, and it is to that same degree useless for the critical objective of productively grasping the origin of the Modern and its efficacy. In short, the more that Schmitt's thought develops, the more he brings Spinoza entirely within the modern intellectual paradigm: precisely because Spinoza's thought can't relate critically to modernity and to its origin, Spinoza's critique remains internal to modernity.

This is why, in Schmitt's 1929 essay "The Age of Neutralizations and Depoliticizations," Schmitt mentions Spinoza only as one among many examples of the scientific metaphysics typical of the heroic age of Western rationalism,[24] while in *The Concept of the Political* (1932) he mentions Spinoza only incidentally, noting that Spinoza is, like Hobbes and Samuel von Pufendorf, a modern philosopher of the State and that he, like them, theorizes the state of nature.[25] Squeezed in this way into the paradigm of modern rationalism, Spinoza is then subjected to Schmitt's genealogical criticism, with the result being a verdict of guilty: Spinoza, Schmitt finds, is on the wrong side, deprived of energy. Indeed, whereas Schmitt's Hobbes has two faces (just like the Modern itself, of which Hobbes is, for Schmitt, the eponymous hero), Schmitt's Spinoza is destined to embody just one: that of the thinker who is responsible, almost in the manner of a scapegoat, for the critical, individualistic, and formalistic drift of modernity (which are of course not the same thing, but in Schmitt's view abstract formalism leaves room for a "bad" sort of concreteness, that of the subject). And Schmitt tries to underline Spinoza's negative role in intellectual and political Western history by emphasizing—as much in the Nazi era as later on—that Spinoza belongs to the Jewish "race."[26]

Schmitt's argumentative line is here quite simple. First, he credits Strauss with having proven, with his 1930 text, that Spinoza depends on Hobbes, and with having understood that the opposition between religion and politics is typically Jewish (one that makes sense, Schmitt notes, only in a Christian context).[27] After criticizing Catholicism for its theory of the *potestas indirecta*, Schmitt then proceeds to concede that Hobbes is indeed responsible for the modern distinction between religious interiority and politics—but only as a means to the end of concreteness. For Hobbes, Schmitt argues, this distinction had the objective of silencing religious dissents by concealing them in the private sphere. Another of Hobbes's objectives, Schmitt continues, was to turn religious unity—achieved by the king thanks to the principle of *cujus regio, ejus religio* [whose is the realm, his is the religion]—into the basis and the main goal of political unity. What Spinoza does—this first "liberal Jew," Schmitt says, using a definition that came from Strauss—is creep into that distinction and completely upset it. Spinoza accomplishes this in chapters 19 and 20 of his *Tractatus Theologico-Politicus*, where he brings the distinction between religious interiority and politics to the foreground in order to turn interior subjective reserve—which is, remember, in Schmitt's reading of Hobbes, merely defensive—into the critical and offensive beginning of a political philosophy that privileges the individual and his freedom, and that moves State politics to the background.[28] According to Schmitt, therefore, the individualistic face of the Modern originates in Spinoza's overturning of the Hobbesian paradigm (which Spinoza also, to be clear, continues) and then proceeds on a liberal-constitutionalist path that distinguishes, above all, between public right and private morals (which are always also decidedly universal in scope). On the German side, in the field of the juridical doctrine of the State and of its relations with the individual, this line of thought goes from Christian Thomasius to Kant and to Goethe, going through Pufendorf as well as Christian Wolff. It is a crack within the "modern crystal of politics,"[29] a weakness that is exploited and developed with special acuity and acrimony by Enlightenment Jews such as Moses Mendelssohn (whose strategy was understood and attacked by Johann Georg Hamann), or by pseudo-conservatives such as Friedrich Julius Stahl. The result is that the State is forced to legitimize itself merely as exterior form and pure legality, so that the nonneutral legal State proposed by Robert von Mohl becomes nothing more than a mere machine, an abstraction that now even its enemies, the Bolsheviks, can invoke.[30] All because of the Jews, in other words, the "legal State" is no longer a political concept.

We are in front of one of the worst passages of Schmitt's intellectual and political biography: the transformation of his traditional cultural anti-Semitism, rooted in his Catholicism, into a weapon for regrounding politics on the basis of race and for excluding and persecuting the "stranger." Until this point, Schmitt's cultural anti-Semitism had not significantly determined his thought. Schmitt's thought was always, of course, characterized by a polemical attitude he derived from anti-Semitic counterrevolutionary authors (such as Charles Marraus). But for a long time that attitude was not openly or mainly directed against Jews, instead directing itself against the thinkers who were more involved with the immanentistic and intellectualistic drifts of the Modern (up to and including the Hegelian left).[31] The truth is that, in 1938, Schmitt openly submitted himself to Nazism. Since the end of 1936, the Nazi regime had strongly suspected him not only because of power struggles in the highest levels and within the Ministry of Justice, but also for Schmitt's basic inability to assimilate, despite his own efforts, the regime's *völkisch* ideology.[32] Schmitt nevertheless dedicated himself to serving that regime, albeit opportunistically, and only in 1944 did he begin to "prudently" distance himself from this decision. During the Nuremberg trials and in his *Ex Captivitate Salus* (1945),[33] he tried to justify his decision as a necessity, both objectively (because of the irreparable fall of Weimar) and subjectively (for having been made a de facto prisoner of the dynamic politico-juridical contradictions of Modernity). In some instances, he even tried to construe his decision as harmless: "in the years 1933–36, I betrayed myself and the dignity of my thoughts less than Plato betrayed himself and his thoughts with his trip to Sicily," Schmitt would write in 1947.[34] Really, however, Schmitt's racist and totalitarian positions, which consciously placed themselves beyond the decisionism and the risky modernity that are the general signature of Schmittian thought, were in line with positions expressed by Schmitt in 1936,[35] on the necessity to discriminate against Jewish jurists because of their fragmentation of the compactness of German doctrine.[36] Racism and totalitarianism are therefore much more than a mere detail in Schmitt's human, political, and intellectual experience.[37] They nevertheless cannot be taken as the only keys for the understanding of his thought, both before and after his conspicuous Nazi phase. Schmitt's thought is certainly suffocated by racism (eventually becoming a *politische Biologie*)[38] and is reinterpreted and distorted in Nazi terms. But before and after this phase, Schmitt's thought kept, and still keeps, important heuristic cues—cues that exist side by side with his anti-Semitism, to be sure, but even more so with his authoritarianism and often factious antiliberalism—that can be extracted with great caution. These cues are contained in texts by Schmitt that need to be interpreted, not embraced with naïveté and enthusiasm; nor, however, do their ideological or polemical elements necessarily make them "homicidal."

In Schmitt's reconstruction of Modernity there is, without question, a historiographic mistake: he reads the history of Jewish emancipation in Germany as if the *Atheismusstreit* [atheism dispute] never happened, and hence as if that emancipation were an inescapable consequence of a linear history set into motion by Spinoza, in whose thought democracy, liberalism, and atheism follow one another according to necessity (a typical counterrevolutionary style of forced argumentation) rather than as a series of tormented choices and treacherous crossroads. There is no doubt, then, that Schmitt's thesis about Spinoza's liberal critique operating a "private" destruction of politics is a misunderstanding of the very essence of Spinoza's thought. But it is also here, lying precisely in the debris of Schmitt's misunderstanding, that we can find the seeds of Reinhart Koselleck's interpretation of the relations between morals and politics during the Enlightenment, and of the interior origin of the very modern reason that constitutes public space.[39]

Along the same lines, in his *Glossarium*—a text written between 1947 and 1951, rich in intelligence but also saturated by rancor and fury, a work full of intuition but also of self-pity—Schmitt reintroduces his harsh anti-Semitism, and once again interprets Spinoza as the first of the Jews to creep inside the German people ("and until that's understood, there is no salvation").[40] This reintroduction must be distinguished, however, at least from an intellectual point of view, from Schmitt's clever observation that, unlike Hobbes, "Spinoza is not Baroque" but is instead "uncritical."[41] With this claim, Schmitt seems to situate Spinoza alongside Machiavelli[42]—he seems to maintain that Spinoza is not able to grasp, on account of his immanentism, the originary structure of modern power (which is to say, of *Herrschaft*), namely, that modern power relies on a decision for representation, on a façade suspended over the nothingness of the death and life of creatures. Modern sovereignty certainly does include a core of mere power (*Macht*), a power that is consistent with its intimate legal positivistic nature, with its essence of statualistic legality aimed only at the protection of the individual. However, Hobbes subsumes this sovereignty within a metaphilosophy, in a thought that does not rest on that power, that does not consider it the ultimate "reality," and as such allows for a reading that is stereoscopic and thrown into relief [in rilievo]: because it is a "political theology" in a Schmittian sense (a politics based on the conscious decisionistic-representative evacuation of divine foundational substance) Hobbes's doctrine displays an epochal concreteness, not merely a legal efficacy. Precisely because Hobbes is Baroque—because of his representation of politics in the image of the Leviathan, whose reasoning is for Schmitt that of an ungrounded decision[43]—he can access a "substantial" publicity and legitimization that do not coincide with the nexus between power, legality, and individuals. It is the Baroque façade that reveals the self-awareness of modern power, thus turning it into sovereignty and allowing it to function as katechon with regard to its machinic-automatic drift. Spinoza, in Schmitt's view, is foreign to all this: his political theology is uncritical because it is too integral, because it tries to do without transcendence, because it is closed within immanence, within the "stupidity" that characterizes the automatism of substance-nature-God.[44] In this sense, Schmitt's view of Spinoza ends up being quite similar to his view of Machiavelli: Spinoza was not Baroque because of his excessive "naturalism," which is completely foreign to every political theology.

Schmitt's judgment on Spinoza hence seems to oscillate between the accusation of immanentistic pantheism (a charge that has long roots in counterrevolutionary thought, especially that of Juan Donoso Cortés) and that of liberal and individualistic hypercriticism (and here Schmitt is quite close to Strauss's essay of 1930). This subjectivist hypercriticism is not true criticism, in Schmitt's view, because it is not a true political theology; indeed, despite its individualism, it perfectly complies with the technical and automatic dynamics of the Modern. On this point, Schmitt diverges from Strauss: for the latter, it is exactly because Spinoza does not exercise political theology that he cannot completely adhere to the nihilistic destiny of Western reason. In fact, in Strauss's view, Spinoza instead dissociates himself from this destiny thanks to the criticality of the philosopher, as distinct from that of the common individual.

There exist two notions of "concreteness" in Schmitt: one that's Nazi and substantialist and another that's decisionist and representative (Baroque, attributable to the "true" political theology). In Schmitt's view,

Spinoza—whether a liberal Jew or an evil political theologian—is an enemy to both. Unlike Strauss, Schmitt cannot attribute any criticality at all to Spinoza, because for Schmitt true criticism is not "critique," but "true" political theology, which is to say, that peculiar nexus that opens up between *exception* and *excess*, on the one hand, and *norm*, on the other (and this whether the excess is that of the sovereign decision over the exception, with regard to the norm, or alternatively, that of the absent Idea relative to its representation). Schmitt certainly cannot genealogically connect this nexus either to "his" Spinoza (in relation to whom one should not speak of exception but of liberal individualistic critique or uncritical political theology of immanence) or to today's Spinoza (whose politics is relation and whose "excess" is collective power).[45] Above all, what testifies to Schmitt's distance from Spinoza is that Spinoza's name never appears in a crucial text like *Political Theology*, even though Spinoza is an obvious reference. Schmitt, in short, excludes Spinoza from "true" political theology.

In his 1978 essay "The Legal World Revolution,"[46] which would be the last that he would publish during his life, Schmitt returned in passing to his old analogy between the relation between *natura naturans* and *natura naturata* in Spinoza and the relation between *pouvoir constituant* and *pouvoir constitués* in Sieyès. Here Schmitt declares that the political theology implicit in this analogy no longer can be understood by contemporary juridical and constitutional science; in its place, he prefers to use the less esoteric Weberian conception (in particular the notion of charismatic power). Keeping in mind that Schmitt's late works must be interpreted with even more attention than his other works, because they often privilege allusions and rhapsodic references over rigorous intellectual coherence, we nevertheless may observe that Schmitt's affirmation seems to grant to Spinoza a theologico-political framework that places him at the very core of the modern democratic doctrine of constitution. At the same time, however, even this observation should be interpreted in light of Schmitt's distinction between the political theology of immanence and "true" decisionistic-representative political theology (which faces the absence of transcendence). As such, we may read Schmitt's last reference to Spinoza as a signal that, in his old age, he was distancing himself from Sieyès and his "non-Baroque" democratic theory of constituent power, the theory that so fixed Schmitt's attention in *Constitutional Theory*.

3. The Meaning of the Two Readings of Spinoza

Strauss and Schmitt never directly agreed or fought about Spinoza. Their "true" authors remain, respectively, Maimonides and Hobbes. Still, the causes and consequences of their diverging interpretations of Spinoza deserve to be analyzed. Besides the fact that both Strauss and Schmitt privilege Spinoza's *Tractatus Theologico-Politicus*, and that they both miss, in different ways and for different reasons, the topic of the power of the multitude, there is no question that Strauss and Schmitt have two very different ideas of Spinoza. For Strauss, Spinoza is, apparently, a liberal-democratic Jew who is defeated by totalitarianism, but who is, above all, a modern philosopher of great significance who was able to escape from the cage that shackles theory directly to practice. On this view, Spinoza's critique resists reason's tendency to saturate the space of experience, and to confuse itself with religion and with politics (and on this reading Spinoza is close to the *philosophia perennis*). For Schmitt, Spinoza is a liberal Jew who is ultimately victorious, at least insofar as his bad criticism corroded the already precarious concreteness of modern politics, thus activating its liberal and normativistic drift. Both Strauss and Schmitt therefore think that critique is Spinoza's chief characteristic. For Schmitt, however, Spinoza's criticism is completely immanent to the Modern, and is indeed the corruption of the Modern, whereas for Strauss it is, perhaps, a truly philosophical criticism, one that can be attained by reason only before the enigmatic presence and absence of the Law. For Schmitt, Spinoza makes concreteness impossible, which is bad; for Strauss, he makes compactness impossible (and "compactness" here means the closure of political space, the coincidence of Religion, Philosophy, Politics), which is good. Faced with the criticism opened up by Spinoza's philosophy, both Schmitt and Strauss thus raise their defenses. In Schmitt's case, we see total, radical refusal. On Strauss's part, we see partial measures designed to ascribe the power of criticism only to the philosopher and not to society. Strauss rejects the topic of the power of the multitude because it is too destabilizing, and Schmitt rejects it because—unlike the constituting power of the people, to which he is indeed tempted to connect it—the power of the multitude cannot be captured in the form of sovereignty, within the dialectic of institution and exception.

From a systematic point of view, Schmitt's and Strauss's different interpretations of Spinoza are born not only from the very great differences in their understanding of Hobbes, but also, even more generally, from their different way of conceiving modernity and its relations with transcendence. Both, in fact, deny the possibility of a political grasp of the Truth, whether in the form of liberal rational mediation, or in the form of revolutionary eschatology. Both, in other words, conceive of the Modern as the absence of transcendence. This absence, however, presents itself and acts in different modes for each thinker. Schmitt grasps it with reference to a peculiar political theology, the one he sees in Hobbes and that he further elaborates in the direction of decisionism and representativism (which are far from a foundationalist political theology of the Catholic type).[47] Strauss, by contrast, believes that this absence must be filled, exoterically, by addressing the people to "natural" and religious elements that must be interpreted in a tolerant and stabilizing way.[48] Esoterically, meanwhile, the absence of transcendence manifests itself for the philosopher as the Shadow of the Law. It's a limit to philosophical reason that is also, and at the same time, the source of philosophy's critical power—a power that is grounded on the Jewish ban on the image, up to and including the Baroque image of an absence suspended over the void of death.[49]

What's at stake in these readings of Spinoza—who is for both Schmitt and Strauss above all, if not exclusively, a liberal—is the essence and the limits of modern political philosophy, and it is precisely in the field of political theology, via Spinoza, that the distance between Schmitt and Strauss on this point becomes most apparent. It's within this field that both thinkers grasp the triumph of modern reason (its victory over tradition) and that both come to analyze the limits of modern reason (its dependence on tradition, and its self-enclosed structure). It's also within this field that both perceive the inability of modern reason, and the politics deriving from modern reason, to justify itself (a point that Weber already had grasped with great intuition in "Science as a Vocation"[50]). But Schmitt reduces political theology to genealogy, resolving it in a theory of the Modern as an always already incomplete process of secularization, and thus too in the individuation of both the spasm of decision (of the originary dead spot in which reason and nonreason effectively touch each other) and the compulsion for form and representation, which constitutes the other face of the Modern. Spinoza, whether understood as a liberal critic or as a thinker of the multitude, is necessarily alien to this concept of political theology. For Strauss, by contrast, every political theology is in general denied by the aporetic relationship between faith and reason (of which there are more than traces in Spinoza), truth and history, ancient and modern, and above all Law (that of which one cannot make an image) and modern rationalistic philosophy. For Strauss, the latter could be critical, and it could rend the veil of every idolatry—up to and including that of modern humanism and its technical and potentially antihuman sides—but, taken on its own terms, it is nothing but a new political theology, one that is no longer overt but now merely inverted.

Strauss's critique of the Modern, in the multiple levels in which it is articulated, can be interpreted from a methodological point of view as a refusal of modernity's *Selbverständnis* [self-understanding]. For Strauss, the Modern is neither original nor new; it is little more than the reversal of the ancient relationship between law and juridical order—or, put a bit differently, it subjectifies the objectivity of premodern natural law.[51] It consists of the same traditional relationship between philosophy and morals,[52] only now in a minor key: the Modern substitutes the *summum bonum* of classical political reason (the good at which politics aims) with a *summum malum* (an evil that politics needs to avoid). Strauss even interprets Machiavelli (who is, of course, quite foreign to rationalism and political theology) as a philosopher who impiously overturns the relation between Good and Evil, who consequently is unable to exit the traditional nexus between politics and the Good, and who therefore arrives at a peculiarly non-Christian political theology, which Strauss sums up with the formula *Deus sive fortuna* [God or luck].[53]

Strauss, in other words, theologizes modern atheism in order to maintain that modernity has failed to exit the theologico-political apparatus of tradition, and that modernity can only overturn this apparatus through a similar relation of foundation and saturation—a relation that no longer would take place between theology and politics, but now between philosophy and politics. His critical thinking consists in showing that even modern reason is not immune from the same closure of political space, and the same perversion of critical power, that also plagued antiquity and Christianity with tyranny and fundamentalism. From this philosophical point of view, Strauss shares the protest of other Jewish intellectuals—such as, for instance, the first thinkers of the Frankfurt School (but some aspects of this critique also pertain to Hannah

Arendt)—with the crucial qualification that Strauss's protest is issued in a nondialectical, politically stabilizing, and nonrevolutionary frame, one that aims at esoterically recuperating ancient natural law while at the same time disclosing its aporias. Like Strauss, Max Horkheimer, Theodor Adorno, and also Arendt grasped reason—understood as mediation between subject and object—as the origin of a movement that inevitably allowed the rational external object (first nature, and then God) to be assimilated by a rational subject (the modern individual) who then would position himself as the center from which the cognitive and constructive power of reason would radiate, but who also would permit this very same power of reason to become autonomous from the subject, and to morph into an impersonal machine of domination. Strauss's specific difference from these intellectuals consists in the way he puts into play a true transcendence (although, again, not mainly through Spinoza). For Strauss, the true transcendence is the Law that cannot be represented, that indeed forbids images of God as well as the representation of man as God. This is the Law that keeps reason open by returning it to its own critical power, but now, above all, in order to use that power primarily against itself—not as a social and political energy, but as a prerogative that belongs only, and exclusively, to the philosopher.

While Schmitt's critical power resides in his perception of the originary and aporetic coexistence of reason and nonreason, Strauss's thus resides in the perception of the failure of the world before the Truth, which we should not mistake for a triumph of Reason (reason, remember, is not truth but criticism) but instead should accept as Law (conceived neither as religious foundation nor, in standard Enlightenment manner, as simple superstition). The power of these two critiques of the Modern nevertheless goes hand in glove with the weaknesses that, in the end, reveal their dependence on the very same conceptual horizon they criticize. On the one hand, we witness Schmitt unable to renounce extremist reaffirmations of the Modern (even when they take the form of the horrible modalities of Nazism). On the other hand, we see Strauss retreat from the public use of critical reason, and withdraw into the distinction between philosopher and city (which, however prudent, is nevertheless intellectually weak). Remaining within the horizon of modern domination and its confutation, neither thinker grasps or reveals—beyond the simple sympathy or antipathy that informs their interpretations—the power of Spinoza, his unity of theory and praxis, which is not so much magnificent as disenchanted, atheist, and participative. Their struggle against the secular, bourgeois world and their hand-to-hand combat with the Modern are at one and the same time also conflicts with Spinoza, and those conflicts manifest themselves through their readings of Spinoza. But the essence of Spinoza's thought either escapes them, or they are not interested in it. For both Strauss and Schmitt, Spinoza is not a propellant; he is, in the end, repellant.

....

CHAPTER 5

SCHMITT AND THE GLOBAL ERA

The Nomos of the Earth, Schmitt's key text among his international works, has raised worldwide attention also among nonspecialists, but especially among jurists and political theorists.[1] The event that stimulated the international attention for this text was its English translation, released over fifty years after the original publication. The numerous interpretations of Schmitt's internationalist works appear as an implicit sign that Schmitt's capacity to analyze international relations is supposed to be still current and effective. Beginning already in the twenties, Schmitt's thought had focused on the theory of the Grossraum, on the land-sea relationship, and on the concept of nomos. His intellectual trajectory seems to describe phenomena that also and especially today remain a privileged object of attention: the vanishing of the balance between land and sea; the triumph of universalist political features (technics, capitalism, humanitarianism, international law) over those determined by space (such as the State); the crisis of the distinctions between peace and war, between criminal and enemy, and the return of topics such as the just war and the criminalization of the defeated; the affirmation of the conflictual sides of politics, often in nonmediated and absolute forms (such as the logic of friend and enemy), which often acquire a religious background (political theology); the new political relevance of non-State entities (terrorism), and in general, the weakening of the distinction between public and private, between social and political; and the possibility of reformulating the international order around clearly defined "Great Spaces" (or, as we call them today, "civilizations").

This chapter grapples with the following question: can Schmitt's thought function as a politico-theoretical master-key to access both the twentieth and the twenty-first centuries? In today's world, can Schmitt's thought explain unlimited conflict as much as imperial order?

1. Methodological Questions

There's no doubt that Schmitt's thought offers a critical outlook on modern political forms (States) and their equilibria (in international law) and that it focuses on their crisis, which was well under way during the twentieth century. Nor is there any doubt that this critical outlook is present in Schmitt's works dedicated to internal politics just as much as those dedicated to international politics, since both are structured around the same intuition—namely, that during modernity, conflict is what makes order possible, and that excess [dismisura] is the measure of politics. However, simply because Schmitt analyzed the crisis of the State, of its juridified sovereignty, and of the international relations formalized around the State as he experienced them, it does not necessarily follow that his thought is an adequate tool to understand the current shape of the crisis of the State and international relations. In fact, the categories of the political thought of any author are born, remain valid, and should be analyzed historically—genealogically, if you will—with reference to the concrete challenges to which the intellectual endeavor is meant to answer and that, in turn, produced it. These categories do not identify only the content and the proposals, but also the origin, the destination, and the orientation of the cultural frameworks that shape them. Thus, in order to prove that Schmitt's thought is adequate for reflecting on the contemporary world, or to affirm that today's dynamics happen in a Schmittian form, and that today's issues can be solved in a Schmittian way, it is not enough to note the external similarity between the object of his thought (crisis) and contemporary political experience. One must also ask if we are facing the same crisis, and if Schmitt's categories come from (and are oriented to) political and intellectual experiences that we can recognize as ours in the contemporary world. Hence, it is important to perform both a genealogical analysis of Schmitt's thought and a structural comparison between the crises of the political entities in the twentieth and in the twenty-first century.

Skipping this step is to risk lazily relying on categories suggested by someone else, however original in their own time their ideas may have been. The risk is that we might simply move from one type of dogmatism to another, from the instrumental use of one system of thought to another, just because it appears more fashionable or more politically correct (this might even happen to Schmitt's thought).

The point is then to take measure of what is alive and what is dead in Schmitt's thought—or, better, to recognize which elements from our time of crisis can be deciphered through Schmitt's analysis of the crisis of his time, and which cannot. Lastly, it is worth noting that evaluations of the capacity of systems of thought to explain contemporary times are very different from judgments regarding their intrinsic acuteness or historical relevance.

2. Schmittian Questions

Schmitt's thought is a reflection that is theoretically determined: it is an extreme deconstruction of modern political theory, and it is an exposition of the originary risk—the Void-of-Order, the conflict—that is immanent to modern political theory. This is true both with regard to internal politics, for the theories of the exception, the decision, and the "political" (which is a genealogical reinterpretation and complication of Hobbes's theory of the rational State); and with regard to international politics, for the theory of the *nomos* and of the partisan (which are genealogical complications of geopolitics and State-based international law). The prominence of the conflictual element in Schmitt's political thought—for him, the enemy plays a necessary role in constituting and maintaining order, whether in the theory of the "political," in the theory of the decision (which originates in secularized political theology), or in the theory of constituent power—is not an apology for absolute conflict. Its function is to orient the political system to the order—political unity—inherent in modern political theory and Schmittian thought alike. For Schmitt, however, conflict is neither fully instrumental for order nor fully subordinate to it. Conflict is instead the endless, internal, and originary perturbation of order and hence endlessly undetermines the very order that also originally determines.

2.1 From the point of view of "internal" politics, Schmitt's thought is able to access the two sides of the Modern—both the modern compulsion to order (the co-implication of order and conflict) and the disjunction in principle between the idea of order and its concrete realization—and as such is able to accept that political form is destined not only for cogency but also for originary unfoundedness. In his access to this aporia, Schmitt sees, in fact, the condition of possibility for all political forms. The unfounded and disquieted political form (which, according to Political Theology, is created by decision) has its origin in the fact that the "substantial form" of the Church—which realizes in praxis the complexio oppositorum thanks to the representation of Christ— is well founded from the theological point of view, and is the model for political representation (as Schmitt says in Roman Catholicism and Political Form). However, at the same time, in the modern era, substantial form becomes impossible to achieve even for the Church, forced as it is to decide on the conflictual opposites that traverse modernity (understood as a technico-economical age). Hence, even as the State can and must preserve the impulse to form that derives from the theological tradi- tion, so too must it also secularize that impulse. It must also, in other words, transform the substantial foundation of politics (which by now is lost, just as modern politics lost the mediation of the pope through which the Church operates) into concretized points, into the absolute contingencies on which the decision then operates. Instead of being "well founded," therefore, modern politics now originates from (and is open to) the Void-of-Order. This is why modern politics can only be an "answer to a challenge," a response to the disorder that is able to create a condition of concrete order only if it first neutralizes the nihilism of disorder by incorporating it; and only if, without any Aufhebung, it turns disorder into the very center of its orientation and determination. The incorporation is indeed the decision on the exception—the immedi- acy that is the truth and the last image of modern rational mediation, although now turned into act of will rather than act of reason (since reason is not the foundation but at best the result of political action). According to Political Theology, modern constructionism realizes in the decision that its foundation is not the individual or collective reason, but the Void-of-Order—or, in a word, conflict.[2]

The fact that conflict is Void-of-Order (and not just Nothing) implies that conflict is not the same as absolute disorder. Instead, the concept of the "political" around which Schmitt labors at the end of the twen- ties, insofar as it consists of the relationship between friend and en- emy, is the permanent presence of conflict at the origin of order, and, through the decision, the permanence of conflict within order. This is true both for the State and for international relations. Schmitt's concept of the "political" is hence radical and determined conflict—conflict that is always in some relation to order, and that is always potentially morphogenetic. It is a lack that both demands and instigates ordering by a political decision (which is why the political functions both in terms of destructuring and, at the same time, in terms of structuring, why it is not only crisis but also order). In this way, modern political form, insofar as it openly poses the problem of the "political," is governance together with sovereign decision, material constitution together with constituent power. It is not at all neutral order; it is determined by an originary conflict, and it is continuously oriented by this conflict. It is, in short, an architectonic nihilism.[3]

For Schmitt, the spatial difference between inside and outside is strategic: it constitutes modern politics and corresponds to the distinction between enemy and criminal, war and peace, police and army. But in order to confine disorder to the outside and pacify the inside, the State must recognize, preserve within itself, and manage its own originary disorder. In order for the State to be closed—to be able to posit boundaries, to separate order and disorder—it thus must be open onto the "political." It must be able, in other words, to activate, by deciding on the exception, the compulsion toward form and the co-implication of order and disorder.

In Schmitt's thought, the difference between inside and outside is also central to the thesis that there exists a dialectic of the Modern— namely, that the Modern is exposed to an endogenous "drift" that tries to remove its originary nihilism, while actually pushing that very nihilism out of control. In fact, the processes of secularization, from which political modernity is born, produce political energy that is oriented to form: these processes generate the absolute State, which is capable of neutralizing religious conflicts and of building a structured political order on the basis of a clear distinction between inside and outside, between police and war. In this way, the absolute State identifies an "area of focus" (or Zentralgebiet)—primarily the theological—in which its conflicts can develop, and which must be depoliticized through the sovereign decision that, drawing from "the political," creates order. This is the principle, both excluding and ordering, of cujus regio ejus religio ("whose is the realm, his is religion"). This very same concrete political order, however, calls into being a society (Enlightenment and revolutionary in the eighteenth century, bourgeois in the nineteenth century, democratic in the twentieth) that sees the State as an enemy to be defeated or limited. This happens precisely because the State allows for a free and adequate development of the rational, individual, and universal logics of the Modern. This historical development transfers conflict to new spheres (morals, economy, technics), which are ever more capable of subtracting themselves from the State and its neutralizing political action, and ever more animated by the (unsuccessful) ideological claim to self-regulation on the basis of individual and collective reason. The State itself thus gives birth to political, ideological, and material forces—a social entwinement of individualism, liberalism, and liberal democracy, of normativism and moralism, of technics, of both capitalist and communist economy—that, in turn, deprive it of its sovereign capacity for order. These forces replace concreteness with indeterminate universality, and try to replace the "political" with the forces of economy, juridical order, and technics (a tendency that has defined the State from the moment of its Hobbesian origins, as Schmitt maintains in *The Leviathan in the State Theory of Thomas Hobbes*). The logics of the Modern proceed from the concrete to the abstract, from being determined to being universal, from the political to the social.

These same logics spell the defeat of the sovereign decision by bourgeois reason. For Schmitt, the latter is defined by the liberal faith that discussion can expel conflict completely from political action, which instead can rely on rational hypotheses of automatic pacification. On the basis of this faith, society—and above all the political organizations born within society, such as the parties and advocacy groups that define democracy in general—invades the State and ends up turning its claim to stability and form into a source of mobilization and formlessness. This results in the situation that Schmitt, writing in 1931–32, defined as the "total State of weakness." To this terminal crisis of the State's political capability corresponds not only its internal lack of efficacy (its death due to the pluralism of politicized social forces) but also the end of its external capacity (its death due to the loss of the distinction between inside and outside). This "intermediate situation"—this *Zwischenlage* of the State, which is now suspended in indecision between peace and war—is the disposition [*Stimmung*] that marks the age of the crisis of the State.

To oppose these developments, Schmitt will polemicize not only against Kelsen's normativism but also against the constitutionalist logics of liberalism. Schmitt insists that faith in the disappearance of the "political" is in fact part of the logic of a moral and juridical fight against politics—a fight that, in fact, turns itself precisely into a political conflict, a war against war. For Schmitt, the claim of eliminating disorder—of completely avoiding any Void-of-Order—expresses nihilism to the highest degree. Wherever there is an attempt to realize a crystal-clear political form—a form purified of any opacity—precisely there the most radical absence of form instead will manifest itself.

The major objective of Schmitt's works, during the first part of his mature phase (1919–32), is to oppose the politico-juridical drift brought forth by modern nihilism—this drift from concreteness toward abstraction—in order to delay it and to fight it from within. Schmitt's aim during this phase is to renew the capacity of the Modern to produce concreteness. During these years, he didn't pursue this aim in a reactionary way; he instead treated the Modern's highest points of crisis as occasions for insights into the ways the danger itself might also contain the possibility for a *katechon*. In other words, Schmitt sought to derive the limits for modernity's drift toward immanence from within the limiting and formative power of the processes of immanence themselves (which remained open to transcendence without also seeking a "foundation" for politics in religion). But as a means to the end of concreteness, Schmitt employed different strategies throughout the course of his life, always interpreting the State as a determinate case of modern political form. In his search to find other possible modes of concrete political form (which, he thought, must be rescued from the drift of the Modern)[4] Schmitt also thought beyond the State. As a part of this difficult theoretical itinerary, Schmitt always accepted both faces of the Modern—the disconnection and co-implication in principle between Idea and reality. In truth, however, his trust in the possibility of realizing such an order decreased over the years, especially in the aftermath of World War II, which was the most "conservative" phase of Schmitt's thought—the phase most marked by disenchantment.

2.2 Also in the background of Schmitt's analyses of "external" politics there is the crisis of the State, which was caused by forces and contradictions operating within modern society. Schmitt's point of departure in these analyses is the crisis of Statual sovereignty, which in his view is no longer able to produce a concrete political form, a form adequate to new historical developments. As such, his analyses are directed toward the search for a new *katechon* for the dynamics of the Modern.

Schmitt's first polemical objective already was clear in 1925, when he produced his first formulation of the critique of the Society of Nations.[5] Schmitt's target in this essay is Genevan universalism, which he saw as the politico-juridical projection of individualism, liberalism, and normativism—and the projection, as well, of their claim to eliminate the "political" from internal and external politics. In Schmitt's evaluation, these developments were manifestations of the crisis (by now irreversible) of modern sovereignty's spatial essence, which is to say, the distinction between inside and outside. The collapse of this distinction, in Schmitt's view, created a confusion between war and crime: with the peace of Versailles—and with the League of Nations in Geneva— war ceased to be a right of State sovereignty. It instead became a crime under international law, according to which the winners may respond with "just war" and with discriminatory punishments against the defeated. The resulting universalism represented the international scene as a smooth and homogeneous space that could be fully subjected to a single morality and a single law. In actuality, however, Schmitt argued, this space was precisely functional to forces (the Anglo-Saxon powers and their economic potential) whose political action consisted in the persecution and moral stigmatization of their enemies. On this view, the League of Nations is an instrument of "indirect" politics, useful for protecting the winners and their plunder, and for punishing the defeated. Its universalism is actually imperialism, an instrument of war camouflaged as an instrument of peace. Schmitt would never abandon this evaluation of universalism; nor did he ever cease considering every proposal for just war as moralistic and discriminatory.

Even so, not all of Schmitt's interpretations of international political relations departed from the crisis of the State sovereignty, the obsolescence of the relation between inside and outside, and the progressive disappearance of the awareness that the "political" is inescapable. Starting with *The Leviathan in the State Theory of Thomas Hobbes*, and going all the way to his final text, "The Legal World Revolution,"[6] Schmitt also advanced a second interpretation of the Modern, of the State, and of international politics. His first interpretation of the Modern, as we have seen, focused on the decision, the exception, sovereignty, political theology, the "political," the constituent power, the concrete order; his second interpretation, meanwhile, analyzed the spatial dimension of politics, the opposition between earth and sea, the concept of *nomos* and of *jus publicum europæum*.

In this second phase of his oeuvre, Schmitt adopted a mode of thought that was openly postdecisionistic: in his attempt to escape the trap of modern nihilism, Schmitt sought to think the origin of politics using categories that were uncompromised by nihilism, and to conceive an order that would be born not from the Void-of-Order but instead from some kind of Measure. Even so, these two theoretical gazes did not constitute two alternative outlooks on the Modern, but instead remained complementary. Like Schmitt's first interpretation of the origin and drift of modernity and statuality, his second hinged on an idea crucial to Schmitt's thought, namely, the insight that political order is made possible through disorder and conflict, and can only be effective and concrete to the extent that it incorporates and conveys disorder. During Schmitt's second phase, this leitmotiv is articulated differently than in his first phase: in *Land and Sea*, for example, it calls forth an interpretation of the Modern that grasps its origin not only in the process of secularization of the conceptual framework of theology, but also in the spatial revolution that occurred after the discovery of the American continent opened Europe up to a new (earthly) world, which produced a disequilibrium within the spatial horizon that defined traditional European politics (the *respublica christiana*), forcing Europe to reorganize the political space of the globe around the "amity lines" [English in the original], while at the same time projecting it on the vastness of the oceans.[7]

The continental European State, according to Schmitt, derives its origin and its political centrality from a decision for politics in its territorial and closed sense, which is to say, from a decision for the sovereignty of the State, and from the resulting capacity of the State to relate itself to other territorial States. These relations may even assume the form of war: understood as a sort of mutual recognition, war itself allows for an unintentional but nevertheless significant structural and functional limitation on war. Instead of being understood as a *bellum justum* (a "just war"), as necessarily was the case in a theological context,[8] war now becomes understood as a *bellum utrimque justum* (a "just war for both sides") that exists between the regular armies of sovereign States, which for just this reason are each understood as *justi hostes* ("just enemies") to one another.[9] In its historical concreteness, however, the European

State exists only within the continental system of the States (the *jus publicum europæum*), which is necessarily balanced by the British maritime State. The British decision in favor of the sea (which began during the Elizabethan age) allowed for the creation of a political form that was not politico-territorial (with the house as its symbol) but simultaneously individualistic and technico-artificial (with the ship as its symbol). This unlimited political form carried with it an enmity that was equally unlimited. In fact, naval warfare would be conducted much differently than was terrestrial warfare: it would tend much more to the absolute and to nonrecognition of the enemy. In maritime war, the enemy would be characterized above all as a pirate, an irregular figure who could be criminalized as the enemy of all humanity. Already in the 1930s,[10] Schmitt understood that the pirate was far from an obsolete subject: to the contrary, the Anglo-Saxon powers' renewed attention to the figure of the pirate, which went so far as to turn the pirate into a political figure, signaled a historico-political tendency to remove all of the limits that hitherto had restrained conflict and to criminalize the supposed "piratic" German concept of total war.

To be sure, during the phase when modernity was still capable of effective political forms—the era of the *jus publicum europæum*, which ran from 1605 to 1900 (or, more precisely, from 1713 to 1918)[11]—it was constituted by an equilibrium between the continent and the United Kingdom, between the territorial State and the maritime State.[12] But aside from this felicitous but mythological (or at least stylized) construction of the category of *jus publicum europæum*, the contribution of *The Nomos of the Earth* is Schmitt's recognition that this originary equilibrium is also, at the same time, a form of disequilibrium. This implies that the external political order is not natural but oriented, and that the very political existence of the European States and their system is made possible on account of a difference imposed by Europe between itself and the rest of the world (which is to say, the line between friendship and enmity that distinguishes the Old World from the New). European civilization exists only because it was able to conquer, occupy, and divide up the New World, and to confine absolute enmity "over there," in the space of the non-State. The limitation of war to the European States, which recognize one another as *hostes aequaliter justi* [equally just enemies], is made possible by the unlimited wars waged against the natives in America (and in Asia and Africa), and also among the European States outside of the European continent.[13]

This nexus of equilibria (between land and sea, individual and State, politics and technique, all of which together constitutes Europe) and disequilibria (between Europe and the rest of the world) is the *nomos* of the earth (its concrete and oriented order) in the era of the *jus publicum europæum*. The concept of *nomos* as orientation and ordering does not then have to do with some sort of originary rootedness that is somehow naturally free from nihilism. Not at all: it indicates how measure is born from what is beyond measure [*dismisura*], how political forms emerge from originary violence, how concrete order is oriented not by a harmony but by a "cut" and a partitioning that creates a political space, and how political spaces generate normality derived not from a norm (*nomos* is not "law") but from a concrete act of differentiation. *Nomos*, in other words, is the originary opening that closes political form without also pacifying it, and that indeed continues to determine it.[14]

Despite the antinihilistic intent of his late intellectual elaboration, and precisely because his aim was to be politically "concrete," Schmitt did not then succeed in thinking an origin of politics that would be outside the power of the Void and free from the compulsion to form. Because the *nomos* subtracts from the earth in a mode that is nevertheless oriented to the earth—because it imposes boundaries on the earth, because its action makes earth enter politics and thence removes it from nature—it reveals the return of a structure that is deeply ingrained in Schmitt's thought. This structure, which is also present in his theory of the "political," involves the compulsion to form together with the co-implication and disconnection in principle between order and contingency, the search for a *katechon*, and the recognition of originary crisis. In each and every case, *nomos* is, for Schmitt, not universalistic: the destiny of politics is to remain particular.

In Schmitt's view, the elements of the crisis of the *jus publicum europæum* are the infinite vectors that are born within the State, in the juridical and moral as well as individual and social claims to subtract the State from the "political." To this list we must add the unilateral development of the "marine" element—which, as with technics, interprets every space as a smooth surface on which to exercise the rationalistic, calculating, and manipulative power of *homo faber*. The crisis of modernity consists in the fact that political form is swamped by the combined dispositions of very different entities, functions, and forces (such as rationalism, individualism, technical power, moralism, and normativism), all of which share a common tendency toward indeterminacy: through their action, any ordinative difference is washed away in a smooth and potentially unifiable space. It follows that universalism as such is tendentially discriminatory, since it reads the exception (and also the difference) as "error," injustice, immorality, or as a wrecker of unity that is unworthy of existence and must therefore be removed. With a dubious theoretical move, Schmitt holds Kant's theory of the *injustus hostis* responsible for offering the most powerful justification of the discriminatory dimension of philosophico-moral universalism: as Schmitt would tell it, Kant relaunched the just wars of the theologians, thus conferring great efficacy and legitimacy on the discriminatory wars of the twentieth century.[15]

On Schmitt's reading, the crisis of the *jus publicum europæum* is certainly endogenous, insofar as it marks the triumph of the side of the Modern that's merely ordinative and abstract, and that causes the loss of political "concreteness." While reconstructing the trajectory of the crisis, Schmitt underlines that "the first long shadow that fell upon the *jus publicum europæum* came from the West," and in particular from the United States.[16] With this declaration, Schmitt distinguishes between a European and continental modernity (healthier, in his view) and an Anglo-Saxon modernity (the carrier of a taint that has spread around the world). This is the ideological and doctrinaire side to Schmitt's thought, which often needs to assign responsibility to an entity (Jews, liberals, Anglo-Americans) for dynamics that in fact constitute one side of the deep structure of the Modern. This side subsides after World War II (although it remains in the speeches he gave in Spain in the 1960s). In the final phase of the Weimar Republic and in the second, internationalist, phase of his work during the Nazi years, Schmitt made a point of emphasizing the birth of the discriminatory just war and the moralistic confusion between enemy and criminal. The responsible were the Anglo-Saxon powers operating in the smooth world space, in which the indirect political action can have free play. Furthermore, Schmitt analyzes the Monroe Doctrine, recognizing its politico-juridical essence as an instrument for the self-justification of the sovereign power of the American empire; he also takes into consideration the conceptual works that have integrated and substituted Monroe's (such as those focused on the economical intervention, the moving of the line of the Western Hemisphere).[17] Through analyses like this, Schmitt claims with remarkable argumentative force that the transition from isolationism to interventionism is just a variant of the American exceptionalism. Already in his 1938 essay "Über das Verhältnis der Begriffe Krieg und Feind" (On the relation between the concepts of war and enemy), Schmitt interpreted discriminatory war as a result of the confusion between war and peace—which is to say of the "intermediate situation" [Zwischenlage] into which the modern effort to distinguish clearly war from peace (through the decision of the State) had fallen. The Zwischenlage is a liminal situation that Schmitt accepts as the disposition [Stimmung] of the era, but he does not want to leave it to be managed by Anglo-Saxon empires and their universalistic moralism.[18] His motivation for this position is based on the tendency of the Anglo-Saxon empires to criminalize war and in turn to generate an openly nihilistic war—a "just war" that assumes the form of discriminatory war, that involves nonmilitary spheres (economy, propaganda), and that affects entire populations, who then are considered to be "guilty."

Schmitt reacts against this emerging spatial organization—defined by a refusal of the concreteness of the "political," by indirect and despatialized politics, and by absolute and moralistic war—by accepting the challenge of poststatuality. This is why, in 1939, he proposed the two concepts of Reich and Grossraum. The latter certainly does indicate a space formed by a hegemonic political command that carries with it the organizing principle of the State; but, more than the State, it has a capacity to give life to a concrete political order, and an awareness of the need to govern a plurality of national organisms in its interior (which would then be hierarchized by Empire into a "Great Space" that excludes foreign, external powers).[19] With this concept, Schmitt aims to respond to the indirect imperialism of maritime, technical, liberal, and democratic universalisms—expressed, above all, in the juridical formalism of the League of Nations[20]—which were unaware of any concreteness, and thus unable to escape the condition of the "intermediate situation." His response to indirect imperialism is direct Empire, which entails a reterritorialization of politics (which is also a direct totalization of politics) and an open affirmation of the logics of political unity (derived from the State, even if rearticulated in a poststatual form as imperial "totality").[21] Along these lines, Schmitt contrasts concrete total war to discriminatory total war (which he sees as a new modality of the old *potestas indirecta*). Total war is waged at first by the total State, which is newly able to distinguish inside and outside, peace and war.[22] Later, it's waged by Empires, which, with the total hostility of which they alone are capable (a hostility that is at the same time political, ideological, social, economical, cultural, technical), recognize and accept the "political" without camouflaging it in moral or juridical forms. With this recognition, these same Empires actuate the origin of a new concrete political form: a "political total war" that could even allow for the neutrality of third parties, which obviously would be inconceivable insofar as war were presented as the sanction of a crime or as the conflict of Good and Evil.[23]

Schmitt's criticism of Genevan universalism—that it is vague about the settings, contents, and modalities of Empire—was shared by some of the writers of his time. But the way Schmitt thought the Reich—which was an important topic for the Conservative Revolution, and which Schmitt faced not in a mystic-spiritual way, but politically[24]—was met with doubt both by the most statalist jurists and by the most orthodox theoreticians of Nazism. For the former, Schmitt's concept of the Reich was too undetermined; for the latter, it was not only too traditionally statual but also too respectful of the plurality of ethnicities that inhabited the "Great Space" (and thus too not sufficiently attentive to the vital needs, in a biological sense, of the German people and of actions that were necessary in order to empty "living space" [*Lebensraum*], and in order to make room for the "master race" [*Herrenvolk*]).[25] However, the defeat of the Third Reich was due less to technico-military dynamics and much more to the fact that, as Schmitt grasped only partially and belatedly, Nazi Germany entailed the degeneration of the State and the Modern, much more than the form of a new order. It was, in fact, much more unrestrained in its nihilism, in its lack of any *katechon*, and much more discriminatory than its enemies as well. In any event, its defeat implied the failure of the theory of the Great Imperial Spaces, at least in its totalitarian form, and left open the question of a new *nomos* of the earth.

It is impossible not to notice just how partial Schmitt's theoretical, narrative, and argumentative system is when interpreted in historical and epochal terms. During the postwar years, Schmitt built up the cornerstones of his self-interpretation as the last jurist of the European tradition. He also built up the myth, or at least the stylization, of the *jus publicum europæum* as an epoch of classical statuality—defined by clear and distinct political forms, and characterized by the restraint of war as the outcome of the reciprocal recognition of equal sovereign States. All of this serves, needless to say, to deprecate the moralistic, technological, and ideological universalism of anti-German positions during World War II. Schmitt's point about the elision of just war from the modern political logics is of course true, but it is also only a partial truth, since this elision is just one among many logics of the Modern (one that was really in effect only for a few decades during the eighteenth and nineteenth centuries, before it was interrupted by the great revolutionary crisis).[26] Indeed, Schmitt's assimilation of any just war to total war and thence too to discriminatory war was an idea that was useful to a "positive" evaluation (as "concrete") of the imperial total war waged by the Third Reich. After the war, meanwhile, it was useful for the complaint about just war expressed by the Allies against Germany, and about the dehumanization of the defeated enemy carried on in the name of humanity.[27]

2.3 Schmitt saw no *nomos*, no spatialized political order, in the confrontation between the United States and the Soviet Union, between East and West, that characterized the Cold War.[28] In Schmitt's view, the late-modern and poststatual principle of the *cujus regio ejus industria* ("whose is the realm, his is the industry"),[29] which founded the postwar world, did not have the ordinative value of the modern principle of *cujus regio ejus religio*. To Schmitt's way of thinking, the superpowers were incapable of taking on the role that once belonged to States: their confrontation in the Cold War had little to do with harmony or order.[30] It did not create a historical concrete order, and didn't even allow for the circular return of an identical metahistorical or natural polarity between land (which should have been the East) and sea (the West). The global dualism of the aftermath of the Second World War was actually the historical and real development, intrinsically contradictory and polemical, of a precise structural aspect of modernity: the British decision for an existence that was naval and thus also technical (to which twentieth-century war added an aerial dimension, thus emphasizing even more the loss of the political centrality of the land). From this decision, Schmitt believed, there derived two "superstructures": bourgeois political economy, on the one hand, and Bolshevik proletarian Marxism, on the other.[31] As Schmitt already had noticed in *Roman Catholicism and Political Form*, each of these superstructures was hostile to the other only insofar as each—armed with a progressive philosophy of history that legitimated its own claim to overcome its competitor—declares itself the most suitable option for developing all of the potentialities for human liberation, and for the domination of nature, contained in modern technics and in the economy technics enables. Capitalists and Communists—who, according to Marxism, are enemies because of the contradiction of their political economies—are thus, for Schmitt, siblings. They are certainly two universalisms caught up in a war with one another for world domination, but both are the children of only one universalism, only one of the modalities of the Modern: the "naval" modernity consisting of civil society, faith in progress, and limitless technics. Both, indeed, are unrelated to modernity's other modality: the sovereign-territorial State (which is, in turn, enslaved by technics, to which, however, it itself gives birth, as Schmitt indicated in his book on Hobbes). In *L'unità del mondo*, Schmitt will thus write that "today an iron curtain separates the East and the West, but the electric waves of a unique philosophy—progressivism—cross the curtain and create a sort of invisible communication."[32]

The world divided in two is, for Schmitt, a disoriented world ("the earth does not have an Eastern and a Western pole")[33] because it is too homogeneous and characterized by a fundamental categorical unity. As such, the aftermath of World War II doesn't appear to him to be either a real One or even a real Two. Instead, the planetary opposition of East and West appears to Schmitt as a figure of the One at war with itself (which he mentions in *Political Theology II*).[34] Even so, Schmitt knows that the real postwar political challenge is produced by the noniterability of this opposition, and at the same time by the insuperability of the technico-industrial horizon, the new destiny of the world. Technics may produce a unity of categorical horizons, but in Schmitt's view it can't produce a political unity of the world, and it can't elaborate political forms, either. To the contrary, within the unity produced by technics, conflicts turn out to be even more acute: technics, as Schmitt suggested in "The Epoch of Neutralizations and Depoliticizations," may provide an arena for political conflict, but it provides no key for conflict's solution or formal composition. The world unified by technics is therefore a world that is conflictual, unstable, and shapeless, as shown even just by the overlapping of multiple political spaces, as in the American case (the territory of the United States, the Western Hemisphere of the expanded version of the Monroe Doctrine, the sphere of defense of NATO, the space of the economical and cultural influence of the United States, the space of the UN).[35] Even this situation can be described as an "intermediate situation" suspended between war and peace: both enemies wage war with each other in every way but with weapons, and both carry universal and discriminatory political demands (even if under opposed flags). From both sides, therefore, the Cold War is thus revolutionary war, a war that is anything but clear and distinct.[36] In his last essay, Schmitt therefore would see the true legitimacy of the era in progress, a principle so strong that it could give birth to mutually exclusive ideologies and could use the forces of the State, not to mention its legality, to actuate a constant world revolution, one that obeys the logics and the dynamics of progress and of technics and of its "industrial grip" (Industrie-Nahme) on the world.[37]

It is within this bad unity, defined by the shared horizon of technics and the theory of Progress, that the opposition between East and West emerges, and is described by Schmitt as "a war in which the dualism of two fronts manifests itself as a clear distinction between friend and enemy."[38] Just one line further, Schmitt declares that "if unity is what's good, then duality is what's bad and dangerous. As St. Thomas says: binarius numerus infamis" [number two, evil number].[39] We should interpret this to be Schmitt saying that, in the aftermath of World War II, when conflict was well known especially in its absolute and irreconcilable form, if one tries to define the Cold War conflict as "political" (and Schmitt does try to do just this, perhaps for lack of a better option), one realizes immediately that, even though the Cold War does allow for a clear distinction between friend and enemy, in this situation the "political" is ultimately incomplete, confused, deprived of its formative forces. As a consequence, the Cold War is not a war in the classic-modern sense of the word (and, in fact, no war of the twentieth century meets this description). If anything, it is a "global civil war."[40] The conflict between East and West is thus still an "intermediate situation," since its intensity, which admittedly is considerable, nevertheless cannot produce an ordinative configuration. To the contrary, it is much more likely to allow for even more extreme forms of conflict. Only the victory of one of the two rivals could allow for a solution for such an extreme and unresolved dualism. Schmitt contemplates the possibility of a resolution of this sort, but he does not hold it in high regard, given that "the survivor would become the only dominator of the world."[41]

Schmitt interprets the conflict between "East and West," in short, as a historical question born at a specific point in the epoch of the crisis of the Modern—a crisis characterized by the Modern's continued search for a *katechon*, or a *nomos* of the earth, that would be post-European without also being universalistic, solely American, or solely Soviet. What this means is that, in Schmitt's view, the Modern continues to look for new forms of political order even at a time defined by a general attempt to dominate the world through technics. Despite Schmitt's description of the *katechon* as a "Christian conception of history," it is for him a form that remains indeterminate with respect to its content, so long as the latter expresses the (antihistoricistic) exigency of stopping the dynamics of modern immanentism and of thinking history as "the settling of the eternal within the course of time."[42] After the Second World War, Schmitt's internationalist proposal remains focused on the notion of Great Space, and continues to aim at allowing for the emergence of the force of the "political," which is not only conflictual but also ordinative. From the viewpoint of the *nomos*, this implies the recuperation, within a world dominated by the naval and by the indistinct and uniform dimension of technics, of the element of political differentiation related to land. Needless to say, Schmitt does not during this phase emphasize certain other elements of his thought (such as "political total war" and of the exclusion of the foreign presence) that he placed in the foreground during his Nazi phase in his effort to delineate the Great Space and Empire.

What he does instead is to entrust to the emergence of a plurality of Great Spaces the possibility of establishing a "new law of nations," understanding this plurality in terms of "third forces" (the British Commonwealth, the Arab world, India, Europe, China). The plurality of these Great Spaces would be the new *nomos* of the earth that would follow the era of the *jus publicum europæum*. A new *nomos*, certainly, but one founded on a principle of equilibrium explicitly similar to that around which the statalistic and Eurocentric *nomos* of modernity structured itself.[43] In *Die Ordnung der Welt nach dem zweiten Weltkrieg*, meanwhile, Schmitt's strategy is to indicate that the "dualistic" phase of the postwar period, which cannot give spatial order to the world, is being replaced by a "pluralistic" phase, in which the new *nomos* is produced by the "partition of the earth into regions that are more industrially developed and less industrially developed, along with the question of who gives help to whom, and also who accepts help from whom."[44] It's as if Schmitt (influenced by the French economist François Perroux)[45] had foreseen the evolution of the principle of *cujus regio, ejus oeconomia* (or *industria*), which had founded the politics of the Cold War, and which, in turn, had divided the world into the space of the market economy, on the one hand, and the space of the command economy, on the other. It's as if he also intuited a tendency toward the reorganization and redistribution of world space along lines that would be not dual but now plural. This world would be reorganized into Great Spaces (with an interior hierarchically divided between rich and poor) determined by *nomos* understood with reference to two of its semantic and logic roots: *das Weiden* (production) and *das Teilen* (partition) (the third root, of course, is *das Nehmen*, "taking").[46] With this argument, Schmitt seems to have had in mind the rivalry between the United States and the Soviet Union to establish connections and areas of influence in the economy and the politics of developing countries. He might have also been considering the growing power of the Third World, resulting from anti-European anticolonialism, as a force that could break the symmetry of the confrontation between East and West.[47]

In *Theory of the Partisan*, Schmitt proposes yet another modality for respatializing politics. Here Schmitt sketches an outline for the last figure of effective political subjectivity—the partisan, a figure of both enmity and order. The partisan's main characteristics are by now well known: the partisan has an intense political character; is not a private person (as was the pirate) but is bound to a larger group of combatants; is not a soldier in an army, but an irregular, and thus is the carrier of a specific spatiality and mobility that is different from that of the State; and is "telluric," or bound to land—even if the partisan has been identified as a revolutionary figure, he is oriented at least since Clausewitz to the defense of a concrete territory and spatialized institutions).[48] Understood in this way, the partisan—"the last sentinel of the earth"[49]—is the carrier of an enmity that is authentic, historical, and determined, intense but still limited, and consequently is part of the concept of "political." The partisan, certainly, is a figure for the danger and mortal risk inherent in political action, but it also signifies a specific knowledge of politics: the knowledge of one's concrete and real enemy, and of the concrete political space in which the enemy acts. The partisan is thus quite different from the pirate: because the latter's irregularity belongs to the land, and not to the technico-naval world, the partisan ultimately retains reference to regularity.[50] In fact, to the extent that the partisan turns the "intermediate situation" into concreteness, he functions as a *katechon*.

What this means is that the figure of the partisan is determined by real political enmity and by the real political spatiality of historical context. For instance, even if Mao conceives world politics in terms of Great Spaces (being hostile to American imperialism), he's not touched by the old European (Statal) limitation imposed by the categories of enmity and of war. Hence he assigns the partisan—who is irregular and who is related to the land—almost the whole weight of war, leaving regular armies only a small portion. For Mao, the war of liberation from an invader is first of all ideological, a civil war limited to the national territory ("at least for now," Schmitt adds). In the European context of the conflict between Germany and the Soviet Union in World War II, by contrast, Schmitt conceived of the partisan as subordinate to the State army, whose front subsequently became the line of partition between East and West Germany.[51]

Thus even though Mao's partisan is more dynamic and aggressive than is his Stalinist counterpart, he's nevertheless much more spatially determined and consequently more political (in Schmitt's sense) than the Leninist partisan (who is less related to the State than is the Stalinist partisan) had the potential to be: the Leninist partisan may be a "revolutionary activist," but he's much more abstract and undetermined because less bound to the land.[52] Indeed, Schmitt holds that it was Lenin who—despite his own good knowledge of his concrete historical enemy, the bourgeoisie—initiated the figure of the professional revolutionary whose ties to a totalitarian and revolutionary party, engaged in a world civil war (hence not limited to the national territory), and transformed his real enemy into an absolute enemy, which in turn became the object of limitless hostility.

This potential development is the first radical transformation of the figure of the partisan, which is ordinative to the extent that he carries concrete hostility, and changes his concrete hostility into a mere passive execution of ideologico-nihilistic logics. For Schmitt, technics is also responsible for the transformation of the partisan into an unlimited and nihilistic figure. If the partisan loses his connection to the land, and hence too the possibility of orienting his irregularity toward regularity, and if the partisan becomes a political combatant in the industrial age, he will find himself among weapons rendered so destructive by techno-logical developments that legitimizing their use requires that the enemy at which they are aimed be completely evil and inhuman.[53] Thus it is that technics promotes the adoption of moral logics that convey the values and the components of nihilism—logics that, in actual fact, call forth an immense increase of enmity, even as they simultaneously formally negate that same enmity. The annihilation of the Valueless brought forth by the Value is never presented as real "war" or "hostility," which means that it is not directed against an enemy having the same dignity (a *justus hostis*). It is instead presented as the execution of an objective deliberation, as the liquidating consequence of a deadly logical axiom.[54]

Schmitt denies that this absolute and unlimited hostility, this nihil-ism unconnected to any concreteness or orientation in the form of real enmity, coincides with the "political": "the core of the political is not en-mity per se, but the distinction between friend and enemy, and the pre-supposition of friend *and* enemy."[55] This partisan, no longer defensive but now aggressive on a world scale, is also an irregular—not because he's related to the risks of the "political," but because he expresses the absolute disorder of technics, its destructive force, which is responsive to any kind of conflict and violence whatsoever. Even so, Schmitt per-ceives this partisan, who cannot be a *katechon*, only as an extreme prob-lem: Schmitt focuses most of his attention on the partisan's adaptability to the world of technico-industrial civilization, as an actor who is sub-ordinated to the superpowers and to their absolute war, and who may be able to carve a space for its more circumscribed war in the interstices of the superpowers. Schmitt even imagines that cosmonauts and astro-nauts may become the partisans fighting in the future space battles.[56]

2.4 In the aftermath of the Second World War, as in his other phases, Schmitt's internationalist thought includes high levels of ideology. His thought must therefore be handled carefully: it's never neutral, and it's always oriented to some or another political position. It also should be noted, however, that, beyond a few verbal liberties, Schmitt's thought does not express naïve calls for immediate "grounding," nor does it present naturalist political paradigms, not even in the direction of geo-politics. Politics for Schmitt is always action: it can be ordering action or destructive action, naïve or self-aware, ideological or concrete, but it is never "nature" (or automatism).

Another important point is that Schmitt shares a system of ideas with authors (from Heidegger to Löwith, from Voegelin to Strauss and even Jünger) who, between the 1940s and 1950s, do not recognize themselves intellectually in any of the protagonists of the clash of civilizations then under way. These thinkers do not line up completely either with the Soviet Union or even with the United States, because in the superficial dualism of this rivalry they discover an identical theoretical framework: the two enemies produce two versions of the same type of relationship between human societies and nature, history, or politics. In political terms, these authors act in a sense that is more or less conservative: they situate themselves within the political dynamics of Western civilization in order to warn it about its own nihilism, its own contradiction and drifts, and of course its Eastern enemy.

Within this intellectual milieu, Schmitt stands out on account of his realism, since he recognizes the political relevance, however temporary, of the clash between East and West. He not only poses that clash in a determined historical phase (and not within the whole development of Western metaphysics) but also makes an effort to find a political solution to the problem of the Great Spaces. He's thus able to grasp the way the *jus publicum europæum* is dissolving due to the progressive disappearance of the political spatiality of the modern State. His analyses allow him to recognize both the crisis of the modern State and the impossibility of juridical universalism (of the United Nations). They also allow him to grasp the transformations of war caused by the changing relation between space and politics, the morphogenetic impotence of the triumphant technics that unify the world, and the incapacity of the imperialistic duopoly of the United States and the Soviet Union to generate a political form.

To be sure, Schmitt's analyses also make him suspicious of the suggestions coming from those who, like Jünger (who openly detached himself from Schmitt's pluralistic hypothesis), trust the "world State" as "the point toward which the political organization of the humanity tends, and which will seal politically the globalization that was already initiated by technics and by the world economy."[57] A perspective like this relies on a literary imagination, which Schmitt does not share, that can see the Earth and not Man as the main actor of a great metamorphosis that, through technics, changes the State into a "world State" at the point where organicity converges with organization. Schmitt's position is also far from Kojève's and from his view of the end of history in a "universal homogenous State" (prefigured by the world domination of the United States). Schmitt's differences from Kojève remain noticeable despite their similarities on the issues of colonialism and the "Latin Empire," and despite their epistolary exchange, their encounters, and their attempts to generate a dialogue (whose real objective was the interpretation and overcoming of Hegel's philosophy of history).[58]

Aside from their ideology, Schmitt's analyses have two obvious limitations. First, they are analyses of his present and not ours: Schmitt, we should recall, died in 1985, in the era of the Cold War and under conditions where East and West opposed one another. Schmitt's analyses, unsurprisingly, rely on many of the categories and problems specific to his time. For example, in his interpretation of the Cold War's international organization as ideological (which allows him to produce his criticism of the concept of West as American and not European), as well as intrinsically unstable and conflictual, it becomes clear that Schmitt still sees danger in the universalistic ideologies and horizons opened during the age of technics by the triumph of the modalities of the "sea." His objective is then to rebalance this dimension (but not to completely substitute it) with a politics of land, and with a respatialization of politics more generally. Second, his view of international relations—however much it may be directed beyond the State, to Empire (or Great Spaces), and to the partisan—nevertheless remains consistently oriented toward interpretations that relate any irregularities and exceptions to regularities or normalities that are in some way their complement. For Schmitt, therefore, the "intermediate situation" is a specific modality of the relation among States that needs to be addressed and resolved with a specific response (namely, Great Spaces). Similarly, according to Schmitt, discriminatory war serves the interests of a specific "naval" power, the United States, so the partisan must be backed up by the regularity of an army and of a *nomos* of the earth. Schmitt's thought is always determined concretely, thinking conflict merely as a phase internal to order. Put simply, he is always in search of a *katechon*. Schmitt's internationalist thought adds to this ordinative and reconstructive mode: it gives us insights into the formation of an unleashed conflictuality (of a technico-ideological sort), even as it expresses the suspicion that even the respatialization of politics might be unproductive and absurd as a possible response to this situation. Schmitt, however, does not investigate this suspicion any further, leaving us the task of generating an effective interpretation of our times, that mass of phenomena and dynamics we now call "globalization."

3. Global Questions

To conclude, I will argue that the global age presents itself discontinuously when compared with the modern era: whereas the latter viewed the world as a vast but definable space, today's world is at once smaller and more infinite or indefinite, infinitely complex and uncontrollable. The essence of globalization is "global mobilization,"[59] an intense and chaotic set of processes that open up and break through all defined spaces.[60] However, the global era is characterized not only by a paradoxical spatiality that is at once multiform and multidimensional, but also by a new relation with time: in the global age, events interconnect in ways that are not consecutive but simultaneous, and thus frustrate the possibility of establishing relations that are chronological and causal. The present is not then determined by history. Quite the opposite: not only does it lack a historical structure in the proper sense of the term, it also lacks any orientation toward tradition, progress, or planning. If the modern era contained elements of nihilism that remained somewhat controlled and structured, in the global era nihilism has become pandemic.

3.1 From an economic standpoint, the characteristics of the global era cannot be easily interpreted spatially. The global era is marked not only by the end of the command economy, but also by the displacement of Fordism with Toyotism, flexibility, "just in time" production strategies, the dispersion of sites of production, financial "deregulation," the prevalence of finance in the real economy, the emergence of migrant workforces at the margins of the law or outside of it, and lastly by a network of financial fluxes and immaterial wealth. Today's world economy, like the economy that gave birth to capitalism, is dependent on other parts of the world; today, however, the world economy presents traits of immediacy and simultaneity that are completely new and that seem increasingly to emancipate the economy from the category of space, whose terms no longer seem to govern economic functions. Global cities, for example, are not spaces in any rigorous sense; they are nodes in a network of relations that are exposed immediately to the logic of the planetary economy, and they exceed from within the territory of the

State in which they find themselves, resulting in a new configuration of the geo-economy organized around districts and economic regions. Above all, the three "worlds" of the Cold War have disintegrated, together with the rivalry between the first two to create areas of economic influence in the third. The Western world (what used to be called the "first" world) has today become the only world. In place of these geographical distinctions, it is today possible to find pockets of the "first" world in the "third," and vice versa. Moreover, China, India, Brazil, Japan, Korea, and Singapore have reorganized the world's economic map, which is no longer either dual or legible on the basis of coexisting Great Spaces that are fixed and coordinated. None of this should imply, of course, that global economic space is either unified or smooth, or that it functions as a stage for capitalism's unlimited progress. Far from it: its apparent unity is not unified but fractured, punctuated by pockets of misery and degradation. Its only geographically legible lines are those inscribed by oil and gas pipes, which remain bound to the territory; but much political turbulence during these years will have been channeled along just these lines.

3.2 The political phenomena of the global age also differ from those of the Cold War. The sun has set on the modern age, when the State held a monopoly of politics; the late-modern age, defined by the rivalry between two superpowers, also has disappeared. The unity of the world that some thinkers (including Schmitt, in his own way) foresaw behind the Cold War's postwar political dualism now has openly manifested itself. This unity does not, however, imply the political unification of the world. The unity produced through globalization is defined less by the smooth space of technics than by the disappearance (or, better, obfuscation) of the connection between politics and space. Violence today is not constrained to a determinate territory or confined to the exterior by State or superpower; it instead circulates in a manner at once free and random. The attacks of September 11, 2001, can be interpreted as a watershed between two phases of globalization: the apparently peaceful one of the 1990s and the openly violent one that followed the attack of the Twin Towers. September 11 can be interpreted as the event that brought to light the violent logics and tendencies immanent to the dynamics of globalization, which previously had been concealed by liberal and progressive ideologies. As a matter of fact, 9/11 is emblematic of the fact that today it is no longer possible to draw a clear distinction between inside and outside. Today, therefore, we face not only the disappearance of the exterior (the space of war in the classical sense) caused by universalistic tendencies (such as those of the United Nations and its ideology), which proposed to frame the world as a single interior devoid of political conflict (and which would have transformed conflict into a crime to be punished by police action). We also face the disappearance of the interior: for the terrorist, every part of the planet is, potentially, immediately exposed to absolute hostility and is, therefore, in some way external to itself. Conversely, for the United States, every part of the planet is a possible theatre for the "War on Terrorism." The increasing inoperativity of distinctions between the inside and the outside (not to mention between civilians and military personnel, between "private" individuals and "State" actors) plunges politics in the global era into twilight, resulting in confusion in the distinctions founded on this spatial distinction (such as those between peace and war, norm and exception) and in an experience where everything appears along the same indistinct continuum. Today, in other words, the "intermediate situation" between war and peace, between rule and exception, has become the norm. It follows from this that it is no longer possible today to make any concrete reference to regularity, order, or even neutrality, for there is no longer any concreteness or regularity with reference to which irregularity could derive its strategic value of destruction and reconstruction.

Global war is our name for this new condition. With this term we designate a situation in which violence manifests itself in the world in a way, and at a pace, that no longer can be mapped geographically as a traditional wartime "front," but only according to logics of instantaneity and punctuality. Under these conditions, every part of the planet is immediately exposed to an ongoing global flux of violence. This flux of violence dissolves the mediations of politics and of the territorial state, which today can no longer distinguish internal from external. From a political standpoint, in fact, global mobilization means that anything can happen anywhere and at any time. Global war does not then take place in a striated space defined by political powers, or even in a smooth space opened by technics. It takes place without any causal relation to space whatsoever, since the only possible relation to space under these conditions is immediacy. Put more precisely, global war is what happens when space, which today operates on non-Euclidean properties, is traversed not by boundaries but by fractures that allow for radically different spaces and times (the caves of Afghanistan and the Twin Towers, archaic tribal societies and hypermodern global cities) to be placed into relations of immediate communication with one another. This paradoxical spatiality is not determined by some sort of disequilibrium between land and sea: even though one certainly could say that the global age is the era of the liquefaction of the land, it would be more exact to say that it is the era in which the relevance of these two primordial spaces is almost completely lost. It also would be off the mark to attribute this loss to the new relevance of air space, since this novelty was already in effect during the terminal phase of modernity. It would be better to attribute it to the emergence of a hyper-complex global space—a space in which land and sea alike are crossed by currents, waves, and flows, by terrorists who act as though they were pirates, and by the electronic web, whose virtual but effective dimensions host the immediate mediations, the actions and reactions, that exemplify global disorder.

Global space, on this reading, is a space in which multiple spaces and multiple times coexist with one another, entering into a situation of immediate connection and constant short-circuit with each other. The infinite polydimensional wars specific to this space, meanwhile, constitute global war. The latter is not then limited to exclusively military and regular warfare; but nor is it limited to asymmetric war between terrorists and counterterrorists, either. It extends to include the entire complex of economic and financial wars, wars over and through information, wars for the control of drug commerce and migration, and wars among "private" companies and mafia groups. Today's "intermediate situation," in other words, consists of more than just the relation between terrorism and counterterrorism, as if aside from this one gray zone the classical forms of politics and modern wars remained intact. In fact, the latter are increasingly outdated and inapplicable (or at the very least residual, since any war between States today would be influenced by the logics of global war). In global space, the forms of war and politics born around the partial spaces tend to deteriorate into global war. Wars for land (such as that between Palestinians and Israel), apparently "tribal" wars (which, as in Africa, are actually determined by mining resources), wars for independence (such as Chechnya's war against Russia) all tend to become eradicated from their contexts and become moments of global war. Even potentially "telluric" partisans today increasingly become terrorists without space. Global war is not of course reducible to terrorism; it's the tendency for all wars to become terrorism, under conditions where the global age allows no space for any other evolution.

If we now examine the global war not from the angle of the space in which it appears, but from that of its determining causes (the subjectivities that want to polemically affirm their identity), or from the angle of the role of religion in today's politics, we encounter parameters that only apparently seem to confirm Schmitt's hypotheses. In fact, the absolute hostility that emerges from the permanent twilight of global war is not exactly the "political" proper. The terrorist cannot be described using terms that refer to the *hostis*, the partisan, the world revolutionary, or perhaps even the technological partisan. The terrorist is in fact a new category both in subjective terms (he has no friends, only enemies, and is in the most extreme cases his own enemy, giving up his own body and life in an act of suicide) and in objective terms (terrorism has no other strategy but terror, and its hostility prefigures no order other than the imaginary). The religious motivation the terrorist gives for his hostility cannot be called "political theology" (not even in a desecularized sense), since his hostility doesn't have any ordering functions. It's instead an "immediate" and "extreme theology," a paranoid identification with God with the sole aim of drawing conflict on into infinity.[61] In the global age, every claim of rootedness in a tradition is ultimately just a phantasmatic projection: such claims pertain not to history but merely to representation, and religion is here just the language in which absolute conflict is expressed. Holy war, in other words, is not the essence or cause of global war, but simply one among many ingredients of it. Not only does holy war share indeterminacy and elusiveness with global war, but it also turns into its own opposite: diabolical war, war without purpose. Holy war shares this destiny with today's iteration of just war—which is to say, with the war against terrorism and for Western "values," a war that turns into an infinite act of counterterrorism.

Today's "intermediate situation" may then give rise at any time to total terroristic war, total discriminatory war, preventive attack, an act of policing, or a crusade in the name of democracy. Global war and its combatants lack a "cause"—in the double sense of the word. They are without cause in the sense of causality, because any single cause for war interacts immediately with the asystematic totality composed of all causes, thus sharing the paradoxical spatiotemporal characteristics of globality more generally. They are also without "cause" in the sense of motivation by a final cause, ideal, goal, or telos (despite the constant exhortations, in contemporary politics, to defend core values). This is the case not because the cause of terrorism is the same as that of democracy, or because the causes of oppression or injustice are analogous to those of liberty and justice, but because of the way all of these causes take effect under conditions of global space and global war. In the latter, any cause—any political choice or subjectivity—vanishes in an irremediable lack of authenticity, since global space cannot support or contain the "seriousness"—not only the radicality, but also the determinacy—of the "political" (this conflictuality that is also order, this enmity that is also concrete identity, this crisis that is also *katechon* and that retains the potential for morphogenesis). For all their strategic planning, the multiple subjects who participate in global war thus nevertheless cannot manage to render it determinate, and they are reabsorbed into the casual senselessness of globalized violence.

Indeed, since it does not know any distinct area, and since its violence is not generated by a single point, but by the entire surface of the globe, global war has no central sphere, no *Zentralgebiet*. Of course, one sometimes sees certain points where the weight is more concentrated than elsewhere, mainly the areas positioned between the Caucasus and Central Asia, passing through the Middle East. These areas are afflicted by many conflicts: struggles for oil and gas (which obviously involve Westerners), for religion (fundamentalists against moderates and infidels), for land (the questions of Palestine and Chechnya, but also of American military bases). And yet, precisely these struggles are the ones that today have become the most indeterminate, that appear to overlap on one other, and that assume "terrorist" elements, thus functioning as triggers for a permanent and uncontrolled explosion—global war— where the fuel is provided by the very atmosphere of globalization itself. Global war is, in short, *globality as violence*. It is a property of global space; it is the chaotic set constituted of all of globality's internal and international relations (primarily economic and technological); and it is a blind process that is, in reality, controlled by no one. That is what we mean when we say that conflict today has become "automatic." Global war is postmodern nihilism.

3.3 This global disorder, these contradictions of globalization, reveal themselves to be increasingly less "political" and increasingly deprived of any relation with space and order, assuming instead the form of de-constituent conflict, global unrootedness, and permanent exception. In the face of this trend, several political responses have emerged. Let's now consider some of them in the concrete, operating on the assumption that they are often combined with one another.

In the first place, there is the attempt to revive the modern universalism of the United Nations and international law, founded on equality and justice. This entails an effort to turn global war into global peace; in the end, it's only a virtual response, one that's hindered by many limitations, as we will see. The alternative to this revival is a very real proposal—a complex response, founded on a new ideology and strategy designed specifically for the global era. This response differs from the sorts of strategies elaborated in the early nineties (which were focused on unlimited economic progress and on a supposedly smooth world space), and it proceeds along two sides: security and threat, identity and difference.

The main feature of this response is that it turns terrorism into the core of global war, and sees it as the origin of global war's novelty. This is a response that turns the terrorist into its enemy; it also turns the conflict against the terrorist into the new "political" and "central sphere" of our era. Understood in this way, the terrorist is the origin not only of the current crisis but also of a new political order determined by the exclusion of the terrorist by the avenger.

This response implies, in the first place, a tendency at the level of internal politics to bypass the modern State's guarantees of rights in favor of its maintenance of security, whether in the case of single individuals or in the case of the State itself, in an attempt to restore the spatial differentiation between inside and outside by means of the identification, imprisonment, and expulsion of the enemy. The security politics that results is obliged to travel along a two-way street: on the one side, it stabilizes rootedness (by producing legitimizing discourses that allow "us" to discover our ethnic, religious, and cultural "roots"), while on the other side, it pursues conflict (in which "we" oppose ourselves to "them" in a perennial short-circuit between identity and threat, violence and juridical order).[62] At first glance, this would seem to be a constituent use of the exception that is not far from Schmitt's conceptual universe, or at least that can be deciphered through it.

Another strategy, only partly analogous, appears in the domain of international politics. Here too terrorism is painted as a form of evil that contains statual determinations (with reference to countries like Iraq, North Korea, and Iran), and here too it serves to construct an identity (that of "civilization" opposed to "barbarism"). In this strategy, civilization's permanent line of action becomes just war, even preventive war, against an unjust threat and against terroristic barbarianism. Here, however, there are no boundaries: because in principle "civilization" (in the concrete, the United States) coincides with all of humanity, the war-like and police-like actions it conducts in the name of humanity—which, as Schmitt already had noted, are especially intense and discriminatory—are not concerned with the delineation of boundaries or the creation of spatial orders. Those actions propose only to rid the world of the enemies of humanity (specifically terrorists, in a moralistic and discriminatory universalism that has as its objective "regime change" on a global scale). According to this neoconservative theory, which seems to go far beyond classical realism, only a uniformly democratic world is safe and peaceful, truly just, and useful to American interests.[63]

In reality, there is a legible intent woven into this neoconservative ideology (which Schmitt did not in fact influence) that is quite close to traditional political realism. On the terms of this theory, the United States sees itself as the political subject acting as the core of "civilization,"[64] one that is not generically "human," but "Western" (a West guided by America, but one that includes Europe and other allied non-Western countries). Its aim is to reterritorialize politics and globalized war, beginning with a unilateral definition of "terrorism" and from the unilateral recognition of the terrorist enemy against whom it is legitimate to wage absolute and discriminatory war. However, this war, despite all its aggressive aspects, is waged with the intent of constructing a limes [fortified frontier] toward external barbarians, stabilizing internal space by capturing and controlling portions of space in the Middle East and in central Asia (areas that are "unstable" and that, as such, are in need of "stabilization") for the purpose of impeding Chinese projects (a motivation very much in keeping with implicit logic of the Great Spaces). The task is to transform the United States's informal Empire (which emerged during the first phase of globalization) into in a direct and territorial Empire (one that is, in many ways, "traditional").[65] The American response to the attacks of September 11 (the wars in Afghanistan and Iraq, but also Guantanamo Bay and the Patriot Act) seem to amount to an attempt to replace the haziness of the liquid age of the first phase of globalization with the solidity and concreteness of a new iron age—an attempt, in other words, to restore political order, even by means of extrajuridical forms, and to transform global war into constituent war, into a new oriented order. The hallmark of this new order would seem to be a hierarchical relationship, typical of Empire, between center and periphery, between imperial elites and local elites. Its point of orientation would appear to be the physical security of America (brought back to its insular dimension, although not in isolation), the indisputable centrality of America's material and cultural living standards, and the preservation of existing power relations between America (the Western world being its extension) and the rest of the world.[66] All of this would seem to amount to a new *nomos* of the earth, a new orientation for its order. Whether or not this *nomos* really can create effective order is, of course, an entirely different discussion.

4. Conclusions

The suitability of Schmitt's political categories for interpreting global war should be measured both against analyses of actual phenomena and against proposed solutions to the problems at hand.

4.1 From the viewpoint of analytical efficacy, the most typical categories of Schmitt's thought are not entirely fit for the phenomenology of the global war, as Schmitt himself hints in the last phase of his work (in his *Theory of the Partisan* in particular). In fact, Schmitt himself explains how absolute enmity is not the "political" in its whole complexity, and how absolute enmity is to the contrary absolute disorder, since it does not refer to a concrete situation, does not include the possibility of order, and is not an "exception." As we saw, today's immediately polemical and identitarian uses of religion—uses that do not pursue a *cujus regio ejus religio*, or any stabilizing ordering—do not qualify as "political theology"; they are instead "extreme theology." The same is true for the power differences that exist across the planet today (which do not constitute Great Spaces) and for the terrorist (who is not the partisan, since he is connected neither to the land, nor to space, nor to defense). Given the terrorist's absolute and systematic irregularity, his nihilism toward himself, and his exception without norm, we conclude that his hostility is outside of Schmitt's historical and intellectual horizon. The modern age was born from the opening of the oceans, whereas the global age is born of the opening of land (an opening that marks the end of the opposition between East and West). Global mobilization is not a disequilibrium between land and sea (in favor of the technico-naval); it marks their amalgamation in a different kind of space. Global war is not "total war"; it presents a more complex spatiality vis-à-vis the tangle of military and nonmilitary levels, and above all because, contrary to what Schmitt thinks, it is not the political act of a unified political entity (be it total State or Empire) that takes it on consciously, thereby giving it meaning through that entity's own political existence. Global war is instead the unrestrained violence of a plurality of subjects whose motivations and strategies are ultimately undetermined. The global age does not display a *Zentralgebiet* from which some power may neutralize conflicts—it has no such territory precisely because power does not know the "political," which, when deployed in a sovereign and decisionist manner, can generate order. Global war is a conflict that cannot be oriented to any *katechon*.

As such, global war cannot be fully understood through Schmittian categories. It is subtly but decisively something "other," something "postmodern," and if we look closely, we see that Schmitt's discourse refers to something else entirely. His thought runs counter to our conflictual universalism, with its ideological, juridical, and moralist origins that serve forms of political power that, however concentrated, are nevertheless poststatual. Schmitt instead understands ideological terrorism to be in service to the Communist empire, to the League of Nations, and to the "just wars" of Great Britain and the United States. Schmitt certainly had foreseen the "derangement" of those universalisms, and he feared them from the innermost center of his thought, which was focused on determinate political conflicts that remained within spatial politics oriented to concreteness and political unity (even when poststatual). However, the fact that Schmitt turns his gaze away from the technological partisan and his casual and despatialized war leads us to conclude that he has little to say either about the definitive characteristics of the global age and global war (such as its exceptions without norm, or its qualitative novelties of spatiality, temporality, subjectivity, and politics).

The complexity of today's world is, necessarily, lost on Schmitt. He was able to observe it only from the viewpoint of the twentieth-century crisis of the conceptual architectures of modern sovereignty. He thus ignored its most recent challenges (such as biopolitical power) as well as the spaces for action opened by globalization—such as the dialectic between worldwide society (the cosmopolitan universe of the social forces) and international society (the macropolitical dynamics of States and of Empires). He knew nothing about multilevel governance, neomedievalism, or complex spaces; nor could he have made sense of political forms that are not Westphalian, but are instead multilateral and characterized by diffuse political power—hypotheses that are no more daring than those of the neoimperialists.[67]

4.2 If we leave aside the analytical perspective of Schmittian political thought, and move on to the organizational perspective, the problem becomes one of understanding if the attempts to respatialize war, to reduce the complexity of the global age, to interrupt the short-circuit that exists between local and global—if these attempts, conducted with realistic presuppositions (or with the conceit of power's continuing morphogenetic function) stemming from a direct, meaningful knowledge of Schmitt's texts (or, as is more likely, from a direct relationship with the pragmatist juridical tradition and realistic political science) have any possibility of being effective and forming political order. To put it another way: Can global war become a constituent conflict? Can the confusion of peace and war, of juridical order and violence, become the origin of a new political form? In philosophical terms: is an image of the World still possible?[68]

One scenario involves the constitution, whether formal or informal, of a Western territorial Empire led by the United States—one that would not be universal but limited, and that would be capable of marking global space with new borders and institutions. It follows that this scenario would create, in an implicitly Schmittian (because pluralistic) perspective, an international order organized according to Great Spaces. In this case, it should be observed that if the force that Western civilization has been unleashing in its "War on Terror" actually does achieve its aims, partitioning its own enemy-free Great Space; and if global war therefore turns into a spatialized "clash of civilizations," a conflict determined as political relation because of an equilibrium between clearly defined subjects—then, whether directly or indirectly, Schmitt will have been at least partially right. Even so, it should be noted that today the morphogenetic use of force, both internal and external, is being radically called into question: organizing formally sovereign states in hierarchical, imperial relationships is as difficult as preventing the enemy "barbarians" from breaching the empire's borders. Furthermore, the essential element of globalization is a worldwide development of the economy that is ill-suited for the control and confinement demanded by the politics implied in the imperial scenario. Lastly, in order to be such, even a commercial and liberal Empire must be able to employ force effectively, while the practical contradictions and the failures of the American neoimperial action show how difficult this task is.

An efficient State-form is needed as an element of the world governance as an important tool to stabilize local portions of larger global dynamics. Within the territories of the States, the morphogenetic and constituent use of the exception certainly seems to operate according to Schmittian logics that seek to revive a juridical order oriented against an internal enemy. However, States revive these schemes today less as a strategic and sovereign decision, or as an active friend-enemy logic, and more as the outcome of merely functionalist dynamics—something like a "just in time" response to disorder. In addition, since all of this happens primarily in the face of cultural conflicts and their polemic potential, the relation between exception and normality (always absent but always present as ideal) does not institute a concrete order, and only manages to conjure up a trick of the eye: enemies and friends are actually ghosts and projections, who feed on desiderata and aggressive nostalgia. This internal mobilization—which holds together groups through conformism and disaggregation—is the only stability the State is currently able to supply, because it is unable to give form to its own internal space, and unable as well to distinguish it from external space and its contradictions.

The potential ordering responses that emerge through Schmittian categories thus turn out to be mostly dubious: it seems, to the contrary, that attempts to form orders based on decision, exception, restoration of space, and the creation of borders are diluted and even liquefied in globalization. It seems, therefore, that new stabilizing answers are necessary, but that above all we must begin asking new questions about political categories oriented toward different horizons from those offered by Schmitt.

It is certainly true that Schmitt's thought can be used today to demystify the universalistic ideologies of the just war or the war for democracy, or to demonstrate the political value of such wars to the United States. Similarly, we can clearly see that the juridical universalism on which the United Nations was founded is an attempt to legalize and reconcile international politics, but ends up being little more than a manifestation of the desire for humanistic rationalization in the global age, a desire to believe in the theory of human rights and the equality of sovereign states (which maintain their phantasmal existence only within the United Nations). Thus, this humanistic will does not depart from the modern nexus—completely ineffective today—between individualism, statism, and universalism. In order to make this criticism, however, there is really no need to rely on the Schmittian critique of the League of Nations; nor is there a need to theorize, as Schmitt did, a *potestas indirecta* of Anglo-Saxon powers lying behind the international institutions. Quite the opposite: today the United Nations is one of the last organizations that, without rising to the level of a *katechon*, is still capable of rebalancing American power in some way.

It's also not necessary to refer to Schmitt in order to grasp the contradictions of the "War on Terror" (the first phase of the "war for democracy"). The "War on Terror" proposes to wage an absolute war against the terrorist (which would have to be a determined political enemy if it is to be able to constitute the origin of a new political order), whom it frames as an enemy of humanity (that is, an undetermined enemy). This absolute, infinite, and ubiquitous war does not produce any spatial order able to distinguish friends from enemies, or peace from war. The "War on Terror" is not then a path out of global war; it is a part of global war. It amalgamates a terroristic "holy war" with a "just war" against terrorism (despite the very different "values" at play). In this situation, the "civilizations" that should be the actors in this war cannot be determined by any boundaries whatsoever: as such, they do not amount to political orders at all, only phantasms and projections.

It is quite possible that this "intermediate situation" could constitute our future. Whether or not this is so, Schmitt's categories will be able to interpret this configuration only partially. It is certainly true, of course, that for Schmitt political orders are never neutral and fully formalized, and that they draw their efficacy instead from the circulation of conflict within themselves (which can assume different forms). It is also true, however, that the specificity of the Modern—that theologico-political epochality that orients Schmitt's thought—is, understood from Schmitt's perspective, at its end, and that the lines of development of our contemporary age seem characterized instead by an instability, a chaos, and a complexity, free of any element of normality, that preclude them from being read as a confirmation of the lasting efficacy of Schmitt's thought.

4.3 In his pars destruens, Schmitt's thought remains partially effective, as a possible (though hardly unique) antiuniversalist strategy. But in the pars construens—in the combination of decision and concreteness at the interior, and of war and spatiality at the exterior—Schmitt's thought now appears confused and inapplicable. It is not enough that Schmitt thinks radical conflict and the spatialized political order (of Empire) to make his thought useful for our understanding of today's conflicts and need for order. In the global age, the challenge of *planetarische Industrie-Nahme*, of unchecked technological enterprise on a world scale, has extended and intensified to such a point that the very terms of the problem, and thus too the range of possible solutions, have changed. One of these possible outcomes is a radical disorientation of the world by a capitalism unwilling to tolerate its own submission to the constraints imposed by the spatial and territorial logic of imperial Great Spaces.

We must then recognize that, despite appearances, politics today resists interpretation and organization alike—not only in a modern individualist or statist manner, but also within Schmittian coordinates. Schmitt's thought was concerned with an end and with the genealogical deconstruction and the a posteriori construction of an era. What we need today, in this age of absolute hostility and paradoxical spatiality, is a beginning. It's not on the basis of ideological pacifism that we arrive at this conclusion, but only out of realism: global war will not turn back into modern war. As Schmitt himself said, historical truths are true only once.

The problem that we have posed in this chapter is the effectiveness of Schmitt's thought for understanding the political dynamics of globalization, not the strategies and the politics suitable for a globalized age. Regarding the latter, the challenges are both stark and plain. There is a need today to imagine an exit from global war, a peace that would not coincide with the modern unitary order of the State, and to imagine a respatialization of politics that would not move either toward State power, toward the hierarchies of Empire, or toward the moralism, universalism, and discrimination of just war. There is equally a need for a peace oriented toward the combination of a new federalism and a newly effective postmodern cosmopolitan universalism—one that would be different from the Statualist universalism of the United Nations, and that would not be grouped around imperial Great Spaces, but that would emerge around centers of "civil power" that could make it concrete (Europe, in fact, could constitute one of such centers). This is finally a need for politics to confront spatiality in terms of fluid relations, rather than with sovereign gestures that pretend to rebuild borders. This would require that politics be able to think affirmatively about the new relations of movement and velocity that bodies are today experiencing vis-à-vis space (a relationship that can be not only liberating but also enslaving), and that politics learns to recognize the dimension of the mobile and the polymorphous alongside that of the stable and isomorphic.

All of these scenarios, needless to say, remain open and undetermined. If we truly wish to be faithful to the lessons of Carl Schmitt, then our task now is to imagine possible interpretations and solutions to the problems of today's politics—interpretations and solutions that begin where Schmitt's thought ends.

NOTES

....

Editor's Introduction. *Carl Schmitt: An Improper Name*

I would like to thank Alek Gorzewski and Laura Merchant for their insightful comments on and criticisms of an earlier draft of this introduction. Portions of this introduction originally appeared in my introduction to Carlo Galli's *Political Spaces and Global War*, Trans. Elisabeth Fay (Minneapolis: University of Minnesota Press, 2010).

1. Karl Loewenstein, "Observations on the Personality and Work of Professor Carl Schmitt," November 14, 1945, Karl Loewenstein Papers, box 46, folder 46, Amherst College Archives and Special Collections, Amherst, Massachusetts.

2. Karl Loewenstein, "Library of Professor Carl Schmitt," October 10, 1945, Loewenstein Papers, box 46, folder 46, Amherst College Archives and Special Collections. Schmitt's library would be returned to him in 1963.

3. Loewenstein, "Observations on the Personality and Work of Professor Carl Schmitt," 1.

4. Loewenstein, "Observations on the Personality and Work of Professor Carl Schmitt," 2.

5. Loewenstein, "Observations on the Personality and Work of Professor Carl Schmitt," 2–3. A month earlier, Loewenstein put the case more forcefully. "In the opinion of this writer Schmitt qualifies as a war criminal. He is one of the intellectual instigators of Hitlers [sic] acts of aggression and aided and abetted them by his influential authorship. I hardly know of any individual person who has contributed more for the defense of the Nazi regime than Carl Schmitt. I suggest that the case be submitted to the War Criminals Commission for further action" (Loewenstein, "Library of Professor Carl Schmitt").

6. Loewenstein, "Observations on the Personality and Work of Professor Carl Schmitt," 4.

7. Loewenstein, "Observations on the Personality and Work of Professor Carl Schmitt," 4.

8. Loewenstein, "Observations on the Personality and Work of Professor Carl Schmitt," 4.

9. Roberto Racinaro, "Carl Schmitt e la genealogia della politica," *Filosofia politica* 11:1 (April 1997), 130.

10. In the event, Schmitt was not permitted to return to teaching: he was submitted to denazification, but only as a prelude for his "renazification," i.e., his remorseless repetition of the same anti-Semitic thematics that governed his prewar writings. See, on this point, Raphael Gross, afterword to *Carl Schmitt and the Jews: The "Jewish Question," the Holocaust, and German Legal Theory*, trans. Joel Golb (Madison: University of Wisconsin Press, 2007), 230–40. Played out to its logical conclusion, Schmitt's analogy of himself to the eponymous figure of Herman Melville's "Benito Cereno" implies that Schmitt was able to find within himself the magnanimity that allowed him "to forgive" his American judges for condemning him. See, on this point, Adam Sitze, "A Farewell to Schmitt: Notes on the Work of Carlo Galli," CR: *New Centennial Review* 10:2 (2010), 53–54.

11. To clarify the concept of "imputation," a short digression may be useful. In Kant's revealing analysis, which orients itself with reference to the concept of *imputatio* in Roman Law, "imputation [Zurechnung] is the judgment by which someone is regarded *as* the author [als Urheber] of an action, which is then called a deed and stands under law." Kant's recourse to "as" indicates that imputation—this power by which judgment retroactively adds an accountable doer to a deed—is not primarily a juridical phenomenon but is instead an effect of what Kant would call the "productive imagination" (*produktive Einbildungskraft*). Expressed on the terms of Kant's system, this "as" is a sign that imputation derives neither from pure reason nor from pure practical reason, but from the faculty of judgment in its properly aesthetic sense. On Kantian terms, in fact, we may say that imputation is the power by which the faculty of judgment *produces* or *invents* an accountable author, who then in turn functions as that "necessary fiction" in the absence of which the faculty of judgment would not be able to judge at all.

For Nietzsche, meanwhile, it would become perfectly clear that the metaphysics of morals (and not only in the Kantian sense) is a tautology that depends for its intelligibility upon a prior power that is, in essence, extramoral—an aesthetic capacity to invent or imagine something that does not yet exist. In *The Genealogy of Morals*, Nietzsche famously would call the very idea of a "doer" a "supplement" [hinzugedichtet]. For Nietzsche, as for Kant, the "doer" is retroactively added to the deed as its cause through a kind of *poesis* (*Gedicht*: "poem"). As distinct from Kant, however, Nietzsche will underline the *nonnecessity* of this fiction: in Nietzsche's view, the "doer" is an impossible echo, a double of the deed that is subsequent to the deed but that comes to precede the deed itself, a preposterous repetition of the deed that at once *fully accounts for all deeds* and *precludes the possibility of thinking any deed on its own terms*. For Nietzsche, crucially, the exemplary instance of this doubling is the lightning strike—the flash of light and sound that ruptures my experience before I know what has hit me, and for which I then try to account by retroactively positing lightning not only as a flash but also as an agent that is prior to and causative of that flash. From this one may infer that the metaleptic repetition of the deed as a doer is occasioned by something that very much resembles a trauma. This inference, in turn, positions Nietzsche's account of repetition as a homologue to the analysis of *Nachträglichkeit* (afterwardsness) that appears in certain of Freud's writings.

Imputative reading, from this perspective, would seem to imply at least three unthinkables: it would seem to derive its intelligibility from a juridical form from Roman Law (*imputatio*) that it cannot also pose as a problem for thought; it would seem *itself* to produce or invent the very author whose acts and deeds it then calls to account and authorizes itself to judge; and its retroactive invention to this effect would seem to be occasioned by some sort of traumatic event that it cannot then in turn cognize or narrate for itself. To stand at a critical distance from the horizon of imputative reading is not of course to propose a reading of Schmitt that *absolves* his thought of its relation to Nazism, since absolution itself is simply one among many declensions of imputative reading (its negation, to be precise). It is simply to prepare the possibility for a different approach to the reading of Schmitt, one that corresponds to a different way of conceiving the relation between his thought and his Nazism.

See, variously, Immanuel Kant, "The Metaphysics of Morals," in *Practical Philosophy*, ed. Allen Wood, trans. and ed. Mary Gregor (Cambridge: Cambridge University Press, 1996), 381–82, emphasis added; Friedrich Nietzsche, "On the Genealogy of Morals: An Attack," in *On the Genealogy of Morals/Ecce Homo*, trans. Walter Kaufman and R. J. Hollingdale (New York: Vintage Books, 1967), 45, translation modified; and Jean Laplanche, "Notes on Afterwardsness," in *Essays on Otherness*, ed. and trans. John Fletcher (New York: Routledge, 1999), 260–65.

12. Among Schmitt scholars, only Joseph Bendersky has written about this memo in any detail. See Joseph Bendersky, "Carl Schmitt's Path to Nuremberg: A Sixty-Year Reassessment," *Telos* 139 (summer 2007), 6–34; compare the relatively scant treatment in Reinhard Mehring, *Carl Schmitt: A Biography*, trans. Daniel Steuer (Malden, MA: Polity Press, 2014), 409–12. On Bendersky's reading, Loewenstein is a man of *ressentiment*: he is merciless and prejudicial; he is filled with hatred for the German people en masse; he hypocritically consorts with Nazis who were much more committed to Nazism than was Schmitt; and his various defenses of democracy were, ironically, derived from Schmitt (reproduced, Bendersky goes so far as to say, "without attribution"). Bendersky presents a Loewenstein who is, in short, Schmitt's uncanny double: for Bendersky, Loewenstein is a figure who is more "Schmittian" than Schmitt himself, and who embodies all of the intolerable characteristics and traits that present-day critics of Schmitt attribute to Schmitt's work and person. Up to a point, one can see the truth in Bendersky's claim. Loewenstein's argument for the prosecution of Schmitt certainly does seem to rest on

the assumption that for military government to be not only legal but also legitimate, the author of *Legality and Legitimacy* must be legitimately brought before the law. And Loewenstein's halfhearted apology for Schmitt—that Schmitt, a tool, could be as successful a democrat as he was a totalitarian—seems to presuppose the commensurability of democracy and dictatorship, a Schmittian argument with which Loewenstein was well familiar, having written to Schmitt about Schmitt's 1923 book *The Crisis of Parliamentary Democracy*. Yet what this goes to show is not that Loewenstein is a plagiarist, but that Schmitt's thought is dialectizable beyond the limits of his proper name. In its vigorous attempt to defend Schmitt's name against Loewenstein, Bendersky's essay deploys that same dialectizability without also thematizing it as a problem for thought.

13. These dynamics are not, of course, limited to Anglophone scholarship on Schmitt. See, for example, Helmut Quaritsch, "Einleitung: Über den Umgang mit Person und Werk Carl Schmitts," in *Complexio oppositorum: Über Carl Schmitt* (Berlin: Duncker & Humblot, 1988), 13–21. See also the polemics that followed the translation into French, in 2002, of Schmitt's 1938 *Der Leviathan in der Staatslehre des Thomas Hobbes* (in particular Yves Charles Zarka, "Carl Schmitt, nazi philosophe?," *Le Monde*, December 6, 2002, VIII) or the disputes that emerged following the 2011 publication of Jean-François Kervégan's *Que faire de Carl Schmitt?* (Paris: Gallimard, 2011) (in particular the contributions by Olivier Jouanjan).

14. Aristotle, *Rhetoric*, 1.9–14.

15. For Aristotle, unlike Plato, rhetoric is a *technē*: it is a neutral art or skill, a means of persuasion that can be used by anybody who wants to speak convincingly, independently of the relation of those means to philosophic concepts of truth and justice (Aristotle, *Rhetoric*, 1.3.54a). To claim the possibility of using Schmittian concepts as a means of persuasion without reference to those concepts' justice or injustice, truth or falsity, etc. is not then to avoid the reduction of Schmitt's thought to rhetoric; it is to radicalize that reduction, to take it to its most fundamental root and logical conclusion.

16. See, on this point, Sitze, "Farewell to Schmitt," 34–35.

17. Carl Schmitt, *The Concept of the Political*, trans. J. Harvey Lomax (Chicago: University of Chicago Press, 2007), 29; but see Carl Schmitt, *Theory of the Partisan: Intermediate Commentary on the Concept of the Political*, trans. Gary L. Ulmen (New York: Telos Press, 2007), 91; see also Jacques Derrida, *Politics of Friendship*, trans. George Collins (New York: Verso Books, 1997), 87.

18. The English translation of Schmitt's *Nomos of the Earth* in 2003 has contributed to something very much resembling a Schmittian turn in the fields of international relations and geography. See, variously, David Chandler, "The Revival of Carl Schmitt in International Relations: The Last Refuge of Critical Theorists?," *Millennium: Journal of International Studies* 37:1 (2008), 27–48; William Hooker, *Carl Schmitt's International Thought: Order and Orientation* (Cambridge: Cambridge University Press, 2009); Benno Gerhard Teschke, "Fatal Attraction: A Critique of Carl

Schmitt's International Political and Legal Theory," *International Theory* 3:2 (2011), 179–227; Stephen Legg, ed., *Spatiality, Sovereignty and Carl Schmitt* (New York: Routledge, 2011); Claudio Minca and Cory Rowan, *On Schmitt and Space* (New York: Routledge, 2014).

19. On the "cryptic" character of Schmitt's oeuvre, see Kervégan, *Que faire de Carl Schmitt?*, 52. For a reflection on Schmitt's "person," see Carlo Galli, *Genealogia della politica: Carl Schmitt e la crisi del pensiero politico moderno*, 2nd ed. (Bologna: Il Mulino, 2010), xi–xii. See also Gopal Balakrishnan, *The Enemy: An Intellectual Portrait of Carl Schmitt* (New York: Verso Books, 2000), 259; Jan-Werner Müller, *A Dangerous Mind: Carl Schmitt in Post-War European Thought* (New Haven, CT: Yale University Press, 2003), 2; Ellen Kennedy, *Constitutional Failure: Carl Schmitt in Weimar* (Durham, NC: Duke University Press, 2004), 5.

20. On contemporary eclecticism, see Jean-François Lyotard, *The Postmodern Condition: A Report on Knowledge*, trans. Geoff Bennington and Brian Massumi (Minneapolis: University of Minnesota Press, 1984), 76. The classical iteration of eclecticism is more intricate. See, on this point, John M. Dillon and A. A. Long, eds., *The Question of "Eclecticism": Studies in Later Greek Philosophy* (Berkeley: University of California Press, 1988).

21. Louis Althusser, *For Marx*, trans. Ben Brewster (New York: Verso Books, 1969), 66–70, esp. 67n30.

22. See, for example, Carl Schmitt, "International Crime," in *Writings on War*, trans. Timothy Nunan (Malden, MA: Polity Press, 2011), 125–97.

23. Étienne Balibar, "Le Hobbes de Schmitt, le Schmitt de Hobbes," in Carl Schmitt, *Le Leviathan dans la doctrine de l'Etat de Thomas Hobbes: Sense et échec d'un symbole politique*, trans. Denis Trierweiler (Paris: Seuil, 2002), 35.

24. Sitze, "Farewell to Schmitt," 48–49.

25. Sitze, "Farewell to Schmitt," 57. On the problematic of the name in Schmitt's thought, see also Jacques Derrida, *The Beast and the Sovereign*, vol. 1, ed. Michel Lisse, Marie-Louise Mallet, and Ginette Michaud, trans. Geoffrey Bennington (Chicago: University of Chicago Press, 2011), 75.

26. Geminello Preterossi, "L'indeducibilità dell'origine: Tra Schmitt e Hegel," *Iride: Filosofia e discussione pubblica* 3 (1997), 574.

27. Galli, *Genealogia*, xxv–xxvi, xxviii.

28. Galli, *Genealogia*, xxvi.

29. Galli, *Genealogia*, xiv–xv, xxv.

30. Carlo Galli, "Carl Schmitt nella cultura italiana (1924–1978): Storia, bilancio, prospettive di una presenza problematica," *Materiali per una storia della cultura giuridica* 9:1 (1979), 81–160.

31. The "gloss" is a method of legal commentary that emerged in the eleventh century at the University of Bologna, where Galli currently teaches. Roberto Esposito has argued that "Italian philosophy" historically has been "a philosophy of cities—of diverse and multiple territorial centers—rather than states" ("The Re-

turn of Italian Philosophy," trans. Zakiya Hanafi, *diacritics* 39:9 [fall 2009], 57, 59; see also Roberto Esposito, *Living Thought: The Origins and Actuality of Italian Philosophy*, trans. Zakiya Hanafi [Stanford, CA: Stanford University Press, 2012], 1–43). Understood on these terms, Galli's "gloss" of Schmitt is "Italian" to the precise extent that it is not Italian but "Bolognese." Elsewhere I have tried to situate Galli's own political thought with reference to the political space—the internally divided city of Bologna—whence it derives. See Sitze, editor's introduction to Carlo Galli, *Political Spaces and Global War*, trans. Elisabeth Fay, ed. Adam Sitze (Minneapolis: University of Minnesota Press, 2010), lxxviii–lxxxv.

32. Galli, *Genealogia*, xv.

33. Galli, *Genealogia*, xvi.

34. Reviewers of Galli's *Genealogia* have not failed to note Galli's emphasis on the tragic quality of Schmittian thought as one of the hallmarks of Galli's specific contribution to Schmitt scholarship. See Vittorio Dini, "Oltre la mediazione. Origine, decisione, forma: Il 'politico' schmittiano come lettura del Moderno," *Iride: Filosofia e discussione pubblica* 3 (1997), 571, 574; Giovanni Messina, "Genealogia della politica. Carl Schmitt e la crisi del pensiero politico moderno" (Review), *Rivista internazionale di filosofia del diritto* 75:3 (1998), 498; Racinaro, "Carl Schmitt e la genealogia della politica," 127; Danilo Zolo, "Schmitt e la ragione politica moderna," *Iride: Filosofia e discussione pubblica* 3 (1997), 577–78. This is not an emphasis one generally finds in Anglophone scholarship on Schmitt. See, for example, Christian Thornhill, "Carl Schmitt after the Deluge: A Review of Recent Literature," *History of European Ideas* 26 (2000), 225–64; Peter Caldwell, "Controversies over Carl Schmitt: A Review of Recent Literature," *Journal of Modern History* 77 (2005), 357–87.

35. Galli, "Schmit nella cultura italiana," 153.

36. Galli, *Political Spaces and Global War*, 90–94; Carlo Galli, introduction to *Guerra*, ed. Carlo Galli (Rome-Bari: Laterza, 2004), xxv.

37. Galli, *Janus's Gaze*, 99–100.

38. Galli, *Genealogia*, 239–40, 244–45; see Carlo Galli, "Presentazione," in Schmitt, *Cattolicesimo romano e forma politica*, ed. and trans. Carlo Galli (Milan: Giuffrè, 1986), 13–14.

39. Galli, *Genealogia*, 242, 245.

40. Galli, *Genealogia*, 4–5.

41. Galli, *Genealogia*, 11; see Carlo Galli, *Modernità: Categorie e profili critici* (Bologna: Il Mulino, 1988), 8.

42. Carlo Galli, "La 'macchina' della modernità: Metafisica e contingenza nel moderno pensiero politico," in *Logiche e crisi della modernità* (Bologna: Il Mulino, 1991), 113–20.

43. Galli, "Presentazione," 13.

44. Galli, "Presentazione," 24.

45. Galli, *Genealogia*, 254.

46. Carlo Galli, "Carl Schmitt's Antiliberalism: Its Theoretical and Historical Sources and Its Philosophical and Political Meaning," *Cardozo Law Review* 5–6 (May 2000), 1598, 1608–9, 1611; Carlo Galli, "Carl Schmitt on Sovereignty: Decision, Form, Modernity," in *Penser la Souveraineté à l'époque moderne et contemporaine*, vol. 2, ed. G. M. Cazzaniga and Y. C. Zarka (Pisa-Paris: Edizioni Ets-Libraire Philosophoque J. Vrin, 2001), 465.

47. Galli, "Carl Schmitt on Sovereignty," 469, 473.

48. See Carlo Galli, "Il cattolicesimo nel pensiero politico di Carl Schmitt," in *Tradizione e Modernità nel pensiero politico di Carl Schmitt*, ed. Roberto Racinaro (Rome-Naples: Edizioni Scientifiche Italiane, 1987), 21–23.

49. Galli, "Schmitt's Antiliberalism," 1599.

50. Galli, "Schmitt's Antiliberalism," 1604. See also Galli, "Carl Schmitt on Sovereignty," 463–64.

51. Galli, "Carl Schmitt on Sovereignty," 467, 470.

52. Galli, *Janus's Gaze*, xlii.

53. Galli, *Genealogia*, XIII–XIV.

54. Sitze, editor's introduction, lxxii–lxxviii. Compare Theodor Adorno, "The Actuality of Philosophy," trans. Benjamin Snow, *Telos* 31 (March 20, 1977), 127.

55. I discuss this at greater length in "Farewell to Schmitt," 39–41.

56. On *Wiederholungszwang*, see Sigmund Freud, "Beyond the Pleasure Principle" (1920), in *The Standard Edition of the Complete Psychological Works of Sigmund Freud*, vol. 18, trans. James Strachey (London: Hogarth Press and Institute of Psycho-Analysis, 1962), 18–23. See also Jacques Lacan, *The Four Fundamental Concepts of Psychoanalysis*, trans. Alan Sheridan, ed. Jacques-Alain Miller (New York: Norton, 1977), 17–66.

57. On "destituent power," compare Raffaele Laudani, *Disobedience in Western Political Thought: A Genealogy*, trans. Jason Francis McGimsey (Cambridge: Cambridge University Press, 2013), 4; and Giorgio Agamben, "What Is a Destituent Power?," trans. Stephanie Wakefield, *Environment and Planning D: Society and Space* 32:1 (2014), 65–74.

58. In an Anglophone world dominated by neoliberalism, for which opposition to Nazism is constitutive of self-affirmation, the imago of a brilliant but evil Nazi is dry kindling for the transferential relationships that enable all reading. On Nazism as a "field of adversity" constitutive for the formation of neoliberal thought, see Michel Foucault, *Birth of Biopolitics: Lectures at the Collège de France (1978–1979)*, trans. Graham Burchell (New York: Palgrave Macmillan, 2008), 120–33.

59. Galli, "Carl Schmitt nella cultura italiana," 155.

60. Carl Schmitt, "Premessa all'edizione italiana," in *Le categorie del "politico,"* trans. Pierangelo Schiera, ed. Gianfranco Miglio and Pierangelo Schiera (Bologna: Il Mulino, 1972), 25–26.

61. Carlo Galli, "La guerra nel pensiero politico di Carl Schmitt," *La Nottola* 1–2 (1986), 150.

62. Galli, *Janus's Gaze*, xlv–xlvi.

63. On this antinomy, see Barbara Cassin, "Nazi et philosophe, telle est la question . . . ," *Le Monde*, December 6, 2002, VIII.

64. Max Horkheimer and Theodor Adorno, "Preface (1944 and 1947)," in *Dialectic of Enlightenment: Philosophical Fragments*, trans. Gunzelin Schmid Noerr (Stanford, CA: Stanford University Press, 2002), xvi. For Balibar, similarly, the question of Schmitt's Nazism cannot be posed without asking about the place and function of Nazism within European history more generally. See Balibar, "Le Hobbes de Schmitt, le Schmitt de Hobbes," 10, 15. This line of interpretation is very different from the critique of anti-Semitism in the work of Raphael Gross, who cites Adorno approvingly, but without also adopting Adorno's dialectical relation to reactionary thinkers.

65. Galli, "Carl Schmitt nella cultura italiana," 153.

66. Galli, "Carl Schmitt nella cultura italiana," 153.

67. Galli, *Genealogia*, 847–48.

68. Hannah Arendt, *The Life of the Mind*, vol. 1, *Thinking* (New York: Harcourt, Brace, and Jovanovich, 1978), 4–5, 13, 179–80.

69. On this point, see Sitze, editor's introduction, xx–xxv, xxxvii, xlvi–liv.

70. On "reliquification" and "reification," see Theodor Adorno, *Negative Dialectics*, trans. E. B. Ashton (New York: Continuum, 1981), 97. It may be worth adding that Galli, who was a student at the University of Bologna from 1968 to 1972, wrote his *laureato* on Adorno's interpretation of Hegel under the guidance of the philosopher Felice Battaglia (a neo-Hegelian with a marked interest in the Frankfurt School). This resulted in Carlo Galli, "Alcune interpretazioni italiane della Scuola di Francoforte," *Il Mulino* 228 (1973), 648–71.

71. On Galli's relation to *Begriffsgeschichte*, see Sitze, editor's introduction, xiv–xvi.

72. Galli, *Janus's Gaze*, xliv.

73. Theodor Adorno, *History and Freedom: Lectures 1964–1965*, trans. Rodney Livingstone, ed. Rolf Tiedemann (Malden, MA: Polity Press, 2006), 92. Between 1964 and 1966, it should be noted, Felice Battaglia (under whom Galli studied at the University of Bologna) organized a lecture series at the University of Bologna in which a range of German intellectuals, including Theodor Adorno, presented papers. See Albino Babolin, ed., *Filosofi tedeschi d'oggi* (Bologna: Il Mulino, 1967).

74. Carl Schmitt, *Roman Catholicism and Political Form*, trans. G. L. Ulmen (Westport, CT: Greenwood Press, 1996), 5.

75. Galli, *Janus's Gaze*, xliii.

76. See Jean-François Kervégan, "Précis de *Que faire de Carl Schmitt?*," *Philosophiques* 39:2 (autumn 2012), 452. See also Kervégan, *Que faire de Carl Schmitt?*, 71–76, 249–52.

77. Galli, *Janus's Gaze*, xlviii; see also 71; 123. To clarify this claim, a short digression may be useful. In a strictly linguistic sense, *inattualità* is simply the priva-

tive form of *attualità*, which translates literally to "modernity" or "newness," such that "outdatedness" may stand as a rough translation of *inattualità*. But while "outdatedness" captures the sense in which *inattualità* designates a privative modality of *historicity*, it doesn't capture the sense in which *inattualità* also and at the same time designates a privative modality of *concrete reality, effectiveness, or actuality*. To grasp this dimension of the term, it's necessary to pass beyond linguistics not only to *the history of philosophy* but also to *the history of the philosophy of history*.

As Charles Alumni has demonstrated in a brilliant analysis, the term *attualità* emerges through a series of productive mistranslations (or "transductions") internal to the German and Italian Hegelianism of the nineteenth century. When Bertrand Spaventa used *attualità* to translate the German *Wirklichkeit* (actuality) that Hegel made so famous in his infamous 1821 "Preface" to *The Philosophy of Right*, he conflated *Wirklichkeit* with a very different term: *Aktuosität* (actuosity), which for Hegel is not just any actuality but is the most profound mode of actuality possible—the actuality of substance itself. Although a deviation in the strict sense, Alumni shows, Spaventa's conflation ended up creating the conditions for a series of felicitous philosophical innovations—up to and including the idea of "intralinguistic translation" itself (the very mode of Alumni's own analysis). See, generally, Charles Alumni, "Attualità," in *Dictionary of Untranslatables: A Philosophical Lexicon*, ed. Barbara Cassin (Princeton, NJ: Princeton University Press, 2014), 64–71.

The meaning of *inattualità* becomes clearer (and Alumni's analysis is confirmed) when we try to reintroduce *inattualità* into the coordinates of Hegelian modal logic. From this exercise we conclude, first of all, that *inattualità* cannot be understood as *the opposite* of actuality: for Hegel, actuality already implies a constitutive antithesis, and that is possibility (*potentia*). We also conclude that *inattualità* cannot be reduced to the category of the accidental or contingent: to the extent that *inattualità* partakes of actuosity (of which, by way of mistranslation, it would seem to be a privative mode), its accidentality is an expression of substance itself, and thus too of necessity (Alumni, "Attualità," 67). And yet, we also must conclude that *inattualità* can't be reduced to the category of necessity, since Hegel does not think a privative mode of necessity (only for necessity's negation in contingency). Last but not least, we can't understand *inattualità* as a negation of the empirical, sensuous, material world: to the extent that it partakes in actuality (of which it *also*, by way of mistranslation, would seem to be a privative mode), *inattualità* must be assumed to manifest itself in empirical existence, but without also of course being reducible to that existence (since not everything that exists empirically is also *Wirklich* in Hegel's sense, and not everything that is *Wirklich* in Hegel's sense also exists empirically).

In short, just as *attualità* emerges through a mistranslation of Hegelian thought, so too is it impossible to retranslate *inattualità* back into the terms of Hegelian thought. From its errant provenance alone, however, we shouldn't conclude that the term is nonsense: as Alumni suggests, and indeed on directly Hegelian grounds, the term's errancy is precisely also the site of its unwitting truth. Given its lack of roots, the most direct way to spool out this truth is simply to translate *inattualità* to the letter, as the privative mode of *attualità*. On these terms, *inattualità* will designate a mode of actuosity that has *so fully actualized itself*—as the State, for example (but of course this is more than just any example)—that *it is no longer actuosity at all, but is instead actuosity's own potential to not-be*. Expressed in terms of modal logic, *inattualità* thus poses a philosophic problem that is *the obverse* of the familiar Scholastic schema of *unactualized potential* (of *dynamis* that turns into *energeia*, or in Hegelian terms, of an *in sich* that turns into the *für sich*). *Inattualità* would seem to designate the strange phenomenon of an *impotent actuosity*—a mode of actuosity that has *so excessively actualized itself* that it has *exhausted itself* without also, for that exhaustion, *passing out of empirical existence*.

A similar dynamic could be outlined in terms of Hegelian phenomenology, where actuality generally refers to the movement by which self-consciousness finds itself confronted by an alien world, externalizes itself in that world and re-makes it in its own image, and thus returns to itself having redoubled itself in the concrete—because of, not despite, its embrace of its own self-alienation. On these terms, *inattualità* would seem to designate a mode of actuality specific to a subject who no longer has the inner capacity to self-consciously alienate itself in the outer world, who instead confronts a world whose actualization has exhausted self-consciousness's own capacity for actualization, its own ability to grasp that world, and who is thus destined to a future in which the only mode of relating to the concrete reality of its own present (to its *attualità*) is stunned and dejected speechlessness on the one hand or on the other hand sterile but vehement judgments (declarations of what "ought to be" that are furious to the precise degree they are also ineffective and unrealizable). Impotent rage and melancholic shock, not ennui or apathy, would then paradoxically emerge as the phenomenological mode in which *inattualità*—understood as a privative mode of the subject's relation to the concrete reality of its own present—externalizes and manifests itself in experience.

On the subjective side as on the objective side, therefore, *inattualità* would seem to designate those elements of concrete experience that have been *excessively actualized* and *that persist in empirically existing*, but that *no longer have the energy to survive their own negation*, that *no longer are capable of living beyond the experience of their own alterity*, and that *so fully and completely partake in presence that they come to lack any negativity whatsoever*. In the same way that Kafka's "Metamorphosis" closes not with Gregor's disappearance but (as readers of Kafka sometimes forget) with a Grete who, in Gregor's absence, has now strangely "bloomed" or "blossomed" [*aufgeblüht*], so too a certain "excess of life" paradoxically turns out to be the mark of exhausted actuality, of experience that reveals itself to be devoid of the void.

78. Raymond Williams, *Marxism and Literature* (Oxford: Oxford University Press, 1977), 110.

79. Williams, *Marxism and Literature*, 122–23, 126.

80. Adorno, "Actuality of Philosophy," 124, translation modified.

81. Italian historicism, it should be noted, emphasizes an experience of the historical neither as an accurate recollection of dates and times nor as the grand narratives of progress or decline but as aphasia and aporia, as symptomatic blockage and obstacle. See, on this point, Remo Bodei, "Italian: A Philosophy for Non-philosophers Too," in *Dictionary of Untranslatables: A Philosophical Lexicon*, 523–27.

82. Which, it should be said, is in Galli's view an element in Schmitt's thought that is not even specific to Schmitt in the first place. See *Janus's Gaze*, 131–33.

83. See, on this point, Derrida, *Beast and the Sovereign*, vol. 1, 150–52.

84. That this dynamic gives rise to an "ethics" of its own is clear from Giorgio Agamben, "Ethics," in *The Coming Community*, trans. Michael Hardt (Minneapolis: University of Minnesota Press, 1993), 44. On the nameless and the named, see also Giorgio Agamben, *The Idea of Prose*, trans. Michael Sullivan and Sam Whitsitt (Albany: State University of New York Press, 1995), 105–6; Giorgio Agamben, "Pardes: The Writing of Potentiality," in *Potentialities: Collected Essays in Philosophy*, ed. and trans. Daniel Heller-Roazen (Stanford, CA: Stanford University Press, 1999), 205–19.

85. Roberto Esposito, *Categories of the Impolitical*, trans. Connal Parsley (New York: Fordham University Press, 2015); Roberto Esposito, *Third Person: Politics of Life and Philosophy of the Impersonal*, trans. Zakiya Hanafi (Malden, MA: Polity, 2012). For an inquiry into the problem of the "improper" from within the coordinates of this horizon, see Timothy Campbell, *Improper Life: Technology and Biopolitics from Heidegger to Agamben* (Minneapolis: University of Minnesota Press, 2011). For Galli's critique of Esposito, see Carlo Galli, "Roberto Esposito, *Nove pensieri sulla politica* (Review)," *Filosofia politica* 1 (1994), 154–56. For Esposito's response, see Roberto Esposito, "Preface to Categories of the Impolitical," trans. Connal Parsley, *diacritics* 39:2 (summer 2009), 108.

86. In the world of Anglophone neoliberalism, as I have noted earlier, the touchstone of clean conscience is self-conscious opposition to Nazism (and above all opposition to self-conscious Nazis, such as Schmitt). But conscience so construed already has proven itself fully capable of coexisting unself-consciously with horrors born out of its own cherished inner principles. Property rights and the rule of law, which neoliberal thinkers sought to reclaim and to polemically reaffirm against Nazism, double as justifications for contemporary thanatopolitics. On this point, see Alain Badiou, *The Century*, trans. Alberto Toscano (Malden, MA: Polity, 2007), 4–5. Under these conditions, it's useful to recall Hegel's teaching in *The Philosophy of Right*: morality and evil alike spring inseparably from one and the same root, the conviction (*Gesinnung*) of a conscience that is fully self-assured and certain of its own good faith and intentions. See G. W. F. Hegel, *Elements of the Philosophy of Right*, ed. Allen Wood, trans. H. B. Nisbet (Cambridge: Cambridge University Press, 1991), 167–70 (sec. 139).

87. Galli, *Janus's Gaze*, 88.

88. This is the converse of Hegel's 1816 claim about the difference between *political history* and *the history of philosophy*. Political history, Hegel argues, takes as its subject the individual in the concrete particularity of his personality: its questions pertain to the character of historical actors, their natural makeup, genius, passions, energy, their weaknesses. The history of philosophy, by contrast, takes as its subject the "freedom of thinking" that belongs to "the general character of man as man." Here the question is not focused on the person. Quite the opposite: the problem is "thinking itself, devoid of characteristics or properties [*eigentüm-lichkeitslose*]." As a result, philosophy that is fully self-conscious of its essence and basis, that is fully for-itself, will think its historicity *sine nomine*. See G. W. F. Hegel, *Introduction to the Lectures on the History of Philosophy*, trans. T. M. Knox and A. V. Miller (Oxford: Oxford University Press, 1985), 9, translation modified.

Preface

1. Ovid, *Fasti*, trans. Anne and Peter Wiseman (Oxford: Oxford University Press, 2011), 2–8 (1.64–70, 89–288).

2. Carlo Galli, *Genealogia della politica: Carl Schmitt e la crisi del pensiero politico moderno*, 2nd ed. (Bologna: Il Mulino, 2010).

3. See the entry of June 22, 1948, in Carl Schmitt, *Glossarium: Aufzeichnungen der Jahre 1947–1951* (Berlin: Duncker & Humblot, 1991). See also Carl Schmitt, "Premessa" (1963) to "Il concetto del 'politico,'" in *Le categorie del "politico,"* trans. Pierangelo Schiera, ed. Gianfranco Miglio and Pierangelo Schiera (Bologna: Il Mulino, 1972).

Chapter 1. Schmitt and the State

1. See also Friedrich Balke, *Der Staat nach seinem Ende: Die Versuchung Carl Schmitts* (München: Fink, 1996); and Geminello Preterossi, *Carl Schmitt e la tradizione moderna* (Rome-Bari: Laterza, 1996).

2. On which point see Carl Schmitt, *Scritti su Thomas Hobbes*, ed. Carlo Galli (Milan: Giuffrè, 1986). See also Carlo Galli, *Genealogia della politica: Carl Schmitt e la crisi del pensiero politico moderno*, 2nd ed. (Bologna: Il Mulino, 2010), 780–806 (which also offers an overview of secondary literature).

3. This is the title of a 1941 essay subsequently published in Carl Schmitt, *Verfassungsrechtliche Aufsätze aus den Jahren 1924–1954* (Berlin: Duncker & Humblot, 1958), 375–85.

4. Schmitt, "Premessa" (1963) to "Il concetto del 'politico,'" in *Le categorie del "politico,"* trans. Pierangelo Schiera, ed. Gianfranco Miglio and Pierangelo Schiera (Bologna: Il Mulino, 1972), 90.

5. [The English language offers only a single term, "law," to translate two terms that are distinct in Italian. *Diritto*, a rough equivalent to the German *Recht* or the French *droit*, refers to the existence of a system of law in general. *Legge*, meanwhile, refers to particular commands or statutes within that system, and is thus an equivalent to the German *Gesetz* or the French *loi*. This creates a well-known problem for translation. To reduce confusion, we have generally followed the lead of Kevin Attell, who recommends translating *diritto* with the English "juridical order." See Giorgio Agamben, *State of Exception*, trans. Kevin Attell (Chicago: University of Chicago Press, 2005), 27. We have swerved from this rule in three cases. Where Galli qualifies *diritto* in such a way as to render its translation by "juridical order" awkward or senseless (e.g., with terms like *diritto positivo*, *diritto delle genti*, *diritto pubblico*, *diritto internazionale*), we have retained the English "law." We have used the English "juridical order," meanwhile, in those few instances where Galli uses the Italian *ordine giuridico*. Last but not least, in passages where Galli is engaged in especially close commentary on Schmitt, we have followed Schmitt's own lead by translating *diritto* with "Juridical Idea." None of these solutions is intended as a substitute for a comprehensive grasp of the more general problem of translation implied here. For deeper analyses of this problem, see the entries "Law, Right" and "Lex" (by Philippe Raynaud and Jean-Pierre Baud, respectively), in *Dictionary of Untranslatables: A Philosophical Lexicon*, ed. Barbara Cassin (Princeton, NJ: Princeton University Press, 2014), 550–58, 565–70.—Trans. and Ed.]

6. *Katechon* is a term taken from Paul's Second Letter to the Thessalonians. "And you know what is restraining [*to katechon*] him now so that he may be revealed in his time. For the mystery of iniquity is already at work; only he who now restrains [*ho katechon*] it will do so until he is out of the way" (2 Thess. 2:6–7, RSV). On Schmitt's role in shaping this concept, which he used since 1942 in a negative sense, and then in a positive sense until his death, see Galli, *Genealogia*, 275–76, which includes a discussion of the secondary literature. See also chapter 2, note 64 here, and chapter 5, note 17 here.

7. See, in general, Carl Schmitt, *Roman Catholicism and Political Form*, trans. Guy Oakes (Cambridge, MA: MIT Press, 1986).

8. On Schmitt's position within the German Catholic culture, and on the limits and the characteristics of Schmitt's Catholicism, see Manfred Dahlheimer, *Carl Schmitt und der deutsche Katholizismus, 1888–1936* (Paderborn: Schöningh, 1998).

9. Carl Schmitt, *Der Wert des Staates und die Bedeutung des Einzelnen* (Tübingen: J. C. B. Mohr [P. Siebeck], 1914).

10. Schmitt, *Der Wert des Staates*, 53.

11. See David Dyzenhaus, *Carl Schmitt, Hans Kelsen and Herman Heller in Weimar* (Oxford: Clarendon Press, 1997); and Marco Caserta, *La forma e l'identità: Democrazia e costituzione in Hans Kelsen e Carl Schmitt* (Turin: Giappichelli, 2005). See also chapter 2, note 31.

12. See, in general, Carl Schmitt, *Political Theology: Four Chapters on the Concept of Sovereignty*, trans. George Schwab (Cambridge, MA: MIT Press, 1985).

13. [Galli's mention of a "crystal" here is a reference to the diagram of Hobbesian political thought that appears in the long endnote Schmitt appended to section 7 of the 1963 reprint of his 1927 treatise *The Concept of the Political*. Because Schmitt's note has been omitted from the existing English translation of *Concept of the Political* (see George Schwab, introduction to Schmitt, *Concept of the Political*, trans. J. Harvey Lomax [Chicago: University of Chicago Press, 2007], 5n8), we here provide the portion of it to which Galli alludes:

> The much-admired system of Thomas Hobbes leaves a door open to transcendence. The truth that *Jesus is the Christ*, which Hobbes had so often and so strongly confessed as his faith, is a truth of the public faith, *public reason* [English in the original], and public worship in which the citizen participates. In the mouth of Thomas Hobbes, this claim is not merely a tactic of protection, without any purpose or necessity except to bring him security against persecution and censorship. It is also something else, something like the *morale par provision* through which Descartes remained with traditional belief.

Schmitt here makes reference to the Third Part of Descartes's *Discourse on Method*. There Descartes argues that just as one must build a provisional dwelling in which to live while one is tearing down and rebuilding one's own house, so too must one construct a "provisional code of morals" while one is subjecting one's traditional moral system to hyperbolic doubt. The *morale par provision* Descartes then proceeds to outline consists of three maxims: obey the laws and customs of the country in which I live; retain the religion of my childhood; and govern myself through moderation and not excess.

> In the transparent structure of the political system of "The Matter, Form, and Power of the Commonwealth Ecclesiastical and Civil" [the subtitle of Hobbes's *Leviathan*], this truth is more of a keystone, in which public worship presents God with a name under the saying *Jesus is the Christ*. Of course, the gruesome civil war between the Christian confessions immediately raises the question: Who interprets, and enforces in a legally binding manner, this continually interpretable truth? Who decides what true Christianity is? Whence the inevitable *Quis interpretabitur?* [Who is to interpret?] and the incessant *judicabit Quis* [Who is to judge?]. Who mints the truth into a *bona fide* coin? These questions are answered with the maxim *Autoritas, non veritas, facit legem*. The truth does not execute itself; it requires executable commands. These are the *potestas directa*, which—in contrast with the *indirecta potestas*—authenticate the execution of the command, require obedience, and are able to protect those who obey. The result of all of this is a series that runs from top to bottom, from the truth of public worship and obedience to protection of the individual. If we now instead

proceed from the bottom up, beginning with the system of the material needs of the individual, then the series starts with the "natural" need for protection and safety on the part of helpless individuals, and consequently too with their obedience to the commands of the *potestas directa*, and leads in reverse order, but *via* the same route, to the door to transcendence. In this way, we arrive at a diagram, which in its five axes—with the 3–3 formula as its central axis—gives us the following *crystal-system*.

Above

Open for Transcendence

↙	1	Veritas: Jesus Christus	5	↖			
↙	2	Quis interpretabitur?		4	↖		
↙	3	Autoritas, non veritas, facit legem			3	↖	
↘	4	Potestas directa, non indirecta		2	↗		
↘	5	Obœdientia et	1	↗			
↘		Protectio	↗				

→ → → →

Below

Closed; System of Needs

This "Hobbes-crystal" (the fruit of lifelong labor on the big issues in general and on the work of Thomas Hobbes in particular) deserves a moment of reflection and serious thought. Obviously, the first formula (the 1–5 axis) already contains a neutralization of the opposites of inner-Christian religious war. Immediately the question arises whether this neutralization over the framework of the common faith in God could be expanded, so that this first sentence could also read, "Allah is great," or even further to include some of the many contestable truths, social ideals, high values, and principles whose interpretation, implementation, and enforcement have also been a source of strife and war (such as, for example, "Liberty, Equality, and Fraternity," "the good of humanity," or "to each according to needs," etc.). I do not think that Hobbes intended so total a neutralization. But the question here is not about Thomas Hobbes's individual subjective psychology or conviction; it is about a systematic and fundamental problem within his political doctrine as a whole, namely, that in it the door to transcendence is by no means closed. It is the question of the interchangeability or noninterchangeability of the formula, *that Jesus is the Christ* [English in the original].

Carl Schmitt, *Der Begriff des Politischen: Text von 1932 mit einem Vorwort und drei Corollarien* (Berlin: Duncker & Humblot, 1963), 121–23, my translation.—Ed.]

14. See, in general, Carl Schmitt, "The Age of Neutralizations and Depoliticizations" (1929), trans. Matthias Konzen and John P. McCormick, in Schmitt, *Concept of the Political*, 80–96.

15. See chapter 2.

16. See chapter 2.

17. See Ernst-Wolfgang Böckenförde, "The Rise of the State as a Process of Secularization," in *State, Society, and Liberty: Studies in Political Theory and Constitutional Law*, trans. J. A. Underwood (Oxford: Berg, 1991), 26–46.

18. Schmitt, "Age of Neutralizations and Depoliticizations," 88.

19. See, on this point, Carl Schmitt, *Political Romanticism*, trans. Guy Oakes (Cambridge, MA: MIT Press, 1986), 139–40.

20. On Schmitt's critique of liberalism, see Eugenia Parise, *Carl Schmitt: La difficile critica del liberalismo* (Napoli: Liguori, 1995); John P. McCormick, *Carl Schmitt's Critique of Liberalism: Against Politics as Technology* (Cambridge: Cambridge University Press, 1997); *Carl Schmitt's Critique of Liberalism*, ed. David Dyzenhaus (Durham, NC: Duke University Press, 1998); William Scheuerman, *Carl Schmitt: The End of Law* (Lanham, MD: Rowman and Littlefield, 1999); Chantal Mouffe, "Carl Schmitt and the Paradox of Liberal Democracy," in *The Challenge of Carl Schmitt*, ed. Chantal Mouffe (London: Verso, 1999), 38–53; Carlo Galli, "Carl Schmitt's Anti-Liberalism: Its Theoretical and Historical Sources, and Its Philosophical and Political Meaning," *Cardozo Law Review* 5–6 (2000), 1597–1617.

21. See, in general, Schmitt, *Concept of the Political*. For the recent literature on this text, see Carl Schmitt, *Der Begriff des Politischen: Ein kooperativer Kommentar*, ed. Reinhard Mehring (Berlin: Akademie, 2003).

22. For interesting suggestions in this direction, see Eckard Bolsinger, *The Autonomy of the Political: Carl Schmitt's and Lenin's Political Realism* (Westport, CT: Greenwood Press, 2001).

23. Schmitt, *Concept of the Political*, 19.

24. Georg Jellinek, *Allgemeine Staatslehre* (Berlin: Häring, 1900), 173.

25. Carl Schmitt, *Staatsgefüge und Zusammenbruch des zweiten Reiches: Der Sieg des Bürgers über den Soldaten* (Hamburg: Hanseatische Verlagsanstalt, 1934).

26. Carl Schmitt, *Die geistesgeschichtliche Lage des heutigen Parlamentarismus* (München: Duncker & Humblot, 1923). On Schmitt's theory of democracy, see Gaetano Azzariti's acute observations in *Critica della democrazia identitaria: Lo stato costituzionale schmittiano e la crisi del parlamentarismo* (Rome-Bari: Laterza, 2005).

27. Max Weber, "Parliament and Government in Germany under a New Political Order," in *Weber: Political Writings*, ed. Peter Lassman and Ronald Speirs (Cambridge: Cambridge University Press, 1994), 152.

28. Carl Schmitt, *Dictatorship*, trans. Michael Hoelzl and Graham Ward (Cambridge, MA: Polity Press, 2010).

29. Carl Schmitt, *Constitutional Theory*, trans. Jeffrey Seitzer (Durham, NC: Duke

University Press, 2008). See Ulrich Thiele, *Advokative Volkssouveränität: Carl Schmitts Konstruktion einer "demokratischen" Diktaturtheorie im Kontext der Interpretation politischer Theorien der Aufklärung* (Berlin: Duncker & Humblot, 2003).

30. [*Verfassung* here has a double sense in German that is important to note. On the one hand it designates a "constitution" in the political or juridical sense, where "constitution" signifies "a set of basic or fundamental laws." On the other hand it designates a "constitution" in the physical or medical sense, where "constitution" signifies not only the "composition" of a living body but also whether that body is in a better or worse "condition," is in good or bad "shape." A similar doubleness pertains in the case of the English word "state" (which can refer both to a political entity, such as Germany or England, or a physical condition, such as health or sickness) and, similarly, the English word "regime" (which can refer both to a form of politics and a form of life).—Ed.]

31. See Carl Schmitt, *Volksentscheid und Volksbegehren: Ein Beitrag zur Auslegung der Weimarer Verfassung und zur Lehre von der Unmittelbaren Demokratie* (Berlin: de Gruyter, 1927).

32. Carl Schmitt, *Political Theology II: The Myth of the Closure of Any Political Theology* (Cambridge: Polity, 2008), 45.

33. Schmitt, *Constitutional Theory*, secs. 3, 6, 8–10.

34. See, in general, Carl Schmitt, *Die Hüter der Verfassung* (Tübingen: Mohr, 1931); Carl Schmitt, *Legality and Legitimacy*, trans. Jeffrey Seitzer (Durham, NC: Duke University Press, 2004); Carl Schmitt, *Hugo Preuss: sein Staatsbegriff und seine Stellung in der deutschen Staatslehre* (Tübingen, Mohr, 1930).

35. Schmitt's "Concrete Constitutional Situation of the Present" contains some important essays from the late 1920s and 1930s. See Schmitt, *Die Hüter*, 71–131.

36. Schmitt, *Die Hüter*, 62–64.

37. Ernst Jünger, *Die totale Mobilmachung* (Berlin: Junker und Dünnhaupt, 1934).

38. Carl Schmitt, "The Way to the Total State," in *Four Articles, 1931–1938*, trans. Simona Draghici (Washington, DC: Plutarch Press, 1999), 1–18.

39. Carl Schmitt, "Pflicht zum Staat," in *Staatsethik und pluralistischer Staat* (Berlin: Metzner, 1930), 144–45.

40. Schmitt, *Legality and Legitimacy*, 90.

41. Schmitt, *Legality and Legitimacy*, 95–101.

42. Olivier Beaud sensibly observes that even though Schmitt was not a Nazi in 1930–32, he nevertheless did not mean to save the Weimar Republic, but instead to deeply upset it. See *Les derniers jours de Weimar: Carl Schmitt face à l'avènement du nazisme* (Paris: Descartes & Cie, 1997).

43. Carl Schmitt, "Essere e divenire dello Stato fascista," in *Posizioni e concetti: In lotta con Weimar-Ginevra-Versailles: 1923–1939* (Milan: Giuffrè, 2007), 177–86.

44. On the German debates of the 1970s and on recent American scholarship that interprets Schmitt's antiliberalism as conservative support for monopo-

listic capitalism, see Joseph W. Bendersky, "The Definite and the Dubious: Carl Schmitt's Influence on Conservative Political and Legal Theory in the US," *Telos* 122 (2002), 33–47.

45. Carl Schmitt, *State, Movement, People: The Triadic Structure of the Political Unity; the Question of Legality*, trans. Simona Draghici (Corvallis, Ore.: Plutarch Press, 2001), 3–52. See also Carl Schmitt, *On the Three Types of Juristic Thought*, trans. Joseph Bendersky (Westport, CT: Praeger, 2004).

46. On the German debate on the total State, see Carlo Galli, "Strategie della totalità: Stato autoritario, Stato totale, totalitarismo, nella Germania degli anni Trenta," *Filosofia politica* 1 (1997), 27–62.

47. Carl Schmitt, *Völkerrechtliche Grossraumordnung: Mit Interventionsverbot für raumfremde Mächte, Ein Beitrag zum Reichsbegriff im Völkerrecht* (Berlin: Deutscher Rechtsverlag, 1939). On the topic of internationalism, see chapter 5.

48. Carl Schmitt, *The Nomos of the Earth in the International Law of the Jus Publicum Europæum*, trans. Gary L. Ulmen (New York: Telos Press, 2003).

49. Carl Schmitt, *Ex Captivitate Salus: Erfahrungen Der Zeit 1945/47* (Köln: Greven Verlag, 1950), 78.

50. Carl Schmitt, *Land and Sea*, trans. Simona Draghici (Washington, DC: Plutarch Press, 1997).

51. Carl Schmitt, "Die Legale Weltrevolution: Politischer Mehrwert Als Prämie Auf Juristische Legalität und Superlegalität" (1978), in *Frieden Oder Pazifismus? Arbeiten Zum Volkerrecht Und Zur Internationalen Politik, 1924–1978* (Berlin: Duncker & Humblot, 2005), 919–68.

52. Carl Schmitt, *Theory of the Partisan: Intermediate Commentary on the Concept of the Political*, trans. Gary L. Ulmen (New York: Telos Press, 2007), 48–61.

53. Carl Schmitt, *Donoso Cortés in gesamteuropaischer Interpretation: Vier Aufsatze* (Köln: Greven, 1950).

54. Jorge Eugenio Dotti, "Schmitt Reads Marx," *Cardozo Law Review* 21:5/6 (2000), 1473–85. See also Galli, *Genealogia*, 33–56.

55. Schmitt dedicated constant attention to Hobbes in various books and essays, such as *The Leviathan in the State Theory of Thomas Hobbes: Meaning and Failure of a Political Symbol* (1938), trans. George Schwab and Erna Hilfstein (Chicago: University of Chicago Press, 2008) and "Die vollendete Reformation: Bemerkungen und Hinweise zu neuen Leviathan-Interpretationen," *Der Staat* 1 (1965), 51–69. See also chapter 4, note 1.

56. On Schmitt and Hegel, see the scholarship reviewed in Galli, *Genealogia*, 13–33.

57. See, on this point, Carlo Galli, "Nichilismi a confronto: Nietzsche e Schmitt," *Filosofia politica* 1 (2014), 99–119.

58. On Schmitt and Weber, see Gary L. Ulmen, *Politischer Mehrwert: Eine Studie über Max Weber und Carl Schmitt* (Weinheim, Germany: VCH, Acta Humaniora, 1991);

and Catherine Colliot-Thélène, "Carl Schmitt contre Max Weber: Rationalité juridique et rationalité économique," in *Le droit, le politique: Autour de Max Weber, Hans Kelsen, Carl Schmitt*, Carlos-Miguel Herrera (Paris: L'Harmattan, 1995), 205–27.

59. Ernst Jünger, *Der Waldgang* (Frankfurt am Main: V. Klostermann, 1952); Ernst Jünger, *Der Weltstaat: Organismus und Organisation* (Stuttgart: E. Klett, 1960).

60. [Galli here makes reference to Michel Foucault, *Discipline and Punish: The Birth of the Prison*, trans. Alan Sheridan (New York: Vintage Books, 1979), 26 (where Foucault outlines a "micro-physics of power . . . whose field of validity is situated . . . between the great functionings [of the state apparatus] and bodies themselves, with their materiality and their forces" [translation modified]).—Ed.]

61. [For Galli's analysis of political space in the global age, see Carlo Galli, *Political Spaces and Global War*, trans. Elisabeth Fay, ed. Adam Sitze (Minneapolis: University of Minnesota Press, 2010), 102–91.—Ed.]

62. See chapter 5.

63. [Ovid, "Amores," in *Ovid: Heroides, Amores*, trans. Grant Showerman (Cambridge, MA: Harvard University Press, 1921), 492–93. The next line is "et videor voti nescius esse mei" (and I seem not to know my own wishes).—Ed.]

Chapter 2. Schmitt's Political Theologies

1. Beginning with Erik Peterson's "Monotheism as a Political Problem: A Contribution to the History of Political Theology in the Roman Empire," in Peterson, *Theological Tractates*, ed. and trans. Michael J. Hollerich (Stanford, CA: Stanford University Press, 2011), 68–105.

2. This is, however, only a conjectural reading. See, generally, Karl Marx, *Critique of Hegel's "Philosophy of Right,"* trans. Annette Jolin and Joseph O'Malley (Cambridge: Cambridge University Press, 1970).

3. Carl Schmitt, *Political Theology: Four Chapters on the Concept of Sovereignty*, trans. George Schwab (Chicago: University of Chicago Press, 2005).

4. Mikhail Bakunin, "The Political Theology of Mazzini and the International" (1871), trans. Sarah Holmes, *Liberty* 4 (September 18, 1886–June 18, 1887). See also Carl Schmitt, *The Leviathan in the State Theory of Thomas Hobbes: Meaning and Failure of a Political Symbol* (1938), trans. George Schwab and Erna Hilfstein (Chicago: University of Chicago Press, 2008), 6–9.

5. Camillo Ruini, "La nuova 'teologia politica' tedesca," *Il Mulino* 6 (1980), 894–926. See also, more generally, Jean-Claude Monod, *La querelle de la sécularisation: De Hegel à Blumenberg* (Paris: Problèmes et controverses, 2002); Merio Scattola, *Teologia politica* (Bologna: Il Mulino, 2007); Mark Lilla, *The Stillborn God: Religion, Politics, and the Modern West* (New York: Knopf, 2007) (on the fragility of the great modern separation between religion and politics).

6. See, in general, Schmitt, *Political Theology*; Schmitt, *Political Theology II: The*

Myth of the Closure of Any Political Theology, trans. Michael Hoelzl and Graham Ward (Cambridge: Polity, 2008). Antonio Caracciolo, in his introduction to the Italian edition of *Political Theology II*, mentions that the *Nachlass* contains an illegible manuscript of notes for a *Political Theology III*. See Antonio Caracciolo, "Presentazione," in Schmitt, *Teologia Politica II* (Milan: Giuffrè, 1992), v–xxx.

7. For further discussions on this same topic, see Galli, *Genealogia della politica: Carl Schmitt e la crisi del pensiero politico moderno*, 2nd ed. (Bologna: Il Mulino, 2010), 333–459.

8. There are a number of works that are openly oriented on the reconstruction of the entirety of Schmitt's thought starting from the notion of "political theology." See Klaus-Michael Kodalle, *Politik als Macht und Mythos: Carl Schmitts "Politische Theologie"* (Stuttgart: W. Kohlhammer, 1973), and Michele Nicoletti, *Trascendenza e potere: La teologia politica di Carl Schmitt* (Brescia: Morcelliana, 1990). For a Christian interpretation of Schmitt's political theology, focused on authority and revelation as the origin of politics, see Heinrich Meier, *The Lesson of Carl Schmitt: Four Chapters on the Distinction between Political Theology and Political Philosophy* (Chicago: University of Chicago Press, 1998). See also Heinrich Meier, *Carl Schmitt and Leo Strauss: The Hidden Dialogue* (Chicago: University of Chicago Press, 1995). See furthermore Jianhong Chen, "What Is Carl Schmitt's Political Theology?," *Interpretation* 33:2 (2006), 153 (for whom Schmitt's political theology is only methodological and not substantial; in this regard, see also chapter 4, notes 47 and 49). Paléologue's study is also noteworthy for the discussion of the notion of *katechon* (about which see also chapter 1 here). Paléologue sees political theology as polysemic concept, and relates Schmitt to Dostoevsky on the topic of Evil. See Théodore Paléologue, *Sous l'oeil du Grand Inquisiteur: Carl Schmitt et l'héritage de la théologie politique* (Paris: Cerf, 2004).

9. Carl Schmitt, "Schattenrisse," in *Carl Schmitts Kulturkritik der Moderne: Text, Kommentar und Analyse der "Schattenrisse" des Johannes Negelinus*, ed. Ingeborg Villinger (Berlin: Akademie Verlag, 1995), 11–68; Carl Schmitt, *Der Wert des Staates und die Bedeutung des Einzelnen* (Tübingen: J. C. B. Mohr [P. Siebeck], 1914); Carl Schmitt, "The Buribunks: A Historico-Philosophical Meditation," in *Gramophone, Film, Typewriter*, ed. Friedrich Kittler, trans. Geoffrey Winthrop-Young and Michael Wutz (Stanford, CA: Stanford University Press, 1999), 231–42.

10. The element of the "glorious"—which is central to Schmitt's *Roman Catholicism and Political Form*—is absent in *Political Theology* where instead the tragic prevails: decision is here the opposite of the triumphalistic Catholic *complexio oppositorum* and takes place when foundational theological substance is absent. Its horizon is a represented form, while Christ is "present" in the Catholic representative mediation mentioned in *Roman Catholicism and Political Form*. On this point, I diverge from the thesis of continuity between *Political Theology* and *Roman Catholicism*, already present in Hugo Ball, *Carl Schmitt's Politische Theologie* (München: Köselsche Buchhandlung, 1924). See Galli, *Genealogia*, 229–80.

11. Schmitt, *Political Theology*, 5.

12. "Looked at normatively," Schmitt argues, "the decision emanates from nothingness" (Political Theology, 31–32).

13. Adalgiso Amendola, Carl Schmitt tra decisione e ordinamento concreto (Napoli: Edizioni scientifiche italiane, 1999).

14. Schmitt, Political Theology, 15.

15. Schmitt, Political Theology, 13. On Schmitt and the crisis of Weimar, see Galli, Genealogia, 635–729.

16. Schmitt calls the sovereign decision Anfang ["commencement" or "beginning"] in On the Three Types of Juristic Thought, trans. Joseph Bendersky (Westport, CT: Praeger Publishers, 2004), 59–62. In this same text Schmitt also calls it archē.

17. Schmitt, Political Theology, 13.

18. Carl Schmitt, Constitutional Theory, trans. Jeffrey Seitzer (Durham, NC: Duke University Press, 2008), paras. 8, 9, 10, 18.

19. Emanuele Castrucci, "Il logos della potenza," in Logos dell'essere—Logos della norma: Studi per una ricerca coordinata da Luigi Lombardi Vallauri (Bari: Adriatica, 1999), 1–54.

20. Schmitt, Political Theology, 13.

21. Schmitt, Political Theology, 12.

22. See chapters 3 and 4.

23. Schmitt, Constitutional Theory, para. 16.

24. Schmitt, Political Theology, 13, translation modified.

25. Schmitt, Political Theology, 33; Schmitt, Constitutional Theory, 182. See Thomas Hobbes, Leviathan, Or, The Matter, Forme, and Power of a Common-Wealth Ecclesiasticall and Civill, ed. Richard Tuck (Cambridge: Cambridge University Press, 1996), 191. The exact phrase is "The Authority of writers, without the Authority of the Commonwealth, maketh not their opinions Law, be they never so true."

26. Schmitt, Leviathan in the State Theory of Thomas Hobbes, esp. 31, where Schmitt speaks of the "spark of reason (ratio)." In this phase of Schmittian thought, the origin of the Hobbesian State is indeed decisionistic but not its full functioning, because he openly denies that the Hobbesian expression auctoritas, non veritas is a sign of mechanical decisionism. (See p. 44: "This sentence . . . is anything but a slogan of irrational despotism" [Schmitt, Leviathan, 44].)

27. Schmitt, Political Theology, 31–32.

28. Schmitt, Political Theology, 27–38. The theme of the impossibility of mediation between juridical idea and immanence if not through decision, is central in Schmitt beginning with Der Wert des Staates.

29. Schmitt, Political Theology, 32–33.

30. Schmitt, Political Theology, 21, 32. Luigi Cimmino connects this text with the same aporias circulating within the twentieth-century reflection in the fields of philosophy of law and normative ethics. See Luigi Cimmino, "La 'teologia politica' di Carl Schmitt e il problema della normatività," Rivista di filosofia politica 1 (2003), 85–105.

31. Hans Kelsen, *Das Problem der Souveränität und die Theorie des Völkerrechts: Beitrag zu einer reinen Rechtslehre* (Tübingen: J. C. B. Mohr [P. Siebeck], 1920), and Hans Kelsen, "God and the State," in *Essays in Legal and Moral Philosophy* (Dordrecht: Reidel, 1973), 61–82. On the relationship between Schmitt and Kelsen, see Galli, *Genealogia*, 345–47, 393–96, 548–51, 684–88, and chapter 1, note 11. See, furthermore, Jean-François Kervégan, "La critique schmittienne du normativisme kelsénien," in *Le droit, le politique: Autour de Max Weber, Hans Kelsen, Carl Schmitt*, ed. Carlos-Miguel Herrera (Paris: L'Harmattan, 1995), 229–41.

32. Schmitt, *Political Theology*, 32. On the critique of the logic of "competences," of positivism, and of Kelsen, see Schmitt, *Political Theology*, 34.

33. Schmitt, *Political Theology*, 34–35.

34. Schmitt's critique of vitalistic irrationalism, elaborated in *Political Romanticism*, is not weakened by the mention of "concrete life" he does in *Political Theology* (15), which is to be interpreted in the sense of "exception" and "extreme case."

35. Schmitt, *Political Theology*, 37.

36. Sabino Acquaviva and Gustavo Guizzardi, *La secolarizzazione* (Bologna: Il Mulino, 1973).

37. Carlo Galli, "Ordine e contingenza: Linee di lettura del *Leviatano*," in *Contingenza e necessità nella ragione politica moderna* (Rome-Bari: Laterza, 2009), 38–71.

38. Carlo Galli, "La critica della democrazia nel pensiero controrivoluzionario," in *Contingenza e necessità*, 95–134.

39. Especially significant and anticipatory in this regard is G. W. F. Hegel, *Hegel: Political Writings*, ed. Laurence Dickey and H. B. Nisbet (Cambridge: Cambridge University Press, 1999), 6–101, esp. 51–56.

40. See G. W. F. Hegel, *Philosophy of Mind: Being Part Three of the Encyclopaedia of the Philosophical Sciences*, trans. William Wallace and A. V. Miller (Oxford: Clarendon Press, 1971), sec. 552; G. W. F. Hegel, *Elements of the Philosophy of Right*, ed. Allen W. Wood, trans. H. B. Nisbet (Cambridge University Press, 1991), sec. 141 (Zusatz).

41. See, generally, Max Weber, *The Protestant Ethic and the Spirit of Capitalism* (New York: Scribner, 1958).

42. See, generally, Friedrich Nietzsche, *Thus Spoke Zarathustra: A Book for All and None*, ed. Adrian Del Caro and Robert B. Pippin, trans. Adrian Del Caro (Cambridge: Cambridge University Press, 2006); Friedrich Nietzsche, "Anti-Christ: A Curse on Christianity," in *The Anti-Christ, Ecce Homo, Twilight of the Idols, and Other Writings*, ed. Aaron Ridley, trans. Judith Norman (New York: Cambridge University Press, 2005), 1–68.

43. Schmitt, *Political Theology*, 36. On analogy more generally, see Erich Przywara, *Analogia Entis*, trans. John R. Betz and David Bentley Hart (Grand Rapids, Mich.: William B. Eerdmans, 2014); Andreas Marxen, *Das Problem der Analogie zwischen den Seinsstrukturen der großen Gemeinschaften* (Würzburg: Konrad Triltsch, 1938); and Ralph McInerny, *Aquinas and Analogy* (Washington, DC: Catholic University of America Press, 1996).

44. Carl Schmitt, *Dictatorship*, trans. Michael Hoelzl and Graham Ward (Cambridge, MA: Polity Press, 2010), 120–21.

45. Schmitt, *Political Theology*, 36, 42–43. On the use of analogy in Catholic legitimism, see the texts collected in *I controrivoluzionari: Antologia di scritti politici*, ed. Carlo Galli (Bologna: Il Mulino, 1981).

46. Carl Schmitt, "The Age of Neutralizations and Depoliticizations" (1929), trans. Matthias Konzen and John P. McCormick, in Schmitt, *Concept of the Political*, trans. J. Harvey Lomax (Chicago: University of Chicago Press, 2007), 89. ("I consider the strongest and most consequential of all intellectual shifts of European history to be the one in the seventeenth century from the traditional Christian theology to 'natural' science.")

47. On *"silete!"* see Carl Schmitt, *The Nomos of the Earth in the International Law of the Jus Publicum Europæum*, trans. Gary Ulmen (New York: Telos Press, 2003), 121, 126, 259, 239; Carl Schmitt, *Ex Captivitate Salus: Erfahrungen der Zeit 1945/47* (Köln: Greven Verlag, 1950), 70. See also Schmitt's 1963 "Preface," which he wrote for the Italian edition of *Der Begriff des Politischen*, and in which he affirmed the epochality of *"silete!"* (Carl Schmitt, *Le categorie del "politico,"* trans. Pierangelo Schiera, ed. Gianfranco Miglio and Pierangelo Schiera [Bologna: Il Mulino, 1972], 96–97). The same is true in Schmitt's 1965 text "Il compimento della riforma," in *Scritti su Thomas Hobbes*, ed. Carlo Galli (Milan: Giuffrè, 1986), 168. On Gentili, see Carlo Galli, "Alberico Gentili e Thomas Hobbes: Crisi dell'umanesimo e piena modernità," *Filosofia politica* 2 (2007), 213–27.

48. Karl Löwith, *Meaning in History: The Theological Implications of the Philosophy of History* (Chicago: University of Chicago Press, 1949); Eric Voegelin, *The New Science of Politics: An Introduction* (Chicago: University of Chicago, 1962); Leo Strauss, *Natural Right and History* (Chicago: University of Chicago Press, 1953).

49. Kelsen, "God and the State," 82.

50. Schmitt, *Political Theology*, 41–42.

51. Walter Benjamin, *The Origin of German Tragic Drama*, trans. John Osborne (London: Verso, 1998), 65–66.

52. Walter Benjamin, "Theses on the Philosophy of History," in *Illuminations*, ed. Hannah Arendt, trans. Harry Zohn (New York: Schocken Books, 1979), 261. On the relationship between Benjamin and Schmitt, see Carlo Galli, *Genealogia della politica*, 50–52, 399–405. See also Carlo Galli, "Hamlet: Representation and the Concrete," trans. Amanda Minervini and Adam Sitze, in *Political Theology and Early Modernity*, ed. G. Hammill and J. R. Lupton (Chicago: University of Chicago Press, 2012), 60–83.

53. Carl Schmitt, *Hamlet or Hecuba: The Intrusion of the Time into the Play*, trans. David Pan and Jennifer R. Rust (New York: Telos Press, 2009), 59–65.

54. Werner Böckenförde, "The Rise of the State as a Process of Secularization," in *State, Society, and Liberty: Studies in Political Theory and Constitutional Law*, trans. J. A. Underwood (Oxford: Berg, 1991), 26–46. See also Jacob Taubes, "Politische

Theorie und politische Theologie: Bemerkungen zu ihrem gegenseitigen Verhältnis," in *Der Fürst dieser Welt: Carl Schmitt und die Folgen,* ed. Jacob Taubes (München:
W. Fink, 1983), 16–25.

55. Geminello Preterossi, "Prefazione," in Ernst-Wolfgang Böckenförde, *Diritto e secolarizzazione: Dallo stato moderno all'Europa unita* (Rome-Bari: Laterza, 2007).

56. Schmitt, *Political Theology,* 47–52.

57. He later clarified this concept in his 1929 essay "The Age of Neutralizations and Depoliticizations," as well as in *The Concept of the Political,* which Schmitt
wrote in the years between 1927 and 1932, and in his 1938 book *Thomas Hobbes's
Leviathan.*

58. See chapter 1, note 34 here.

59. On Donoso Cortés, see Schmitt, *Political Theology,* 52–66; and Carl Schmitt,
"A Pan-European Interpretation of Donoso Cortes," *Telos* (2002), 100–115.

60. On the counterrevolutionaries, see Schmitt, *Political Theology,* 53–66. The
distinction between *agonikós* and *dogmatikós* is at 57. In this regard, see also Carlo
Galli, "La critica della democrazia nel pensiero controrivoluzionario," in *Contingenza e necessità,* 95–134.

61. See also chapter 1.

62. Schmitt, "Preface to the Second Edition," *Political Theology,* 1–4. On the debates over "political theology" in the 1920s and 1930s, see Galli, *Genealogia della
politica,* 405–20. On the relationship between the reprinting of *Political Theology*
and the Protestant pro-Nazi political theology of the *Deutsche Christen,* see Gross,
Carl Schmitt and the Jews, 47–51, 54–59.

63. See, generally, Schmitt, *The Nomos of the Earth.*

64. See 2 Thess. 2:6–7, RSV; compare chapter 1, note 6. On the role of this concept in Schmitt, see Günter Meuter, *Der Katechon: Zu Carl Schmitts fundamentalischer
Kritik der Zeit* (Berlin: Duncker & Humblot, 1994), and Massimo Maraviglia, *La pen-
ultima guerra: Il "katéchon" nella dottrina dell'ordine politico di Carl Schmitt* (Milan: LED,
2006). See also chapter 5, note 17.

65. See, generally, Carl Schmitt, "Die vollendete Reformation: Bemerkungen
und Hinweise zu neuen Leviathan-Interpretationen," *Der Staat* 1 (1965), 51–69.

66. On this see chapter 1, note 12.

67. On "reoccupation," see Hans Blumenberg, *The Legitimacy of the Modern Age,*
trans. Robert Wallace (Cambridge, MA: MIT Press, 1983), 49 and following (on
Schmitt, see 92 and following). Blumenberg advanced his critique after the first
edition of this work (1966), to which Schmitt provided a response in his 1970 *Political Theology II;* in the second edition, Blumenberg continued his contention with
Schmitt in light of Schmitt's 1970 reply.

68. See Schmitt, *Political Theology II,* 116–30.

69. Peterson, "Monotheism as a Political Problem," 86 and following.

70. See note 1 here.

71. See Helmut Peukert, *Diskussion zur "politischen Theologie": Mit einer Bibliogra-*

phie zum Thema (Mainz: Grünewald-Verl., 1969). See also Robert Spaemann, "Theologie, Prophetie, Politik: Zur Kritik der politischen Theologie," in *Zur Kritik der politischen Utopie: Zehn Kapitel politischer Philosophie* (Stuttgart: E. Klett, 1977), 57–76.

72. Schmitt, *Political Theology II*, 122–23 (to say nothing of the philological correctness of Schmitt's quotation of Gregory of Nazianzo).

73. Schmitt, *Political Theology II*, 70–102.

74. Schmitt, *Political Theology II*, 112–15.

75. Schmitt, *Political Theology II*, 128–30.

76. See also Schmitt's letter to Carlo Galli of November 7, 1979, cited in Galli, *Genealogia* (92), in which he affirms that the modern era, understood as a politico-theological era, is "finished" ("zu Ende ist").

77. Carlo Galli, *Political Spaces and Global War*, trans. Elisabeth Fay (Minneapolis: University of Minnesota Press, 2010), 145–49. See also the special issue on "Teologie Estreme," *Teologia Politica* 1 (2004), and chapter 5 here.

Chapter 3. Schmitt and Machiavelli

1. Carl Schmitt, *Tagebücher: Oktober 1912 bis Februar 1915*, ed. Ernst Hüsmert (Berlin: Akademie, 2003), 163.

2. Schmitt, *Tagebücher*, 163.

3. See, in general, Schmitt, "The Age of Neutralizations and Depoliticizations," (1929), trans. Matthias Konzen and John P. McCormick, in Schmitt, *The Concept of the Political*, trans. J. Harvey Lomax (Chicago: University of Chicago Press, 2007), 80–96.

4. Carl Schmitt, *Dictatorship*, trans. Michael Hoelzl and Graham Ward (Cambridge, MA: Polity Press, 2010), 5–7.

5. See, variously, Schmitt, *Political Theology: Four Chapters on the Concept of Sovereignty*, trans. George Schwab (Chicago: University of Chicago Press, 2005), 46–48; Schmitt, *Die Hüter der Verfassung* (Tübingen: Mohr, 1931), 75; Schmitt, *Legality and Legitimacy*, trans. Jeffrey Seitzer (Durham, NC: Duke University Press, 2004), 8–9, 17–26.

6. Schmitt, *Roman Catholicism and Political Form*, trans. Guy Oakes (Cambridge, MA: MIT Press, 1986), 16.

7. Carl Schmitt, *Politische Romantik*, 3rd ed. (Berlin: Duncker & Humblot, 1968), 81n1. ("Die Staatsphilosophie des Spinoza ist zu sehr von dem rationalistischen Naturrechts ihres zeitlichen Milieus und von Machiavelli beeinflusst, als dass sie ein typischer und konsequenter Ausdruck seiner emanatistischen Philosophie sein könnte[.]")

8. On Schmitt and Spinoza, see chapter 4.

9. Schmitt, "Age of Neutralizations and Depoliticizations," 94.

10. "If one wishes a sect or a republic to live long, it is necessary to draw it back often toward its beginning" (3.1). See Niccolò Machiavelli, *Discourses on Livy*,

trans. Harvey Mansfield and Nathan Tarcov (Chicago: University of Chicago Press, 1996), 209.

11. Schmitt, *Die Hüter*, III.

12. Virgil, *Eclogues, Georgics, Aeneid*, trans. H. Rushton Fairclough (Cambridge, MA: Harvard University Press, 1917) [1.563–64].

13. Niccolò Machiavelli, *The Prince*, trans. Angelo Codevilla (New Haven: Yale University Press, 1997), 61–64.

14. Carl Schmitt, "Machiavelli," *Kölnische Volkszeitung*, June 21, 1927, reprinted in *Staat, Grossraum, Nomos: Arbeiten aus den Jahren 1916–1969*, ed. Günther Maschke (Berlin: Duncker & Humblot, 1995), 102–5.

15. For a discussion of the literature on Nietzsche and Schmitt, see Galli, *Genealogia della politica: Carl Schmitt e la crisi del pensiero politico moderno*, 2nd ed. (Bologna: Il Mulino, 2010), 123–30, 156–61. Carlo Galli, "Nichilismi a confronto: Nietzsche e Schmitt," *Filosofia politica* 1 (2014), 99–119. See also Emanuele Castrucci, "Genealogia della potenza costituente: Schmitt, Nietzsche, Spinoza," *Filosofia Politica* 2 (1999), 245–51.

16. Schmitt, "Machiavelli," 102–5; compare Machiavelli, *The Prince*, 66.

17. Schmitt, *Constitutional Theory*, trans. Jeffrey Seitzer (Durham, NC: Duke University Press, 2008), 255.

18. Schmitt, *Constitutional Theory*, 237.

19. Schmitt, *Constitutional Theory*, 313.

20. See, in general, Schmitt, *Concept of the Political*.

21. Schmitt, *Concept of the Political*, 61.

22. Schmitt, *Concept of the Political*, 59.

23. Schmitt, *Concept of the Political*, 65. This is an implicit reference to chapter 21 of *The Prince*, in which Machiavelli deems it necessary that the prince be "either a true friend or a downright enemy." It also could be a reference to Machiavelli's "Words to Be Spoken on the Law for Appropriating Money, after Giving a Little Introduction and Excuse," in *Machiavelli: The Chief Works and Others*, trans. Allan Gilbert (Durham, NC: Duke University Press, 1989), 1439–43. In this little text, politics appears to be determined by the actual possibility of a mortal enemy.

24. Schmitt, *Concept of the Political*, 66. Schmitt's thesis that Machiavelli was not Machiavellian was also put forward in the 1927 article and returns in Schmitt, *Glossarium: Aufzeichnungen der Jahre 1947–1951* (Berlin: Duncker & Humblot, 1991), 81, 256–57; Carl Schmitt, "Trecento anni di Leviatano" (1951), in *Scritti su Thomas Hobbes*, ed. Carlo Galli (Milan: Giuffré, 1986), 148; and Carl Schmitt, *Dialogo sul potere* (Genova: Il melangolo, 1990), 49.

25. Galli, *Genealogia*, 807.

26. Carlo Galli, "Carl Schmitt nella cultura italiana (1924–1978): Storia, bilancio, prospettive di una presenza problematica," *Materiali per una storia della cultura giuridica* 9:1 (1979), 81–160.

27. See the summary, drawn up by Schmitt himself, of the conference he held

on April 16, 1936, at the Casa di Goethe in Rome (*Lo Stato* 4 [1936], 193–96). See also Carl Schmitt, "Machiavelli," 102–5.

28. See, on this point, chapter 4, note 31.

29. Carl Schmitt, *The Leviathan in the State Theory of Thomas Hobbes: Meaning and Failure of a Political Symbol* (1938), trans. George Schwab and Erna Hilfstein (Westport, CT: Greenwood Press, 1996), 50.

30. Schmitt, *Leviathan in the State Theory of Thomas Hobbes*, 84.

31. Schmitt used this expression referring to Tocqueville. See Carl Schmitt, *Ex Captivitate Salus: Erfahrungen der Zeit 1945/47* (Köln: Greven Verlag, 1950), 27–35. He would use it again later in a February 9, 1967, letter to Armin Mohler. See *Carl Schmitt—Briefwechsel mit einem seiner Schüler*, ed. Armin Mohler (Berlin: Akademie Verlag, 1995), 380.

32. Schmitt, *Leviathan in the State Theory of Thomas Hobbes*, 84.

33. ["San Casciano" was the location where Machiavelli retired after having been expelled from the Florentine political scene as a suspect of a plot to overturn the cardinal Giovanni de' Medici in 1513. Machiavelli referred to his country residence by the name "Albergaccio."—Trans.]

34. See Schmitt's letter to Jünger of March 26, 1974, in which he would identify himself for the first time with the name "San Casciano." See also Schmitt's letters of April 18 and June 6, 1956, in which he would explain this key identification. See Carl Schmitt and Ernst Jünger, *Briefe, 1930–1983*, ed. Helmuth Kiesel (Stuttgart: Klett-Cotta, 1999), 298, 302–4, 305–6. Schmitt refers to "the analogy with Machiavelli's refuge in San Casciano" in his May 12, 1956, letter to Alexander Kojève. See "Alexander Kojève–Carl Schmitt Correspondence," ed. and trans. Erik de Vries, *Interpretation* 29:1 (fall 2001), 111.

35. See Schmitt's letter to Jünger of August 4, 1974, in Schmitt and Jünger, *Briefe, 1930–1983*, 402–3. See also Schmitt's 1982 interview with Fulco Lanchester, in *Un giurista davanti a se stesso: Saggi e interviste*, ed. Giorgio Agamben (Vicenza: Nera Pozza, 2005), 151–83. Also of note is Andreas Koenen, *Der Fall Carl Schmitt: Sein Aufstieg zum "Kronjuristen des Dritten Reiches"* (Darmstadt: Wissenschaftliche Buchgesellschaft, 1995), 19. Regarding his "disciples," Schmitt is probably referring here to Waldemar Gurian, a Catholic émigré who from exile wrote numerous critical pieces against his former teacher, arguing that Schmitt sold himself to the regime. Exponents of the Nazi regime used Gurian's pieces against Schmitt.

36. On Benito Cereno, see Schmitt, *Ex Captivitate Salus*, 24, 78. See also the entry of December 18, 1941, in Ernst Jünger, *Irradiazioni: Diario 1941–1945* (Parma: Guanda, 1995), 44. On Epimetheus, see Schmitt, *Ex Captivitate Salus*, 55 (with reference to the poet Konrad Weiss and his 1933 *Der christliche Epimetheus*).

37. See Schmitt's note of November 12, 1947 (*Glossarium*, 39). The issue of liberalism as moralistic and individualistic criticism of the *Leviathan* is also in Schmitt, *Leviathan in the State Theory of Thomas Hobbes*, 36.

38. See Schmitt's note of November 24, 1947 (*Glossarium*, 49). Also of interest

is the extemporaneous note of May 6, 1948 (*Glossarium*, 146), where Schmitt refers to Machiavelli's *Discourses on Livy*, 2.26 (191–93), in which the Florentine maintains that it is not possible to weaken the enemy with words. Note also Schmitt's *Gespräch über die Macht und den Zugang zum Machthaber* (Pfullingen: G. Neske, 1954), where he construes the same problem in a Hobbesian light.

39. There is no mention of Machiavelli in Schmitt's *Nomos of the Earth* (1950), *Die Geschichtliche Struktur des heutigen Weltgegensatzes von Ost und West* (1955), *Hamlet or Hecuba: The Intrusion of the Time into the Play* (1956), trans. David Pan and Jennifer R. Rust (New York: Telos Press, 2009), or *Tyranny of Values* (1960), trans. Simona Draghici (Washington, DC: Plutarch Press, 1996). In 1963, Schmitt mentions Machiavelli briefly in his polemic on the theory of war between Clausewitz and Fichte. See Carl Schmitt, *Theory of the Partisan: Intermediate Commentary on the Concept of the Political*, trans. Gary L. Ulmen (New York: Telos Press, 2007), 45.

40. Wilhelm Dilthey, *Gesammelte Schriften*, bk. 2, *Weltanschauung und Analyse des Menschen seit Renaissance und Reformation* (Leipzig: Teubner, 1923), 31. Schmitt cites this text without complete agreement in *Concept of the Political*, 59.

41. Friedrich Meinecke, *Die Idee der Staatsräson in der neueren Geschichte* (München and Berlin: R. Oldenbourg, 1924). See Carl Schmitt, "Zu Friedrich Meinecke Idee der Staatsräson" (1926), in *Positionen und Begriffe: im Kampf mit Weimar, Genf, Versailles (1923–1939)* (Berlin: Duncker & Humblot, 1988), 45–51.

42. Gerhard Ritter, *The Corrupting Influence of Power*, trans. F. W. Pick (Hadleigh, Essex: Tower Bridge Publications, 1952). See also Carlo Galli, "Il volto demoniaco del potere? Alcuni momenti e problemi della fortuna continentale di Machiavelli," in *Contingenza e necessità nella ragione politica moderna* (Rome-Bari: Laterza, 2009), 5–37.

43. On Schmitt and Machiavelli, see also Galli, *Genealogia*, esp. 270–71, 577, 772.

44. On this point, see Galli, *Political Spaces and Global War*, trans. Elisabeth Fay, ed. Adam Sitze (Minneapolis: University of Minnesota Press, 2010), 38–41.

45. See Galli, *Genealogia*, 333–459; see also chapter 2 here.

46. See, in general, Schmitt, *The Crisis of Parliamentary Democracy*.

47. For Schmitt, Machiavelli is alternative to, and not just prior to, modern rationalism, a thesis that emerges because Schmitt suspects his similarity to Spinoza—although for bad reasons.

Chapter 4. Schmitt, Strauss, and Spinoza

1. See, generally, Carl Schmitt, *The Leviathan in the State Theory of Thomas Hobbes: Meaning and Failure of a Political Symbol*, trans. George Schwab and Erna Hilfstein (Westport, CT: Greenwood Press, 1996).

2. Leo Strauss, *The Political Philosophy of Hobbes: Its Basis and Its Genesis*, trans. Elsa Sinclair (Chicago: University of Chicago Press, 1996); Leo Strauss, "On the Basis

of Hobbes' Political Philosophy," in *What Is Political Philosophy?* (Glencoe, Ill.: Free Press, 1959), 170–96. On Strauss's interpretation of Hobbes's thought, in addition to the works quoted in the previous note, see Carlo Galli, *Modernità: Categorie e profili critici* (Bologna: Il Mulino, 1988), 227–36.

3. On Nietzsche, see Leo Strauss, "Jerusalem and Athens: Some Preliminary Reflections," in *Studies in Platonic Political Philosophy* (Chicago: University of Chicago Press, 1985), 147–73; and Leo Strauss, *Natural Right and History* (Chicago: University of Chicago Press, 1953), 26, 195–96, 252–53.

4. Leo Strauss, "Notes on Carl Schmitt, *The Concept of the Political*," in Schmitt, *The Concept of the Political*, trans. J. Harvey Lomax (Chicago: University of Chicago Press, 2007), 81–108. On this work, see Galli, *Genealogia della politica: Carl Schmitt e la crisi del pensiero politico moderno*, 2nd ed. (Bologna: Il Mulino, 2010), 780–86; Heinrich Meier, *Carl Schmitt and Leo Strauss: The Hidden Dialogue*, trans. J. Harvey Lomax (Chicago: University of Chicago Press, 1995); Miguel Vatter, "Taking Exception to Liberalism: Heinrich Meier's *Carl Schmitt and Leo Strauss: The Hidden Dialogue*," *Graduate Faculty Philosophy Journal* 2 (1997), 1–22.

5. Riccardo Caporali has discussed the indeterminate and enigmatic character of Strauss's relationship with Spinoza. See Riccardo Caporali, "Postfazione," in Leo Strauss, *La critica della religione in Spinoza* (Rome-Bari: Laterza, 2003), 265–66.

6. See, generally, Leo Strauss, *Spinoza's Critique of Religion*, trans. E. M. Sinclair (New York: Schocken Books: 1965). For an overview on Strauss as a reader of Spinoza, see Caporali, "Postfazione." Of special importance are Carlo Altini, *Leo Strauss: Linguaggio del potere e linguaggio della filosofia* (Bologna: Il Mulino, 2000), 40–53 and 219–26, and Carlo Altini, "Oltre il nichilismo: Ritorno all'ebraismo e crisi della modernità politica in Leo Strauss," in Leo Strauss, *Filosofia e Legge: Contributi per la comprensione di Maimonide e dei suoi predecessori*, ed. Carlo Altini (Firenze: Giuntina, 2003), 37–75; Stefano Visentin, "El profeta y la moltitud: Notas sobre Strauss, lector de Spinoza," *Res publica* 8 (2001), 127–48; Claudia Hilb, *Leo Strauss: El arte de leer: Una lectura de la interpretación straussiana de Maquiavela, Hobbes, Locke y Spinoza* (Buenos Aires: Fondo de Cultura Económica, 2005), 259–314. Finally, see also Heinrich Meier, *Leo Strauss and the Theological-Political Problem*, trans. Marcus Brainard (Cambridge: Cambridge University Press, 2006); and Mauro Farnesi Camellone, *Giustizia e storia: Saggio su Leo Strauss* (Milan: Franco Angeli: 2007), 67–88.

7. Caporali, "Postfazione," 283–84.

8. See, generally, Caporali, "Postfazione." See also Camellone, *Giustizia e storia*, 75.

9. Leo Strauss, "How to Study Spinoza's Theologico-Political Treatise," in *Persecution and the Art of Writing* (Glencoe, Ill.: Free Press, 1952), 142–201; Leo Strauss, "Preface to the English Translation," in *Spinoza's Critique of Religion*, trans. E. M. Sinclair (Chicago: University of Chicago Press, 1997), 1–31.

10. Strauss, "How to Study Spinoza's Theologico-Political Treatise," 143–44.

11. Strauss, "How to Study Spinoza's Theologico-Political Treatise," 184–93.

12. Strauss, "How to Study Spinoza's Theologico-Political Treatise," 163, 190–91.

13. Strauss, "Preface," 16.

14. Strauss, "Preface," 18.

15. Strauss, "Preface," 18–21.

16. Strauss, "Preface," 29–30.

17. See, generally, Leo Strauss, *Philosophy and Law: Contributions to the Understanding of Maimonides and His Predecessors*, trans. Eve Adler (Albany: State University of New York Press, 1995). See also Leo Strauss, *The Argument and the Action of Plato's Laws* (Chicago: University of Chicago Press, 1975).

18. In the sense that the primacy of philosophy is, according to Strauss, a logical a priori. See, on this point, Shadia Drury, "The Esoteric Philosophy of Leo Strauss," *Political Theory* 3 (1985), 315–35.

19. On June 23, 1935, Strauss wrote to Löwith, "By the way: I am not an orthodox Jew!" See "Karl Löwith and Leo Strauss: Correspondence," *Independent Journal of Philosophy* 5/6 (1988), 183.

20. Aside from Miguel Vatter ("Strauss and Schmitt as Readers of Hobbes and Spinoza : On the Relation between Political Theology and Liberalism," *CR: The New Centennial Review* 4:3 [Winter 2004], 161–214), see Manfred Walther, "Carl Schmitt et Baruch Spinoza, ou les aventures du concept du politique," in *Spinoza au XXe siècle*, ed. Olivier Bloch (Paris: Presses universitaires de France, 1992), 361–74 (in the face of a liberal and democratic Spinoza, where the main lines of the Modern entwine, stands a Schmitt regarded as a Thomist and natural law philosopher); Thomas Heerich and Manfred Lauermann, "Der Gegensatz Hobbes-Spinoza bei Carl Schmitt (1938)," *Studia Spinozana* 7 (1991), 97–160 (arguing that while Hobbes thinks the logic of the "political," Spinoza—with his circularity between *potentia* and *potestas*—thinks the logic of the social, which is why he is criticized by Schmitt); Emanuele Castrucci, "Genealogia della potenza costituente: Schmitt, Nietzsche, Spinoza," *Filosofia politica* 2 (1999), 245–51.

21. On the difference between the theoretical and the political aspects of Spinoza's atheist pantheistic rationalism, see Carl Schmitt, *Political Romanticism*, trans. Guy Oakes (Cambridge, MA: MIT Press, 1986), 54–55; for Spinoza's relations to Malebranche and Schelling, see Schmitt, *Political Romanticism*, 95–96, 113.

22. Carl Schmitt, *Dictatorship*, trans. Michael Hoelzl and Graham Ward (Cambridge, MA: Polity Press, 2010), 99 (on the difference between Spinoza, who nullifies the individual, the Universe is everything, and Hobbes, for whom the State is everything), 123 (on the similarity of Spinoza and Sieyès).

23. Carl Schmitt, *Constitutional Theory*, trans. Jeffrey Seitzer (Durham, NC: Duke University Press, 2008), 128.

24. Carl Schmitt, "The Age of Neutralizations and Depoliticizations" (1929), trans. Matthias Konzen and John P. McCormick, in Schmitt, *Concept of the Political*, 83.

25. Schmitt, *Concept of the Political*, 59.

26. Schmitt, *Leviathan*, 57–58. The reprinted edition of 1982, which was edited for Hohenheim Verlag (Köln-Lövenich) by Günther Maschke while Schmitt was still alive, is identical to the 1938 original—up to and including its anti-Semitic passages.

27. Schmitt, *Leviathan*, 10–11. It should be noted that it was thanks to Schmitt's support that in 1932 Strauss was able to obtain a scholarship from the Rockefeller Foundation for a project on Hobbes and was thus able to get out of Germany. See, on this point, Altini, *Leo Strauss: Linguaggio del potere e linguaggio della filosofia*, 15.

28. Schmitt, *Leviathan*, 57–58.

29. On Hobbes's "crystal," see chapter 1, note 13.

30. Schmitt, *Leviathan*, 57–63, 69–72.

31. See, generally, Raphael Gross, *Carl Schmitt and the Jews: The "Jewish Question," the Holocaust, and German Legal Theory* (Madison: University of Wisconsin Press, 2007). Gross argues that anti-Semitic polemics accompany the works of Schmitt all along, assuming the form of the oppositions between concreteness and rooting on the one hand and between formal and legalistic universalism, on the other hand. Only during the Nazi era did this polemic take on a specifically "biological" significance.

32. On this event, see Joseph W. Bendersky, *Carl Schmitt: Theorist for the Reich* (Princeton, NJ: Princeton University Press, 1983); Andreas Koenen, *Der Fall Carl Schmitt: Sein Aufstieg zum "Kronjuristen des Dritten Reiches"* (Darmstadt: Wissenschaftliche Buchgesellschaft, 1995); Gross, *Carl Schmitt and the Jews*, 29–30, 68–76; David Cumin, *Carl Schmitt: Biographie politique et intellectuelle* (Paris: Les Éditions du Cerf, 2005), 135–81 (for an in-depth study). For a discussion of the secondary literature and the different interpretations, see Galli, *Genealogia*, 890–96.

33. See "Interrogation of Carl Schmitt by Robert Kempner," *Telos* 72 (summer 1987), 97–129; and "The 'Fourth' (Second) Interrogation of Carl Schmitt at Nuremberg," *Telos* 139 (2007), 35–43. For Schmitt's quotation of Macrobius's dictum "non possum scribere in eum qui potest proscribere" [It's not easy to write against someone who has the power to "write you up"]; his attempt to identify his position with that of an internal emigré; and his comparison between his own experience as a European jurist and the figure of Benito Cereno, see Carl Schmitt, *Ex Captivitate Salus: Erfahrungen der Zeit 1945/47* (Köln: Grevern Verlag, 1950), 21.

34. Schmitt, *Glossarium: Aufzeichnungen der Jahre 1947–1951* (Berlin: Duncker & Humblot, 1991), 18 (entry of September 26, 1947).

35. Carl Schmitt, *On the Three Types of Juristic Thought*, trans. Joseph Bendersky (Westport, CT: Praeger Publishers, 2004), 43–71.

36. Carl Schmitt, "Die deutsche Rechtswissenschaft im Kampf gegen den jüdischen Geist," *Deutsche Juristen-Zeitung* 41 (1936), 1193–99.

37. Yves Charles Zarka, *Un dettaglio nazi nel pensiero di Carl Schmitt* (Genova: Il Melangolo, 2005), where the thesis of the "detail" is turned into a complete nazi-

fication of Schmitt and his "homicidal ideas." For a more balanced account, see Antonino Scalone, *Carl Schmitt e il nazismo: Sviluppi recenti della ricezione schmittiana in Francia* (2008), http://eprints.sifp.it/46/ (accessed March 23, 2014). See also the polemical but informed Alain de Benoist, "Carl Schmitt e la nuova caccia alle streghe," *Trasgressioni* 45 (2007), 85–112.

38. Gross, *Carl Schmitt and the Jews*, 15–76.

39. Reinhart Koselleck, *Critique and Crisis: Enlightenment and the Pathogenesis of Modern Society* (Cambridge, MA: MIT Press, 1988). On this see Vatter's very good contribution ("Strauss and Schmitt"). Vatter, to whom I owe the note about the *Atheismusstreit*, criticizes Schmitt for his completely individualistic reading of Spinoza and for his resulting inability to see Spinoza at the origin of the Enlightenment and Kantian public use of reason.

40. Schmitt, *Glossarium*, 290 (entry of January 12, 1950). For other expressions of anti-Semitism see also *Glossarium*, 17–18 (entry of September 25, 1947).

41. Schmitt, *Glossarium*, 41 (entry of November 15, 1947).

42. Schmitt, *Glossarium*, 39 (entry of November 12, 1947).

43. See Schmitt, *Leviathan*, 32.

44. Schmitt, *Glossarium*, 275 (entry of October 10, 1949).

45. For further reference see André Tosel, *Spinoza, ou le crépuscule de la servitude: Essai sur le Traité Théologico-Politique* (Paris: Aubier Montaigne, 1984); Paolo Cristofolini, *La scienza intuitiva di Spinoza* (Naples: Morano, 1987); Antonio Negri, *Spinoza* (Rome: DeriveApprodi, 1998); Riccardo Caporali, *La fabbrica dell'imperium: Saggio su Spinoza* (Naples: Liguori, 2000); Stefano Visentin, *La libertà necessaria: Teoria e pratica della democrazia in Spinoza* (Pisa: ETS, 2001); Lucia Nocentini, *Il luogo della politica: Saggio su Spinoza* (Pisa: ETS, 2001); Étienne Balibar, *Spinoza: From Individuality to Transindividuality* (Milan: Ghibli, 2002); Roberto Ciccarelli, *Potenza e beatitudine: Il diritto nel pensiero di Baruch Spinoza* (Rome: Carocci, 2003); Filippo Del Lucchese, *Conflict, Power, and Multitude in Machiavelli and Spinoza: Tumult and Indignation* (New York: Continuum, 2009).

46. Carl Schmitt, "The Legal World Revolution," trans. G. L. Ulmen, *Telos* 72 (summer 1987), 87.

47. Galli, *Genealogia*, 333–459; see also chapter 2 here. For an interpretation of political theology as original sin, see Heinrich Meier, *The Lesson of Carl Schmitt: Four Chapters on the Distinction between Political Theology and Political Philosophy*, trans. Marcus Brainard (Chicago: University of Chicago Press, 1998).

48. On its logical and theoretical difficulty, see Roberto Esposito, "Introduzione," in Leo Strauss, *Gerusalemme e Atene: Studi sul pensiero politico dell'Occidente* (Turin: Einaudi, 1998), VII–XLIV.

49. For a polemic against Meier, see Jianhong Chen, "What Is Carl Schmitt's Political Theology?," *Interpretation* 2 (2006), 153–75. Chen argues that political theology—understood as a method and not as an authoritarian acceptance of revelation—constitutes Schmitt's specific political philosophy, which differs from

Strauss's (and on this point Chen is in agreement with Meier). Also see Vatter's pertinent observations in "Taking Exception to Liberalism."

50. Max Weber, "Science as a Vocation," trans. H. H. Gerth and C. Wright Mills, in *From Max Weber: Essays in Sociology*, ed. H. H. Gerth and C. Wright Mills (New York: Oxford University Press, 1946), 129–56.

51. See, generally, Strauss, *Natural Right and History*.

52. Strauss, "On the Basis of Hobbes' Political Philosophy," 16.

53. See, generally, Leo Strauss, *Thoughts on Machiavelli* (Seattle: University of Washington Press, 1958), and Strauss, "Machiavelli," in *History of Political Philosophy*, 3rd ed., ed. Leo Strauss and Joseph Cropsey (Chicago: University of Chicago, 1987), 311 (for Strauss's displacement of Spinoza's *Deus sive natura* [God or Nature] with the formula *Deus sive fortuna*, which Strauss says could express Machiavelli's theology).

Chapter 5. Schmitt and the Global Era

1. Schmitt, *The Nomos of the Earth in the International Law of the Jus Publicum Europæum*, trans. Gary Ulmen (New York: Telos Press, 2003). This topic was covered in the various presentations at the panel "The International Political Thought of Carl Schmitt," section 11 of the Fifth Pan-European International Relation Conference on Constructing World Orders, The Hague, September 11–14, 2004. See also Louiza Odysseos and Fabio Petito, eds., *The International Political Thought of Carl Schmitt* (London: Routledge, 2007).

2. For the bibliography on this, see chapter 2 here.

3. For the bibliography on this, see chapter 1 here.

4. On this point, see chapter 1 here.

5. This was published as a book the following year. See Carl Schmitt, "Die Kernfrage des Völkerbundes," in *Frieden oder Pazifismus?: Arbeiten zum Völkerrecht und zur internationalen Politik 1924–1978*, ed. Günter Maschke (Berlin: Duncker & Humblot, 2005), 73–128. Many of Schmitt's essays dealing with internationalism appear in this collection, as well as in *Staat, Grossraum, Nomos: Arbeiten aus den Jahren 1916–1969*, ed. Günter Maschke (Berlin: Duncker & Humblot, 1995).

6. See, generally, Carl Schmitt, *The Leviathan in the State Theory of Thomas Hobbes: Meaning and Failure of a Political Symbol* (1938), trans. George Schwab and Erna Hilfstein (Westport, CT: Greenwood Press, 1996); Carl Schmitt, *Il concetto d'impero nel diritto internazionale Ordinamento dei grandi spazi con esclusione delle potenze estranee*, ed. L. Vanutelli Rey (Rome: Istituto nazionale di cultura fascista, 1941); Carl Schmitt, *Land and Sea* (1942), trans. Simona Draghici (Washington, DC: Plutarch Press, 1997); Carl Schmitt, *Nomos of the Earth* (1950); Carl Schmitt, "La unità del mondo" (1951), in *L'unità del mondo e altri saggi*, ed. Alessandro Campi (Rome: Pellicani, 1994), 303–21; Carl Schmitt, "La contrapposizione planetaria tra Oriente e Occidente" (1955), in Ernst Jünger and Carl Schmitt, *Il nodo di Giordio: Dialogo su Oriente*

e Occidente nella storia del mondo (Bologna: Il Mulino, 1987¹), 135–67; Carl Schmitt, "L'ordinamento planetario dopo la seconda guerra mondiale" (1962), in *L'unità del mondo e altri saggi*, 321–44; Carl Schmitt, *The Theory of the Partisan: Intermediate Commentary on the Concept of the Political* (1963), trans. Gary L. Ulmen (New York: Telos Press, 2007); Carl Schmitt, "The Legal World Revolution" (1978), trans. G. L. Ulmen, *Telos* 72 (summer 1978), 73–89. On Schmitt's work on international politics, see Carlo Galli, *Genealogia della politica: Carl Schmitt e la crisi del pensiero politico moderno*, 2nd ed. (Bologna: Il Mulino, 2010), 864–89. See also Alessandro Colombo, "L'Europa e la società internazionale: Gli aspetti culturali e istituzionali della convivenza internazionale in Raymond Aron, "Martin Wight e Carl Schmitt," *Quaderni di scienza politica* 6:2 (1999), 251–301; Caterina Resta, *Stato mondiale o "nomos" della Terra: Carl Schmitt tra universo e pluriverso* (Rome: Pellicani, 1999); Felix Blindow, *Carl Schmitts Reichsordnung: Strategie für einen europäischen Grossraum* (Berlin: Akademie, 1999); Günter Maschke, "La unificación de Europa y la teoria del gran espacio," *Carl Schmitt Studien* 1 (2000), 75–85; Nicola Casanova, "*Justissima Tellus*": *Figure dello spazio nel pensiero di Carl Schmitt* (Firenze: Forum per i problemi della pace e della guerra, 2001); Franco Volpi, "Il potere degli elementi," in Schmitt, *Terra e mare: Una riflessione sulla storia del mondo* (Milan: Giuffrè, 1986), 113–49; Alessandro Campi, "Introduzione alla nuova edizione," in Carl Schmitt, *L'unità del mondo e altri saggi* (Rome: Pellicani, 1994), 9–37; Jan-Werner Müller, "Visioni di un ordine globale nell' 'età post-europea'": Carl Schmitt, Raymond Aron e il funzionario dello Spirito del mondo," *Ricerche di storia politica* 2 (2004), 205–26 (reprinted as chapter 6 of *A Dangerous Mind: Carl Schmitt in Post-War European Thought* [New Haven: Yale University Press, 2003], 87–103); Jean-François Kervégan, "Carl Schmitt et 'l'unité du monde,'" *Les Études Philosophiques* 1 (2004), 2–23; Thalin Zarmanian, "Carl Schmitt and the Problem of the Legal Order: From Domestic to International," *Leiden Journal of International Law* 19:1 (2006), 41–67.

7. Schmitt, *Nomos of the Earth*, 86–100.

8. Both in the case of traditional or of a more modern theology. See, for example, Francisco de Vitoria, "De jure belli" (1539), in *De Indis et de jure belli relectiones*, ed. Ernest Nys (Washington, DC: Carnegie Institution of Washington, 1917), 163–87. Compare Schmitt, *Nomos of the Earth*, 101–25.

9. Schmitt, *Nomos of the Earth*, 152–71.

10. Carl Schmitt, "Il concetto di pirateria" (1937), in *Posizioni e concetti: In lotta con Weimar-Ginevra-Versailles: 1923–1939* (Milan: Giuffrè, 2007), 399–404.

11. [These are the dates Schmitt assigns to the beginning and end of the jus publicum Europæum, starting from the treaties of Nymwegen and Utrecht and ending with World War I. See Schmitt, *Nomos of the Earth*, 184.—Ed.]

12. Schmitt, *Land and Sea*, 46–49.

13. Schmitt, *Nomos of the Earth*, 140–213 (pt. 3).

14. For a definition of *nomos* as "spatial ordering" (even if "oriented" renders *Ortung* better), see Schmitt, *Nomos of the Earth*, 71. On the one hand, Schmitt argues

that the concept of *Gesetz* (law) is of Judaic origin, and is opposed to the concept of *nomos* (orientation and ordering), which he says is of Greek-German origin. On the other hand, Schmitt argues against right-wing authors of the Weimar era, such as Wilhelm Stapel and Hans Bogner (to whom one could add Albrecht Erich Günther), who mingled the term *nomos*, which they introduced in political debate, with *Gesetz*, giving *nomos* a biological accent that Schmitt refused. Schmitt's debt to the Protestant right in this area is underlined in Raphael Gross, *Carl Schmitt and the Jews: The "Jewish Question," the Holocaust, and German Legal Theory* (Madison: University of Wisconsin Press, 2007).

15. Schmitt, *Nomos of the Earth*, 168–71. Compare Fabio Vander, "Kant and Schmitt on Preemptive War," *Telos* 125 (fall 2002), 152–66.

16. Schmitt, *Nomos of the Earth*, 227.

17. See Carl Schmitt, "Forms of Modern Imperialism in International Law," trans. Matthew Hannah, in *Spatiality, Sovereignty and Carl Schmitt: Geographies of the Nomos*, ed. Stephen Legg (New York: Routledge, 2011), 29–45; Schmitt, "Cambio di struttura del diritto internazionale" (1943), in *L'unità del mondo*, 177–95. The latter is an important text in which there is already the definition of *nomos*, and which analyzes the transition from a Eurocentric to an Americocentric international law. Schmitt gives further attention to the topic of the Western Hemisphere in "La lotta per i grandi spazi e l'illusione americana" (1942), in *L'unità del mondo*, 171–76. In this text, Schmitt gives the *katechon* a negative value, construing it as the factor of delay of the transition from the Modern to the imperial spatiality of Great Spaces.

18. See, generally, Schmitt, "Forms of Modern Imperialism in International Law."

19. Schmitt, "Il concetto d'Impero," 71–92.

20. See, generally, Schmitt, "Forms of Modern Imperialism in International Law."

21. Schmitt, "Il concetto d'Impero," 80.

22. Carl Schmitt, "Totaler Feind, totaler Krieg, totaler Staat" (1937), in *Frieden oder Pazifismus?*, 481–507.

23. Carl Schmitt, "Stato totalitario e neutralità internationazionale" (1938), in *L'unità del mondo*, 119–24.

24. The concept of Great Space remains political and not geographical, even though Schmitt did consider Karl Haushofer's concept of geopolitics during these years. On this see Mario G. Losano, "La geopolitica nazionalsocialista e il diritto internazionale dei 'Grandi Spazi,'" *Materiali per una storia della cultura giuridica* 35:1 (2005), 5–64.

25. Galli, *Genealogia*, 896–97n17.

26. Gabriella Silvestrini, "Diritto naturale e diritto di uccidere: Teorie moderne della guerra fra modelli teorici e tradizioni di pensiero," *Filosofia politica* 21:3 (2007), 425–52. On revolution, within an argument less remote from Schmitt, see

Eugenio Di Rienzo, *Il diritto delle armi: Guerra e politica nell'Europa moderna* (Milan: Angeli, 2005).

27. Danilo Zolo, *Chi dice umanità: Guerra, diritto e ordine globale* (Turin: Einaudi, 2000), 111–17.

28. See Schmitt, *Glossarium*, 179 (entry of July 16, 1948).

29. Schmitt, "Legal World Revolution," 79.

30. See Schmitt, "Premessa" (1963), in *Il concetto di "politico,"* 99.

31. Schmitt, *La contrapposizione planetaria tra Oriente e Occidente.*

32. Schmitt, "Il concetto imperiale di spazio," in *L'unità del mondo*, 203 [my translation.—Trans.]

33. Schmitt, *La contrapposizione planetaria tra Oriente e Occidente*, 135.

34. Schmitt, *Political Theology II*, 122.

35. Schmitt, *L'ordinamento planetario*, 220–21.

36. Schmitt, *L'ordinamento planetario*, 213.

37. See, in general, Schmitt, "Legal World Revolution."

38. Schmitt, *L'unità del mondo*, 200.

39. Schmitt, *L'unità del mondo*, 200. The German text is not different from the Spanish one, on which the Italian translation is based. See Carl Schmitt, "Die Einheit der Welt," in *Frieden oder Pazifismus?*, 841–52 (esp. 843 together with the editor's notes on 852–71). Schmitt employs the distinction between friend and enemy as a mere description of conflict, even when it becomes absolutely opaque. See Schmitt, "Premessa all'edizione italiana," in *Categorie del "politico,"* 21–26, esp. 25.

40. See Schmitt, "Premessa all'edizione italiana," 25.

41. Schmitt, *L'unità del mondo*, 200.

42. Schmitt, *L'unità del mondo*, 205–8. The citation is from Schmitt, "Tre possibilità di una immagine Cristiana della storia" (1950), in *Un giurista davanti a stesso: saggi e interviste*, ed. Giorgio Agamben (Vicenza: Neri Pozza, 2005), 24–25 (a review of Karl Löwith's 1949 book *Meaning in History*).

43. Schmitt, *L'unità del mondo*, 201.

44. Schmitt, *L'ordinamento planetario*, 221.

45. François Perroux, *La coesistenza pacifica* (Turin: Einaudi, 1961).

46. Schmitt, "Appropriation/Distribution/Production: An Attempt to Determine from Nomos the Basic Questions of Every Social and Economic Order," in *Nomos of the Earth*, 324–35.

47. Schmitt, *L'ordinamento planetario*, 218.

48. Schmitt, *Theory of the Partisan*, 14–22, 40–48. Taking his point of departure from this book, Alberto Moreiras problematizes Schmitt's entire system of thought. In particular, Moreiras considers the ambiguity of the notion of political theology, the oscillation of the relationship between friend and enemy between determination and indeterminacy, and the possibility of framing the partisan in terms of terrorism. Based on these considerations, Moreiras concludes with a ref-

erence to Derrida's thought regarding the overcoming of the logic of the sovereignty (toward a "messianicity" without messianism and political theology). See Alberto Moreiras, "A God without Sovereignty: Political Jouissance: The Passive Decision," CR: The New Centennial Review 4.3 (2005), 71–108.

49. Schmitt, Theory of the Partisan, 71.

50. Schmitt, Theory of the Partisan, 25–28, 70–71, 91.

51. Schmitt, Theory of the Partisan, 59–61.

52. Schmitt, Theory of the Partisan, 28, 49–53, 74–76.

53. Schmitt, Theory of the Partisan, 77–79.

54. Schmitt, The Tyranny of Values, trans. Simona Draghici (Washington, DC: Plutarch Press, 1996).

55. Schmitt, Theory of the Partisan, 91, emphasis in original.

56. Schmitt, Theory of the Partisan, 79–80.

57. See I prossimi Titani: Conversazioni con Ernst Jünger, ed. Antonio Gnoli and Franco Volpi (Milan: Adelphi, 1997), 66–67; Ernst Jünger, Der Weltstaat: Organismus und Organisation (Stuttgart: E. Klett, 1960).

58. On the "universal homogeneous State," see Alexandre Kojève, Outline of a Phenomenology of Right, trans. Bryan-Paul Frost and Robert Howse, ed. Bryan-Paul Frost (Lanham, Md.: Rowman and Littlefield, 2000). On this work, see Giorgio Barberis, Il regno della libertà?: Diritto, politica e storia nel pensiero di Alexandre Kojève (Naples: Liguori, 2003); and Maria Laura Lanzillo, "'Il cappello da cowboy di Molotov': La fine della storia e l'unificazione del mondo in Alexandre Kojève," in L'Occidente sull'Atlantico, ed. Maurizio Ricciardi (Soveria Mannelli: Rubbettino, 2006), 95–114. For Schmitt's correspondence with Kojève, see Alexandre Kojève and Carl Schmitt, "Correspondence," ed. and trans. Erik de Vries, Interpretation 29:1 (fall 2001), 91–114. On this exchange, see Carlo Altini, "La fine del mondo moderno: La crisi della politica nelle lettere di Carl Schmitt e Alexandre Kojève," Filosofia politica 17:2 (2003), 209–22. On Schmitt's relationship with Kojève, see also Galin Tihanov, "Regimes of Modernity at the Dawn of Globalisation: Carl Schmitt and Alexandre Kojève," in Other Modernisms in an Age of Globalization, ed. Djelal Kadir and Dorothea Löbbermann (Heidelberg: Universitätsverlag C. Winter, 2002), 75–93. See also Antonio Gnoli, "Postfazione" to Alexandre Kojève, Il silenzio della tirannide, trans. Antonio Gnoli (Milan: Adelphi, 2004), 253–67. On the end of history in relationship to the United States, see Alexandre Kojève, Introduction to the Reading of Hegel: Lectures on the Phenomenology of Spirit, assembled by Raymond Queneau, trans. James H. Nichols, Jr., ed. Allan Bloom (New York: Basic Books, 1969), 161. ("I was led to conclude from this that the 'American way of life' was the type of life specific to the posthistorical period, the actual presence of the United States in the World prefiguring the 'eternal present' future of all of humanity.") On empire and colonialism, see Alexandre Kojève, "L'Impero latino: Progetto di una dottrina della politica francese (27 agosto 1945)," in Il silenzio della tirannide, 163–210; Alexandre

Kojève, "Colonialism from a European Perspective," ed. and trans. Erik de Vries, *Interpretation* 29:1 (fall 2001), 115–30 (this was a conference talk that Kojève gave on Schmitt's invitation in Düsseldorf on January 16, 1957).

59. This argument is grounded in Carlo Galli, *Political Spaces and Global War*, trans. Elisabeth Fay, ed. Adam Sitze (Minneapolis: University of Minnesota Press, 2010); Carlo Galli, "La guerra globale: Continuità e discontinuità," *Iride* 40 (2003), 433–42; Carlo Galli, "Introduzione a Jünger e Schmitt," in *Il nodo di Gordio: Dialogo fra Oriente e Occidente nella storia del mondo* (Bologna: Il Mulino, 1987), 7–30. See also Alessandro Colombo, *La guerra ineguale: Pace e violenza nel tramonto della società internazionale* (Bologna: Il Mulino, 2006), and Saskia Sassen's extraordinary analyses in *Territory, Authority, Rights: From Medieval to Global Assemblages* (Princeton, NJ: Princeton University Press, 2006).

60. On this point, see Galli, *Political Spaces and Global War*, 113–17.

61. See above, chapter 2, note 77. See also Carlo Galli, "On War and on the Enemy," trans. Amanda Minervini and Adam Sitze, *New Centennial Review* 9:2 (2010), 195–219, esp. 214–17.

62. On the so-called enemy's criminal law see, for example, *Diritto politico e diritto penale del nemico*, ed. Alessandro Gamberini e Renzo Orlandi (Bologna: Monduzzi, 2007). See also, though not strictly limited to the question of terrorism, Lucia Re, *Carcere e globalizzazione: Il boom penitenziario negli Stati Uniti e in Europa* (Rome-Bari: Laterza, 2006).

63. See Jim Lobe and Adele Oliveri, eds., *I nuovi rivoluzionari: Il pensiero dei neoconservatori americani* (Milan: Feltrinelli, 2003); Mario Del Pero, *The Eccentric Realist: Henry Kissinger and the Shaping of American Foreign Policy* (Ithaca, NY: Cornell University Press, 2010); Alia Nardini, "La concezione della guerra secondo il movimento neoconservatore americano," in *La guerra tra morale e politica*, ed. Alia Nardini (Bologna: Bonomo, 2007), 233–78.

64. For the opposite argument, see Shadia Drury, *Leo Strauss and the American Right* (New York: St. Martin's Press, 1999), 94–95, and 178. Drury argues that neoconservatives derive from Strauss and that—since Strauss supposedly drew from Schmitt and his criticism of liberalism—Schmittian elements (such as hatred of pluralism, nationalism, religious foundation of politics, friend-enemy logic) would be present in neoconservatives as well. Drury's argument, though, appears much more ideological than structural, and much more analogic than conceptual.

65. For recent examples of the rich literature on the imperial dimension of the United States, see Vittorio Emanuele Parsi, "L'Impero come fato?: Gli Stati Uniti e l'ordine globale," *Filosofia politica* 1 (2002), 83–113; Herfried Münkler, *Empires: The Logic of World Domination from Ancient Rome to the United States*, trans. Patrick Camiller (Cambridge, MA: Polity Press, 2007), 146–61; and Alejandro Colás, *Empire* (Cambridge, MA: Polity Press, 2007), 158–91.

66. See Alberto Burgio, *Guerra: Scenari della nuova "grande trasformazione"* (Rome: DeriveApprodi, 2004).

67. I am referring to two (of many possible) circles in the most recent debates in international relations. For the first, see Ian Clark, *International Legitimacy and World Society* (Oxford: Oxford University Press, 2007); for the second, see Jan Zielonka, *Europe as Empire: The Nature of the Enlarged European Union* (Oxford: Oxford University Press, 2006).

68. For intellectual exchanges—apparently quite important—between Schmitt and Hans J. Morgenthau, one of the fathers of political realism, see William E. Scheuerman, *Carl Schmitt: The End of Law* (Lanham, Md.: Rowman and Littlefield, 1999), 225–51. See also Alessandro Campi, "Introduzione" to Hans J. Morgenthau, *L'uomo scientifico versus la politica di potenza: Un'introduzione al realismo politico* (1946), trans. Marcella Mancini (Rome: Ideazione, 2005), VII–XXII. Compare the critical and reductive considerations suggested by Joseph W. Bendersky, "The Definite and the Dubious: Carl Schmitt's Influence on Conservative Political and Legal Theory in the US," *Telos* 122 (2002), 33–47.

INDEX

....

Bonald, Louis de, 26, 60
Bossuet, Jacques-Bénigne, 60, 67

Cassian of Imola, 71
Catholicism: counterrevolutionary Catholicism, 26, 67; French reactionary Catholicism, 60; Galli's discussion of, xv, xxv–xxviii, xxxv–xxxvi; internal politics and, 99–103; interpretations and self-interpretations and, 50–57; Machiavelli and, 64–69; Nazism and, 23; political theology of Schmitt and, 34, 42–48; Schmitt's political theory and, 4, 71–73; state and role of, 1–3
Chen, Jianhong, 166n49
Cimmino, Luigi, 155n30
civilization, in global era, 126–28
class struggle, Schmitt's political theory and, 15
Clausewitz, Carl von, 115
Cohen, Hermann, 80, 83
Cold War: internationalist philosophy and, 117–20; Schmitt and, 111–17, 129–34
colonialism, Schmitt and, xxiii, xxvi–xxvii, 115, 119, 130–34
Communism, Schmitt's legacy and fall of, 31–32
complexio oppositorum: in Galli's discussion of Schmitt, xxiv–xxviii; in Schmitt's Roman Catholicism and Political Form, 100, 154n10
compulsions, Galli's discussion of, xxix
Concept of the Political, The (Schmitt), xix–xx, xxxiii, 2, 148n13; Machiavelli and, 65–69; political theology and, 11–12; Spinoza in, 86
concreteness, Schmitt's theory of, 52–57, 90–91; Machiavelli and, 62–69, 76–77; Strauss and, 78–85
conflict, Schmitt's discussion of, 76–77,

99–103, 119–20; global war and, 121–25, 128–34
Conservative Revolution, 110
Constitution of Athens, The (att. Aristotle), xii
constituent power: decisionism and, 36–37; Schmitt's concept of, 9–11, 16–18; secularization and, 44–48
constitutionalism, in Schmitt's political theory, 16–18, 103, 151n30
Constitutional Theory (Schmitt), xx, 37–38, 63, 66–67, 85, 91
contingency, idea and, 48–50
Crisis of Parliamentary Democracy, The (Schmitt), 137n12
criticality, Strauss's concept of, 78
criticism, Spinoza's discussion of, 83, 92–96
Cromwell, Oliver, 27
"crystal-system" of Hobbes, 6, 18, 76, 87, 148n13
cujus regio ejus industria ("whose is the realm, his is the industry"), 111–17
Cusa, Nicholas de, xxiv

Dæmonie der Macht, Die (Ritter), 74
"Das Zeitalter der Neutralisierungen und Entpolitisierunger" (The Age of Neutralizations and Depoliticizations) (Schmitt), 7
decisionist thesis: Galli's discussion of, xx; Kelsen's formalism and, 41; Machiavelli and, 76–77; political theology and, 34–38, 50; Schmitt's political theory and, 7–11, 23–26
democracy, Schmitt's interpretation of, 13–26
Descartes, René, 80, 148n13
dictatorship, 15
Dictatorship (Schmitt): Machiavelli and, 60–62; political theology and, 15, 34, 37, 44; Spinoza and, 85

Teilen (partition), 115
terrorism, in global era, 122–34
"The Actuality [Aktualität] of Philosophy" (Adorno), xxxviii
Theory of the Partisan (Schmitt), xx, 26, 115–17, 128–29
Thomasius, Christian, 87
Three Types of Juristic Thought (Schmitt), xx
Tocqueville, Alexis de, 26
totalitarianism, Schmitt's embrace of, 22–26, 69, 88–91
total State, Schmitt's concept of, 19–22
Tractatus Theologico-Politicus (Spinoza), 87
"tragic drama" (Trauerspiel), 47
"tragicity," Schmitt's concept of, xxiii–xxiv, xxxvii
transcendence: in Schmitt's political theology, 52–57, 93–96; Strauss's view of, 93–96
translation (Übersetzung), 42–48; Schmitt's philosophy and, xxxii, 42
tyranny, Schmitt's discussion of, xli–xlii

"Über das Verhältnis der Begriffe Krieg und Feind" (On the relation between the concepts of war and enemy) (Schmitt), 109–11
United Nations, 126, 132
universalism, in global era, 125–34

Valéry, Paul, 26
Vatter, Miguel, 166n39
Verfassung, 16–18, 76, 151n30
Versailles Treaty, 104

violence: in global era, 121–25; politics and, 14–15
Virgil, 64
Voegelin, Eric, 47, 118
Void-of-Order, 40–42, 48, 99–103
völkisch ideology, 23, 52, 88
Volksentscheid und Volksbegehren (Plebiscite and referendum) (Schmitt), 16
von Mohl, Robert, 87

war: global war, 121–25, 128–34; Schmitt on theory of, 162n39; sovereignty and, 104–11
war crimes, Schmitt linked to, xxi, 135n5
War on Terror, Schmitt's ideology and, 132–34
weakness, State of, 19
Weber, Max, xiv, 15, 28–29, 43–44, 93
Weiden (production), 115
Weimar Republic: failure of, 22–26, 29, 88; Reserve Constitution of, 20–22, 35, 52; Schmitt and, xxi–xxii, 18–19, 71–73, 151n42
Wert des Staates und die Bedeutung des Einzelnen, Der (The value of the State and the meaning of the individual) (Schmitt), 4–7, 67
Wilhelmine academic science, 29
Williams, Raymond, xxxvi
Wolff, Christian, 87
"Words to Be Spoken on the Law for Appropriating Money, after Giving a Little Introduction and Excuse" (Machiavelli), 160n23

Zwischenlage (intermediate situation), 102–3, 109–11, 113–17